3rd Edition

Ventures 4

STUDENT'S BOOK

Gretchen Bitterlin ▪ Dennis Johnson ▪ Donna Price ▪ Sylvia Ramirez

K. Lynn Savage (Series Editor)

CAMBRIDGE
UNIVERSITY PRESS

CAMBRIDGE
UNIVERSITY PRESS

University Printing House, Cambridge CB2 8BS, United Kingdom

One Liberty Plaza, 20th Floor, New York, NY 10006, USA

477 Williamstown Road, Port Melbourne, VIC 3207, Australia

314–321, 3rd Floor, Plot 3, Splendor Forum, Jasola District Centre, New Delhi – 110025, India

79 Anson Road, #06–04/06, Singapore 079906

Cambridge University Press is part of the University of Cambridge.

It furthers the University's mission by disseminating knowledge in the pursuit of education, learning and research at the highest international levels of excellence.

www.cambridge.org
Information on this title: www.cambridge.org/9781108449588

First published 2008
Second edition 2014

20 19 18 17 16 15 14 13 12 11 10 9 8 7 6 5 4

Printed in Dubai by Oriental Press

A catalogue record for this publication is available from the British Library

ISBN 978-1-108-45062-1 Workbook
ISBN 978-1-108-44947-2 Online Workbook
ISBN 978-1-108-68517-7 Teacher's Edition
ISBN 978-1-108-44923-6 Class Audio CDs
ISBN 978-1-108-45054-6 Presentation Plus

Additional resources for this publication at www.cambridge.org/ventures

AUTHORS' ACKNOWLEDGMENTS

The authors would like to acknowledge and thank focus-group participants and reviewers for their insightful comments, as well as Cambridge University Press editorial, marketing, and production staffs, whose thorough research and attention to detail have resulted in a quality product.

The publishers would also like to extend their particular thanks to the following reviewers and consultants for their valuable insights and suggestions:

Barry Bakin, Instructional Technology, Los Angeles Unified School District, Los Angeles, CA;

Jim Brice, San Diego Community College District Continuing Education, San Diego, CA;

Diana Contreras, West Valley Occupational Center, Los Angeles, CA;

Druci J. Diaz, Hillsborough Country Public Schools, Tampa, FL;

Linda Foster, Instructor, Hillsborough County Schools Adult Education Department, Tampa, FL;

Margaret Geiger, M.Ed., Dallas, TX;

Ana L. Herrera, San Jacinto Adult Learning Center, El Paso, TX;

Cindi Hartmen, ESL Instructor, San Diego Continuing Education, San Diego, CA;

Patrick Jennings, Tomlinson Adult Learning Center, St. Petersburg, FL;

Lori Hess-Tolbert, Frisco, TX;

AnnMarie Kokash-Wood, Tomlinson Adult Learning Center, St. Petersburg, FL;

Linda P. Kozin, San Diego Continuing Ed, San Diego Community College District, San Diego, CA;

Caron Lieber, Palomar College, San Marcos, CA;

Reyna P. Lopez, Southwest College, Los Angeles, CA;

Rosemary Lubarov, Palo Alto Adult School, Palo Alto, CA;

Lori K. Markel, Plant City Adult and Community School, Plant City, FL;

Mary Spanarke, Center for Applied Linguistics / Washington English Center, Washington, DC;

Rosalie Tauscher, Fort Worth ISD Adult Ed, Fort Worth, TX;

Timothy Wahl, Abram Friedman Occupation Center, Los Angeles, CA;

Delia Watley, Irving ISD Adult Education and Literacy, Irving, TX;

Andrea V. White, Tarrant County College, Arlington, TX;

Sandra Wilson, Fort Worth Adult Education, Fort Worth, TX

SCOPE AND SEQUENCE

UNIT TITLE TOPIC	FUNCTIONS	LISTENING AND SPEAKING	VOCABULARY	GRAMMAR FOCUS
Welcome pages 2–5	▪ Exchanging information ▪ Discussing study habits and strategies	▪ Listening to people talk about study habits and strategies ▪ Asking about study habits and strategies ▪ Talking about classmates' study habits and strategies	▪ Study habits and strategies	▪ past continuous and simple past ▪ simple past and present perfect
Unit 1 **Personal information** pages 6–17 Topic: **Ways to be smart**	▪ Describing personal strengths ▪ Expressing opinions ▪ Expressing agreement and disagreement	▪ Asking about aptitudes ▪ Discussing multiple intelligences ▪ Giving opinions	▪ Adjectives and adverbs ▪ Multiple intelligences ▪ Prefixes and roots	▪ Nouns, verbs, adjectives, and adverbs ▪ Noun clauses with *that* ▪ *so* and *that*
Unit 2 **At school** pages 18–29 Topic: **Planning for success**	▪ Inquiring about educational opportunities ▪ Describing educational goals ▪ Describing successful people	▪ Asking about courses and classes ▪ Discussing how to continue one's education ▪ Discussing obstacles and successes	▪ Education and careers ▪ Educational requirements	▪ The present passive ▪ Infinitives after the passive ▪ *be + supposed to* and *be + not supposed to*
Review: Units 1 and 2 pages 30–31		▪ Understanding a conversation		
Unit 3 **Friends and family** pages 32–43 Topic: **Parents and children**	▪ Discussing appropriate behaviors at home and school ▪ Using polite forms of language	▪ Asking about rules at home and at school ▪ Asking questions indirectly ▪ Talking about past events and experiences	▪ Rules and expectations ▪ Word families	▪ Indirect *Wh-* questions ▪ Indirect *Yes / No* questions ▪ *say* and *tell* with reported speech
Unit 4 **Health** pages 44–55 Topic: **Stressful situations**	▪ Discussing stress ▪ Expressing necessity and lack of necessity ▪ Making suggestions ▪ Expressing past regrets	▪ Asking about stress ▪ Discussing ways to cope with stress ▪ Giving advice about past actions	▪ Stress and ways to cope ▪ Suffixes	▪ *should, shouldn't, have to, don't have to* ▪ *should have* and *shouldn't have* ▪ *must* and *may / might*
Review: Units 3 and 4 pages 56–57		▪ Understanding a phone conversation		
Unit 5 **Around town** pages 58–69 Topic: **Community involvement**	▪ Describing volunteer responsibilities ▪ Describing a sequence of events ▪ Describing repeated actions in the past and present	▪ Asking about volunteer activities ▪ Discussing personal experiences of volunteering or helping people ▪ Discussing schedules	▪ Volunteerism ▪ Positive and negative words	▪ Clauses with *until* and *as soon as* ▪ Repeated actions in the present and past ▪ Contrasting *used to* and *be used to*

READING	WRITING	LIFE SKILLS	PRONUNCIATION
▪ Reading a paragraph about bad weather	▪ Writing sentences about your partner	▪ Discussing study habits and strategies for learning English	▪ Pronouncing key vocabulary
▪ Reading an article about multiple intelligences ▪ Skimming to predict what a reading is about	▪ Writing a descriptive paragraph about a primary intelligence ▪ Using a topic sentence and supporting details	▪ Using a dictionary ▪ Reading and understanding a visual diagram	▪ Pronouncing key vocabulary
▪ Reading an article about an immigrant family ▪ Scanning to find specific information	▪ Writing a descriptive paragraph about a successful person ▪ Using specific details such as facts, examples, and reasons	▪ Using a dictionary or thesaurus to identify synonyms ▪ Reading and understanding a chart about the location of vocational classes	▪ Pronouncing key vocabulary
			▪ *-ed* verb endings
▪ Reading an article about barriers between generations ▪ Noticing words that repeat to get an idea of what a reading is about	▪ Writing an expository paragraph about a difference between generations ▪ Using a transition within a paragraph	▪ Using a dictionary ▪ Reading and understanding a chart ▪ Interpreting census bureau information	▪ Pronouncing key vocabulary
▪ Reading an article about stress ▪ Relating the title and section heads to personal experience	▪ Writing a descriptive paragraph about how to cope with stress ▪ Using causes and effects to organize a paragraph	▪ Reading and understanding a bar graph ▪ Discussing stress in the workplace	▪ Pronouncing key vocabulary
			▪ Contrasting intonation of direct and indirect *Wh-* questions
▪ Reading an article about volunteers ▪ Using context clues to guess if the meaning of a word is positive or negative	▪ Writing a descriptive paragraph about someone who made a difference ▪ Making writing more interesting by including details that answer *Wh-* questions	▪ Reading and understanding ads for volunteer positions ▪ Discussing volunteer activities	▪ Pronouncing key vocabulary

UNIT TITLE TOPIC	FUNCTIONS	LISTENING AND SPEAKING	VOCABULARY	GRAMMAR FOCUS
Unit 6 **Time** pages 70–81 Topic: **Time and technology**	▪ Expressing agreement and disagreement ▪ Giving opinions and reasons	▪ Talking about time-saving devices ▪ Discussing the advantages and disadvantages of technology	▪ Technology and time-saving devices ▪ Words with multiple definitions	▪ *although* ▪ Contrasting *because* and *although* ▪ *so* and *such*
Review: Units 5 and 6 pages 82–83		▪ Understanding a radio interview		
Unit 7 **Shopping** pages 84–95 Topic: **Buying and returning merchandise**	▪ Explaining problems with a purchase ▪ Discussing preferences ▪ Explaining mistakes ▪ Asking for information about store policies	▪ Asking about returning merchandise ▪ Asking about store policies ▪ Talking about shopping mistakes ▪ Describing people, places, and things	▪ Buying and returning merchandise ▪ Compound nouns	▪ *who*, *that* and *which* as the subject of an adjective clause ▪ *that* as the object of an adjective clause ▪ Clarifying questions
Unit 8 **Work** pages 96–107 Topic: **Success at work**	▪ Giving advice ▪ Making suggestions ▪ Explaining job responsibilities ▪ Describing the duration of an activity	▪ Discussing work schedules ▪ Talking about workplace problems and their solutions ▪ Asking questions about work experiences	▪ Job responsibilities and skills ▪ Prefixes and roots	▪ Contrasting present perfect and present perfect continuous ▪ Adjectives ending in *-ed* and *-ing* ▪ Polite requests and offers
Review: Units 7 and 8 pages 108–109		▪ Understanding a class lecture		
Unit 9 **Daily living** pages 110–121 Topic: **Saving our planet**	▪ Describing environmental issues and concerns ▪ Giving advice ▪ Making suggestions ▪ Describing actions one can take	▪ Asking questions about "saving our planet" ▪ Discussing causes and effects of environmental problems ▪ Discussing actions that could help the environment	▪ The environment ▪ Antonyms	▪ Present unreal conditional ▪ *since* and *so* ▪ Contrasting present real and present unreal conditionals
Unit 10 **Free time** pages 122–133 Topic: **Celebrations**	▪ Describing future possibility ▪ Describing actions based on expectations ▪ Expressing hopes and wishes ▪ Comparing customs and celebrations	▪ Asking about and comparing wedding customs ▪ Discussing possible and hypothetical holiday plans ▪ Talking about hopes and wishes	▪ Celebrations ▪ Words with multiple meanings	▪ Contrasting future real and future unreal conditionals ▪ *hope* and *wish* ▪ Tag questions
Review: Units 9 and 10 pages 134–135		▪ Understanding a street interview		

READING	WRITING	LIFE SKILLS	PRONUNCIATION
▪ Reading a magazine article about the impact of technology ▪ Reading first and last paragraph for main idea	▪ Writing an expository paragraph about a time-saving device or activity ▪ Using advantages and disadvantages to organize a paragraph	▪ Using a dictionary ▪ Reading and understanding a table ▪ Discussing Internet use ▪ Discussing survey results	▪ Pronouncing key vocabulary
			▪ Stressed and unstressed words
▪ Reading a newspaper advice column about return policies ▪ Recognizing synonyms in a reading	▪ Writing a persuasive paragraph about shopping online ▪ Using transition words such as *first*, *second*, *next*, *furthermore*, *moreover*, and *finally* to signal a list of reasons in a paragraph	▪ Reading and understanding a returned-merchandise form ▪ Talking about returning or exchanging merchandise	▪ Pronouncing key vocabulary
▪ Reading an article about hard and soft job skills ▪ Reading an email cover letter to apply for a job ▪ Recognizing quotations and reasons for using them	▪ Writing an email cover letter to apply for a job ▪ Including information about skills and experience in a cover letter	▪ Using a dictionary ▪ Reading and understanding a table about the fastest-growing occupations ▪ Discussing work skills	▪ Pronouncing key vocabulary
			▪ Stressing function words
▪ Reading a fable about how all things in life are connected ▪ Asking questions to identify a cause-and-effect relationship	▪ Writing a paragraph about an environmental problem ▪ Using cause and effect to organize a paragraph	▪ Using a dictionary or thesaurus ▪ Reading and understanding a chart about reasons to "Save our planet" ▪ Discussing ways to help the environment	▪ Pronouncing key vocabulary
▪ Reading an article about special birthday celebrations around the world ▪ Using punctuation as a clue to meaning	▪ Writing a descriptive paragraph about a favorite holiday or celebration ▪ Concluding a paragraph by relating it to your personal life	▪ Using a dictionary ▪ Reading and understanding a recipe ▪ Discussing traditional meals and recipes	▪ Pronouncing key vocabulary
			▪ Linking consonant-vowel sounds

TO THE TEACHER

What is *Ventures*?

Ventures is a six-level, four-skills, standards-based, integrated-skills series that empowers students to achieve their academic and career goals.

- Aligned to the new NRS descriptors while covering key English Language Proficiency, College and Career Readiness Standards, and WIOA requirements.
- A wealth of resources provide instructors with the tools for any teaching situation, making *Ventures* the most complete program.
- Promotes 21st century learning complemented by a suite of technology tools.

How Does the Third Edition Meet Today's Adult Education Needs?

- The third edition is aligned to the NRS' interpretive, productive, and interactive outcomes at each level.
- To help students develop the skills they need to succeed in college and the workplace, *Ventures* 3rd Edition offers a dedicated College and Career Readiness Section (CCRS) with 10 worksheets at each level, from Level 1 to Transitions (pages 136–155).
- Audio tracks and grammar presentations linked to QR codes can be accessed using smartphones (see page x), promoting mobile learning.
- Problem-solving activities added to each unit cover critical thinking and soft skills key to workplace readiness.
- More rigorous grammar practice has been added to Lessons B and C, and more evidence-based reading practice has been added to Lesson D.

What are the *Ventures* components?

Student's Book

Each of the core **Student's Books** contains ten topic-focused units, with five review units. The main units feature six skill-focused lessons.

- **Self-contained lessons** are perfectly paced for one-hour classes. For classes longer than 1 hour, additional resources are available via the Workbook and Online Teacher's Resources.
- **Review units** recycle and reinforce the listening, vocabulary, and grammar skills developed in the two prior units and include a pronunciation activity.

Teacher's Edition

The interleaved **Teacher's Edition** includes easy-to-follow lesson plans for every unit.

- Teaching tips address common problem areas for students and additional suggestions for expansion activities and building community.
- Additional practice material across all *Ventures* components is clearly organized in the *More Ventures* chart at the end of each lesson.
- Multiple opportunities for assessment such as unit, mid-term, and final tests are available in the Teacher's Edition. Customizable tests and test audio are also available online (www.cambridge.org/ventures/resources/).

Online Teacher's Resources www.cambridge.org/ventures/resources/

Ventures Online Teacher's Resources offer hundreds of additional worksheets and classroom materials including:

- *A placement test* that helps accurately identify the appropriate level of *Ventures* for each student.
- *Career and Educational Pathways Worksheets* help students meet their post-exit employment goals.
- *Collaborative Worksheets* for each lesson develop cooperative learning and community building within the classroom.
- *Writing Worksheets* that help literacy-level students recognize shapes and write letters and numbers, while alphabet and number cards promote partner and group work.
- *Picture dictionary cards and Worksheets* that reinforce vocabulary learned in Levels Basic, 1, and 2.
- *Multilevel Worksheets* that are designed for use in multilevel classrooms and in leveled classes where the proficiency level of students differs.
- *Self-assessments* give students an opportunity to reflect on their learning. They support learner persistence and help determine whether students are ready for the unit test.

Workbook

The **Workbook** provides two pages of activities for each lesson in the Student's Book.

- If used in class, the Workbook can extend classroom instructional time by 30 minutes per lesson.
- The exercises are designed so learners can complete them in class or independently. Students can check their answers with the answer key in the back of the Workbook. Workbook exercises can be assigned in class, for homework, or as student support when a class is missed.
- Grammar charts at the back of the Workbook allow students to use the Workbook for self-study.

Online Workbooks

The self-grading **Online Workbooks** offer programs the flexibility of introducing blended learning.

- In addition to the same high-quality practice opportunities in the print workbooks, the online workbooks provide students instant feedback.
- Teachers and programs can track student progress and time on task.

Presentation Plus
www.esource.cambridge.org

Presentation Plus allows teachers to digitally project the contents of the Student's Books in front of the class for a livelier, interactive classroom. It is a complete solution for teachers because it includes the Class audio, answer keys, and the Ventures Arcade. Contact your Cambridge ESL Specialist (www.cambridge.org/cambridgeenglish/contact) to find out how to access it.

Ventures Arcade
www.cambridge.org/venturesarcade/

The Arcade is a free website where students can find additional practice for the listening, vocabulary, and grammar found in the Student's Books. There is also a Citizenship section that includes questions on civics, history, government, and the N-400 application.

Unit organization

LESSON A Listening focuses students on the unit topic. The initial exercise, ***Before you listen***, creates student interest with visuals that help the teacher assess what learners already know and serves as a prompt for the unit's key vocabulary. Next is ***Listen***, which is based on conversations. Students relate vocabulary to meaning and relate the spoken and written forms of new theme-related vocabulary. ***After you listen*** concludes the lesson by practicing language related to the theme in a communicative activity, either orally with a partner or individually in a writing activity.

LESSONS B AND C focus on grammar. The lessons move from a ***Grammar focus*** that presents the grammar point in chart form; to ***Practice*** exercises that check comprehension of the grammar point and provide guided practice; and, finally, to ***Communicate*** exercises that guide learners as they generate original answers and conversations. These lessons often include a *Culture note*, which provides information directly related to the conversation practice (such as the use of titles with last names) or a *Useful language* note, which introduces useful expressions.

LESSON D Reading develops reading skills and expands vocabulary. The lesson opens with a ***Before you read*** exercise, designed to activate prior knowledge and encourage learners to make predictions. A *Reading tip*, which focuses on a specific reading skill, accompanies the ***Read*** exercise. The reading section of the lesson concludes with ***After you read*** exercises that check comprehension. In Levels Basic, 1, and 2, the vocabulary expansion portion of the lesson is a ***Picture dictionary***. It includes a *word bank*, pictures to identify, and a conversation for practicing the new words. The words expand vocabulary related to the unit topic. In Books 3 and 4, the vocabulary expansion portion of the lesson uses new vocabulary from the reading to build skills such as recognizing word families, selecting definitions based on the context of the reading, and using clues in the reading to guess meaning.

LESSON E Writing provides practice with process writing within the context of the unit. ***Before you write*** exercises provide warm-up activities to activate the language needed for the writing assignment, followed by one or more exercises that provide a model for students to follow when they write. A *Writing tip* presents information about punctuation or paragraph organization directly related to the writing assignment. The ***Write*** exercise sets goals for the student writing. In the ***After you write*** exercise, students share with a partner.

LESSON F Another view brings the unit together with opportunities to review lesson content. ***Life-skills reading*** develops the scanning and skimming skills used with documents such as forms, charts, schedules, announcements, and ads. Multiple-choice questions (modeled on CASAS[1] and BEST[2]) develop test-taking skills. **Solve the problem** focuses on critical thinking, soft-skills, and workplace development. In Levels 1–4, ***Grammar connections*** contrasts grammar points and includes guided practice and communicative activities.

1 The Comprehensive Adult Student Assessment System. For more information, see www.casas.org.

2 The Basic English Skills Test. For more information, see www.cal.org/BEST.

UNIT TOUR

The Most Complete Course for Student Success

- Helps students develop the skills needed to be college and career ready and function successfully in their community
- Covers key NRS and WIOA requirements
- Aligned with the English Language Proficiency (ELP) and College and Career Readiness (CCR) standards

The Big Picture

- Introduces the unit topic and creates an opportunity for classroom discussion.
- Activates students' prior knowledge and previews the unit vocabulary.

Unit Goals

Introduces the competencies students will learn.

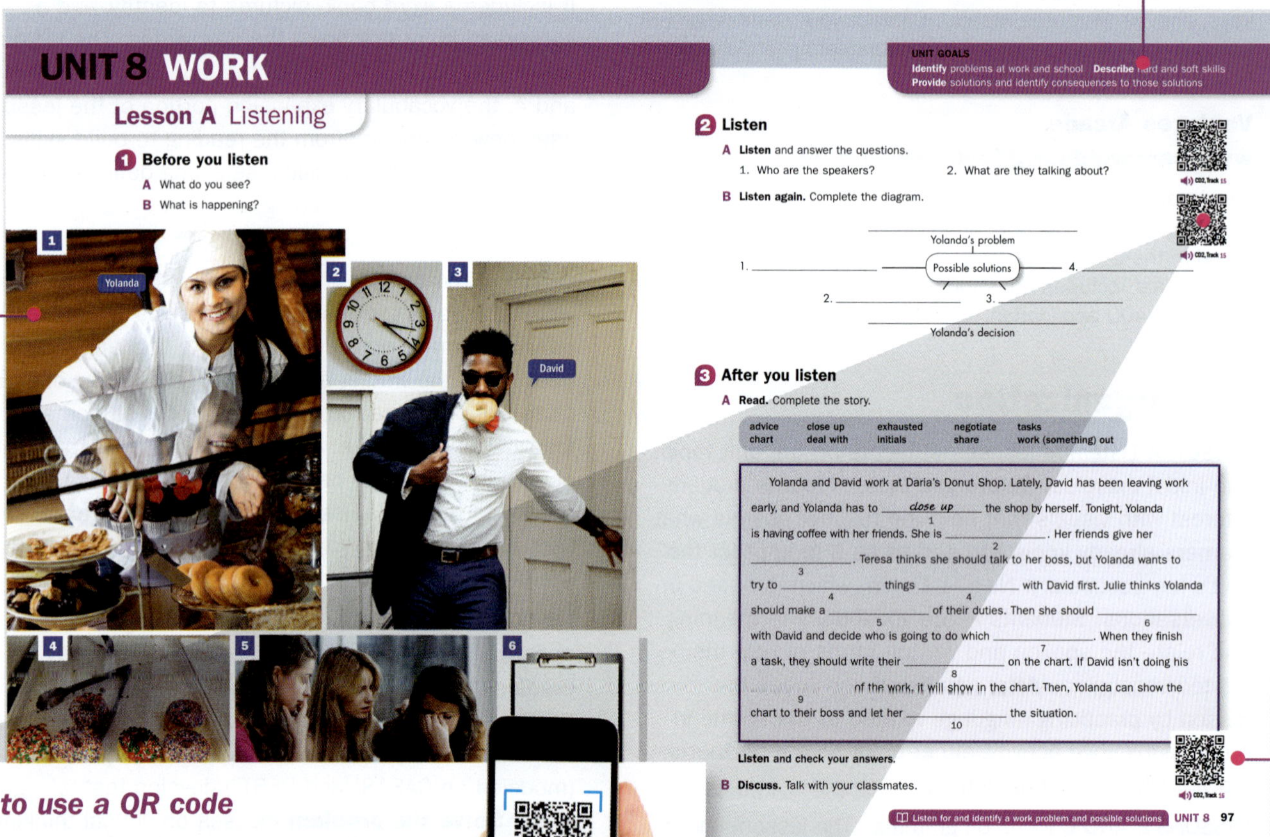
UNIT 8 WORK

UNIT GOALS
Identify problems at work and school **Describe** hard and soft skills
Provide solutions and identify consequences to those solutions

Lesson A Listening

1 Before you listen

A What do you see?

B What is happening?

2 Listen

A **Listen** and answer the questions.

1. Who are the speakers?
2. What are they talking about?

B **Listen again.** Complete the diagram.

3 After you listen

A **Read.** Complete the story.

advice chart close up deal with exhausted initials negotiate share tasks work (something) out

Yolanda and David work at Daria's Donut Shop. Lately, David has been leaving work early, and Yolanda has to *close up* (1) the shop by herself. Tonight, Yolanda is having coffee with her friends. She is ______ (2). Her friends give her ______ (3). Teresa thinks she should talk to her boss, but Yolanda wants to try to ______ (4) things ______ (4) with David first. Julie thinks Yolanda should make a ______ (5) of their duties. Then she should ______ (6) with David and decide who is going to do which ______ (7). When they finish a task, they should write their ______ (8) on the chart. If David isn't doing his ______ (9) of the work, it will show in the chart. Then, Yolanda can show the chart to their boss and let her ______ (10) the situation.

Listen and check your answers.

B **Discuss.** Talk with your classmates.

Listen for and identify a work problem and possible solutions UNIT 8 97

How to use a QR code

- Open the camera on your smartphone.
- Point it at the QR code.
- The camera will automatically scan the code. If not, press the button to take a picture.

* Not all cameras automatically scan QR codes. You may need to download a QR code reader. Search "QR free" and download an app.

3 Easy Ways to Access Audio

- Scan QR codes
- Download from *Ventures* Online Resources: www.cambridge.org/ventures/audio/
- Play from Class audio CDs

Every unit has two grammar lessons taught using the same format.

Grammar Chart

- Presents and practices the grammar point.
- Extra grammar charts online can be used for reference and give additional support.

Grammar Presentation

Animated presentations to watch on mobile devices using QR codes allow for self-directed learning and develop digital literacy.

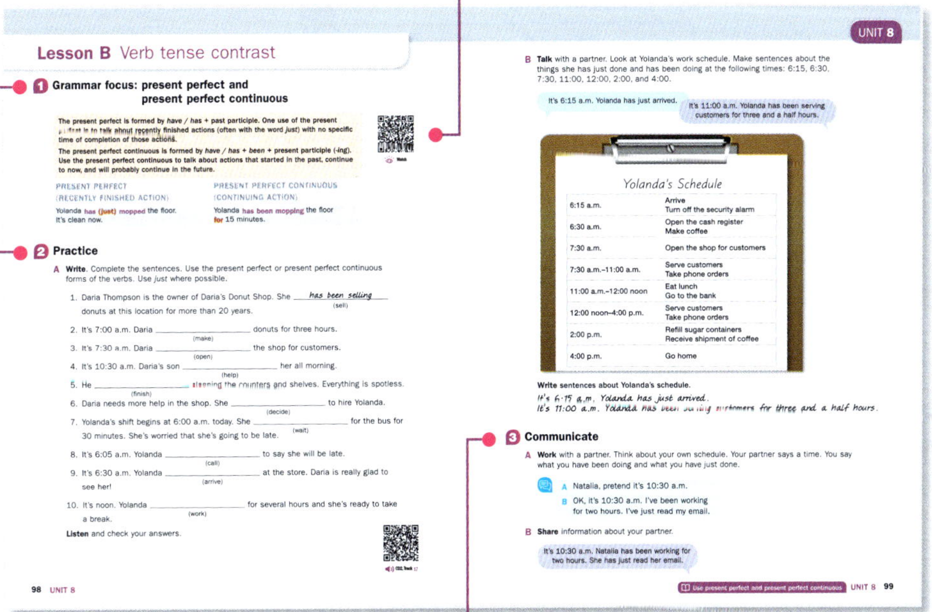

Additional Grammar Activities

Ensures students have the chance to practice more grammar to meet the rigor of CCRS.

Natural Progression

Moves from controlled to communicative activities for students to ask and answer questions about familiar text, topics, and experiences.

Real-life Practice

Engages students and provides meaningful application of the grammar.

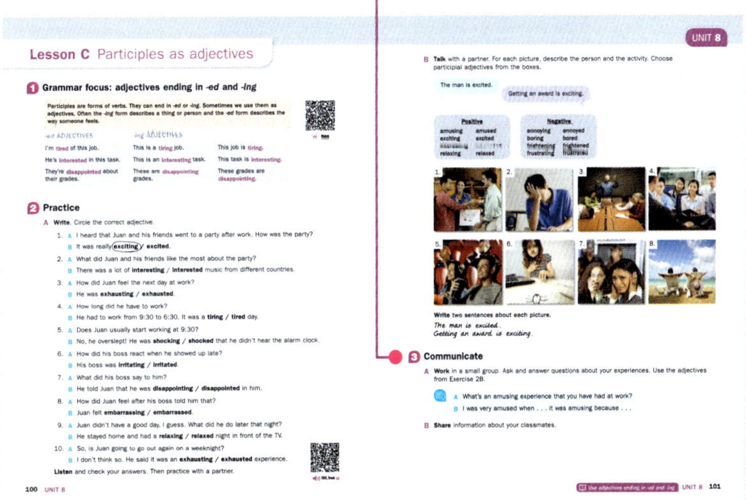

Reading

- Uses a 3-step reading approach to highlight the skills and strategies students need to succeed.
- Combines reading with writing and listening practice for an integrated approach to ensure better comprehension.
- Brings text complexity into the classroom to help students read independently and proficiently.

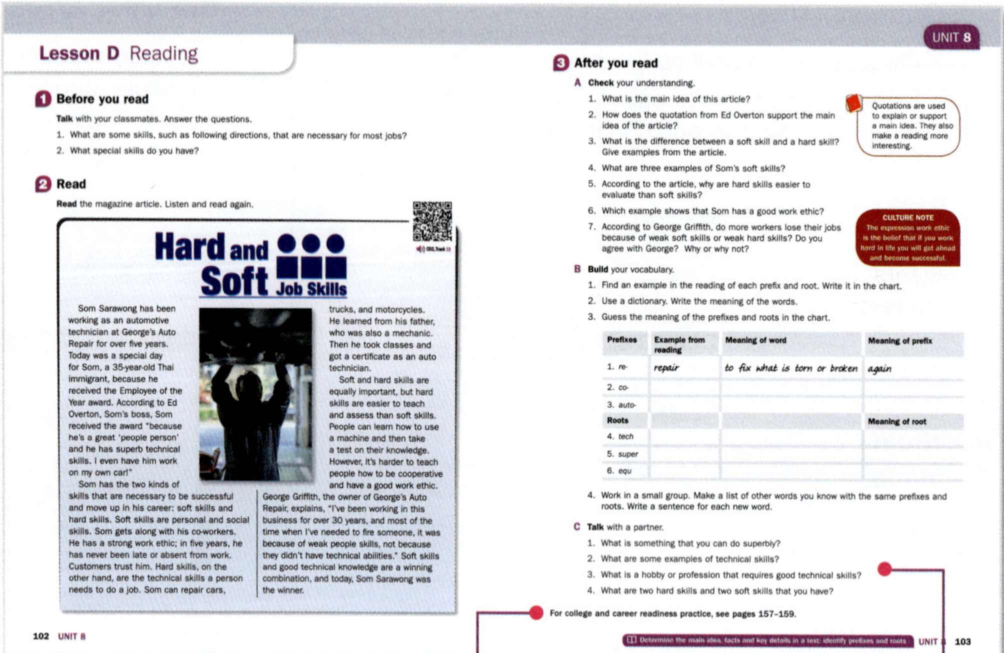

Lesson D Reading

UNIT 8

1 Before you read

Talk with your classmates. Answer the questions.

1. What are some skills, such as following directions, that are necessary for most jobs?
2. What special skills do you have?

2 Read

Read the magazine article. Listen and read again.

Hard and Soft Job Skills

Som Sarawong has been working as an automotive technician at George's Auto Repair for over five years. Today was a special day for Som, a 35-year-old Thai immigrant, because he received the Employee of the Year award. According to Ed Overton, Som's boss, Som received the award "because he's a great 'people person' and he has superb technical skills. I even have him work on my own car!"

Som has the two kinds of skills that are necessary to be successful and move up in his career: soft skills and hard skills. Soft skills are personal and social skills. Som gets along with his co-workers. He has a strong work ethic; in five years, he has never been late or absent from work. Customers trust him. Hard skills, on the other hand, are the technical skills a person needs to do a job. Som can repair cars, trucks, and motorcycles. He learned from his father, who was also a mechanic. Then he took classes and got a certificate as an auto technician.

Soft and hard skills are equally important, but hard skills are easier to teach and assess than soft skills. People can learn how to use a machine and then take a test on their knowledge. However, it's harder to teach people how to be cooperative and have a good work ethic. George Griffith, the owner of George's Auto Repair, explains, "I've been working in this business for over 30 years, and most of the time when I've needed to fire someone, it was because of weak people skills, not because they didn't have technical abilities." Soft skills and good technical knowledge are a winning combination, and today, Som Sarawong was the winner.

3 After you read

A Check your understanding.

1. What is the main idea of this article?
2. How does the quotation from Ed Overton support the main idea of the article?
3. What is the difference between a soft skill and a hard skill? Give examples from the article.
4. What are three examples of Som's soft skills?
5. According to the article, why are hard skills easier to evaluate than soft skills?
6. Which example shows that Som has a good work ethic?
7. According to George Griffith, do more workers lose their jobs because of weak soft skills or weak hard skills? Do you agree with George? Why or why not?

Quotations are used to explain or support a main idea. They also make a reading more interesting.

CULTURE NOTE
The expression *work ethic* is the belief that if you work hard in life you will get ahead and become successful.

B Build your vocabulary.

1. Find an example in the reading of each prefix and root. Write it in the chart.
2. Use a dictionary. Write the meaning of the words.
3. Guess the meaning of the prefixes and roots in the chart.

Prefixes	Example from reading	Meaning of word	Meaning of prefix
1. *re-*	*repair*	*to fix what is torn or broken*	*again*
2. *co-*			
3. *auto-*			
Roots			**Meaning of root**
4. *tech*			
5. *super*			
6. *equ*			

4. Work in a small group. Make a list of other words you know with the same prefixes and roots. Write a sentence for each new word.

C Talk with a partner.

1. What is something that you can do superbly?
2. What are some examples of technical skills?
3. What is a hobby or profession that requires good technical skills?
4. What are two hard skills and two soft skills that you have?

For college and career readiness practice, see pages 157–159.

Determine the main idea, facts and key details in a text; identify prefixes and roots

102 UNIT 8 / UNIT 8 103

College & Career Readiness Section

Builds critical-thinking skills and uses informative texts to help master the more complex CCR standards.

Speaking Practice

Helps students internalize the vocabulary and relate it to their lives.

Writing

- Helps students develop a robust process-writing approach.
- Supports students to meet the challenges of work and the classroom through academic and purposeful writing practice.

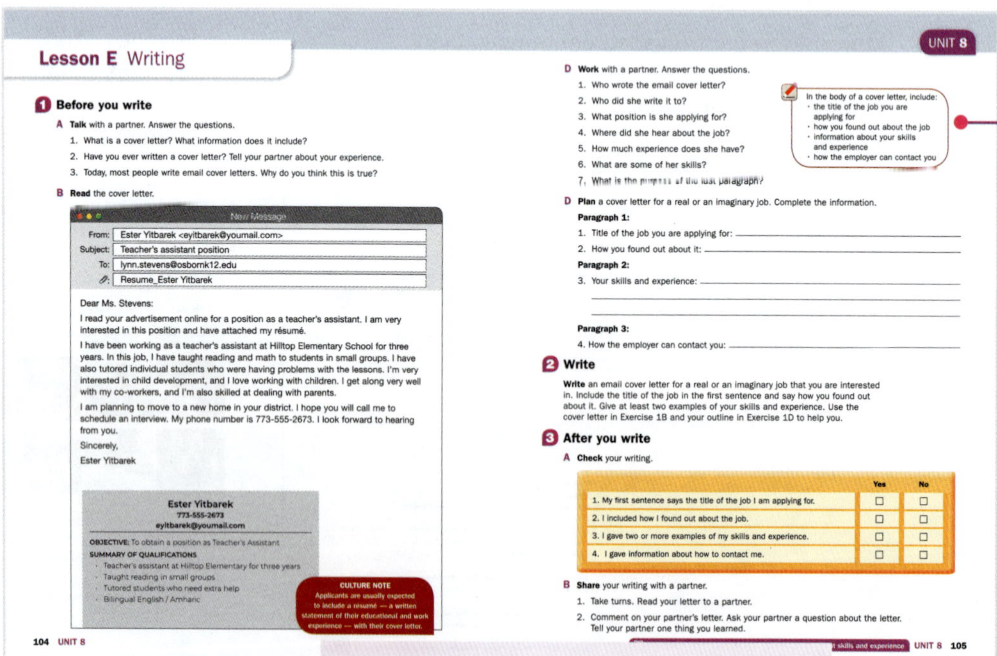

Lesson E Writing

UNIT 8

1 Before you write

A Talk with a partner. Answer the questions.

1. What is a cover letter? What information does it include?
2. Have you ever written a cover letter? Tell your partner about your experience.
3. Today, most people write email cover letters. Why do you think this is true?

B Read the cover letter.

New Message

From: Ester Yitbarek <eyitbarek@youmail.com>
Subject: Teacher's assistant position
To: lynn.stevens@osbornk12.edu
Resume_Ester Yitbarek

Dear Ms. Stevens:

I read your advertisement online for a position as a teacher's assistant. I am very interested in this position and have attached my résumé.

I have been working as a teacher's assistant at Hilltop Elementary School for three years. In this job, I have taught reading and math to students in small groups. I have also tutored individual students who were having problems with the lessons. I'm very interested in child development, and I love working with children. I get along very well with my co-workers, and I'm also skilled at dealing with parents.

I am planning to move to a new home in your district. I hope you will call me to schedule an interview. My phone number is 773-555-2673. I look forward to hearing from you.

Sincerely,
Ester Yitbarek

Ester Yitbarek
773-555-2673
eyitbarek@youmail.com

OBJECTIVE: To obtain a position as Teacher's Assistant
SUMMARY OF QUALIFICATIONS
- Teacher's assistant at Hilltop Elementary for three years
- Taught reading in small groups
- Tutored students who need extra help
- Bilingual English / Amharic

CULTURE NOTE
Applicants are usually expected to include a resumé — a written statement of their educational and work experience — with their cover letter.

D Work with a partner. Answer the questions.

1. Who wrote the email cover letter?
2. Who did she write it to?
3. What position is she applying for?
4. Where did she hear about the job?
5. How much experience does she have?
6. What are some of her skills?
7. What is the [illegible]

In the body of a cover letter, include:
- the title of the job you are applying for
- how you found out about the job
- information about your skills and experience
- how the employer can contact you

D Plan a cover letter for a real or an imaginary job. Complete the information.

Paragraph 1:
1. Title of the job you are applying for: ______
2. How you found out about it: ______

Paragraph 2:
3. Your skills and experience: ______

Paragraph 3:
4. How the employer can contact you: ______

2 Write

Write an email cover letter for a real or an imaginary job that you are interested in. Include the title of the job in the first sentence and say how you found out about it. Give at least two examples of your skills and experience. Use the cover letter in Exercise 1B and your outline in Exercise 1D to help you.

3 After you write

A Check your writing.

	Yes	No
1. My first sentence says the title of the job I am applying for.	☐	☐
2. I included how I found out about the job.	☐	☐
3. I gave two or more examples of my skills and experience.	☐	☐
4. I gave information about how to contact me.	☐	☐

B Share your writing with a partner.

1. Take turns. Read your letter to a partner.
2. Comment on your partner's letter. Ask your partner a question about the letter. Tell your partner one thing you learned.

104 UNIT 8 / UNIT 8 105

Writing Tips

Gives students confidence in writing with easy-to-follow writing tips and strategies.

Document Literacy

Builds real-life skills through explicit practice using authentic document types.

Grammar connections

Contrasts two grammar forms in a communicative way to help with grammar accuracy.

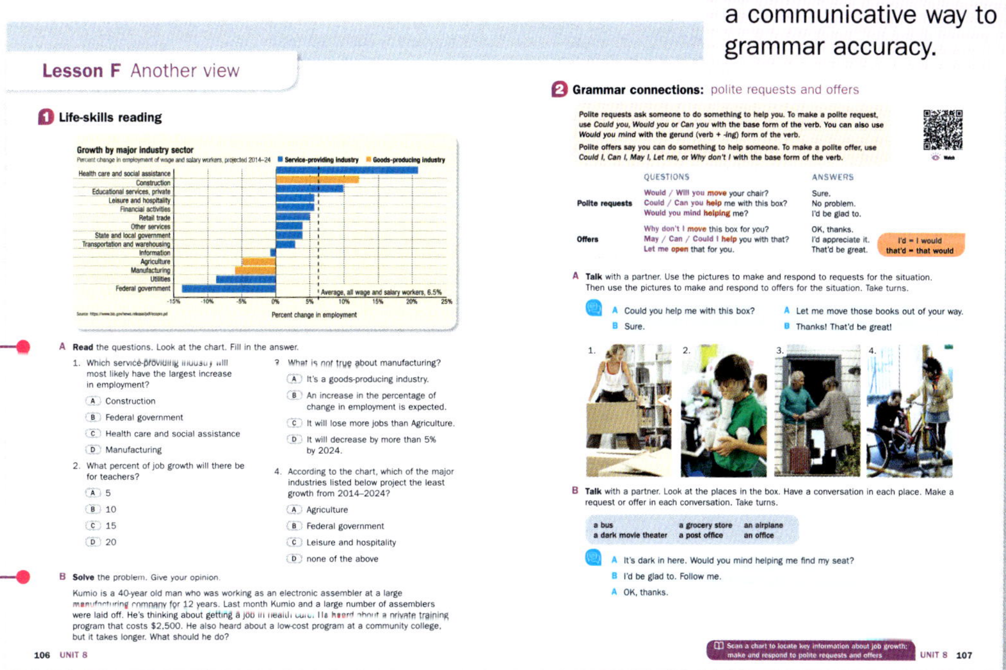

Lesson F Another view

1 Life-skills reading

Growth by major industry sector

A Read the questions. Look at the chart. Fill in the answer.

1. Which service-providing industry will most likely have the largest increase in employment?
   (A) Construction
   (B) Federal government
   (C) Health care and social assistance
   (D) Manufacturing
2. What percent of job growth will there be for teachers?
   (A) 5
   (B) 10
   (C) 15
   (D) 20
3. What is not true about manufacturing?
   (A) It's a goods-producing industry.
   (B) An increase in the percentage of change in employment is expected.
   (C) It will lose more jobs than Agriculture.
   (D) It will decrease by more than 5% by 2024.
4. According to the chart, which of the major industries listed below project the least growth from 2014–2024?
   (A) Agriculture
   (B) Federal government
   (C) Leisure and hospitality
   (D) none of the above

B Solve the problem. Give your opinion.

Kumio is a 40-year old man who was working as an electronic assembler at a large manufacturing company for 12 years. Last month Kumio and a large number of assemblers were laid off. He's thinking about getting a job in health care. He heard about a private training program that costs $2,500. He also heard about a low-cost program at a community college, but it takes longer. What should he do?

106 UNIT 8

2 Grammar connections: polite requests and offers

A Talk with a partner. Use the pictures to make and respond to requests for the situation. Then use the pictures to make and respond to offers for the situation. Take turns.

A Could you help me with this box?
B Sure.

A Let me move those books out of your way.
B Thanks! That'd be great!

B Talk with a partner. Look at the places in the box. Have a conversation in each place. Make a request or offer in each conversation. Take turns.

A It's dark in here. Would you mind helping me find my seat?
B I'd be glad to. Follow me.
A OK, thanks.

UNIT 8 107

Test-taking Skills

Prepares students for standardized tests like the CASAS by familiarizing them with bubble answer format.

Problem-solving Activity

Covers critical thinking and soft skills – crucial for workplace readiness – and helps students meet WIOA requirements.

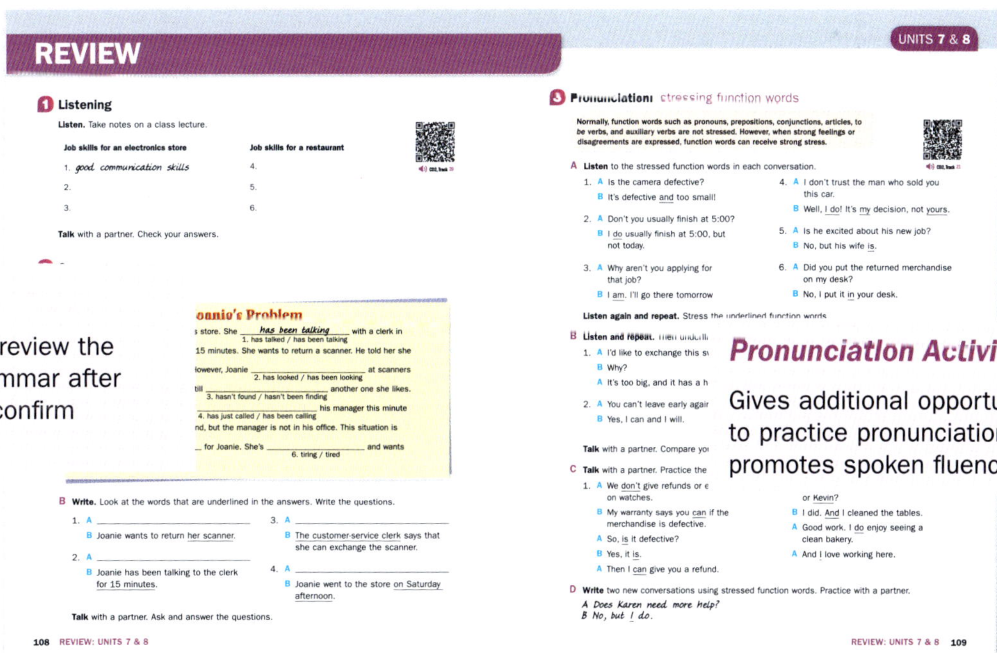

REVIEW

UNITS 7 & 8

1 Listening

Listen. Take notes on a class lecture.

Job skills for an electronics store	Job skills for a restaurant
1. *good communication skills*	4.
2.	5.
3.	6.

Talk with a partner. Check your answers.

B Write. Look at the words that are underlined in the answers. Write the questions.

1. A ______ B Joanie wants to return her scanner.
2. A ______ B Joanie has been talking to the clerk for 15 minutes.
3. A ______ B The customer-service clerk says that she can exchange the scanner.
4. A ______ B Joanie went to the store on Saturday afternoon.

Talk with a partner. Ask and answer the questions.

108 REVIEW: UNITS 7 & 8

3 Pronunciation: stressing function words

A Listen to the stressed function words in each conversation.

1. A Is the camera defective? B It's defective and too small!
2. A Don't you usually finish at 5:00? B I do usually finish at 5:00, but not today.
3. A Why aren't you applying for that job? B I am. I'll go there tomorrow.
4. A I don't trust the man who sold you this car. B Well, I do! It's my decision, not yours.
5. A Is he excited about his new job? B No, but his wife is.
6. A Did you put the returned merchandise on my desk? B No, I put it in your desk.

D Write two new conversations using stressed function words. Practice with a partner.

A Does Karen need more help?
B No, but I do.

REVIEW: UNITS 7 & 8 109

Review Pages

Allows students to review the vocabulary and grammar after every two units to confirm retention.

Pronunciation Activities

Gives additional opportunities to practice pronunciation and promotes spoken fluency.

CORRELATIONS

UNIT	CASAS Competencies	Florida Adult ESOL Low Beginning	LAUSD ESL Beginning Low Competencies
Unit 1 Personal information Pages 6–17	0.1.2, 0.1.4, 0.1.5, 0.1.6, 0.2.1, 0.2.4, 4.1.7, 4.1.8, 4.4.2, 4.5.2, 4.5.5, 4.6.1, 4.7.3, 4.8.1, 4.8.2, 7.1.1, 7.1.4, 7.2.3, 7.2.4, 7.4.1, 7.4.2, 7.4.5, 7.4.9, 7.5.1	5.01.01, 5.01.02, 5.01.03, 5.01.04, 5.03.06, 5.03.10, 5.03.11	A Course: I. 1b II. 5a VIII. 45 B Course: I. 1a, 1b, 1c II. 6a, 6b VIII. 35, 37, 38
Unit 2 At school Pages 18–31	0.1.2, 0.1.5, 0.1.6, 0.2.1, 0.2.4, 2.3.1, 2.3.2, 2.5.5, 2.7.6, 4.1.4, 4.1.7, 4.1.9, 4.4.1, 4.6.1, 4.8.1, 4.8.2, 4.9.1, 6.0.1, 7.1.1, 7.1.4, 7.2.1, 7.2.2, 7.4.1, 7.4.2, 7.4.5, 7.5.1	5.01.01, 5.01.13, 5.03.05, 5.03.06, 5.03.11, 5.03.12	A Course: II. 5a, 5b III. 11a, 11b, 11c, 15 VIII. 42, 43 B Course: II. 5, 9a III. 10a, 10b, 10c VII. 29 VIII. 35, 37, 38, 39
Unit 3 Friends and family Pages 32–43	0.1.2, 0.1.3, 0.1.4, 0.1.5, 0.2.2, 0.2.4, 4.4.3, 4.8.1, 4.8.2, 6.0.1, 6.6.5, 7.1.1, 7.1.4, 7.2.1, 7.2.3, 7.5.1, 7.5.5, 7.5.6, 8.3.1, 8.3.2	5.01.01, 5.01.03, 5.02.08, 5.03.06, 5.03.11, 5.05.01	A Course: I. 1b II. 5a, 6 B Course: I. 2 II. 5, 6a, 7 III. 11 VIII. 37, 38
Unit 4 Health Pages 44–57	0.1.2, 0.1.3, 0.1.4, 0.1.5, 0.2.2, 0.2.4, 4.4.3, 4.8.1, 4.8.2, 6.0.1, 6.6.5, 7.1.1, 7.1.4, 7.2.1, 7.2.3, 7.5.1, 7.5.4, 7.5.5, 7.5.6, 8.3.1, 8.3.2	5.01.01, 5.01.03, 5.03.06, 5.03.11, 5.05.01	A Course: I. 1b B Course: II. 6c VI. 27 VIII. 37
Unit 5 Around town Pages 58–69	0.1.2, 0.1.5, 0.1.6, 0.2.4, 2.7.3, 3.1.3, 3.5.8, 3.5.9, 4.1.4, 4.8.1, 6.0.1, 7.1.1, 7.1.3, 7.1.4, 7.2.1, 7.2.2, 7.4.1, 7.4.2, 7.4.3, 7.5.1, 7.5.2, 7.5.5, 8.3.1, 8.3.2	5.01.01, 5.02.07, 5.03.02, 5.03.06, 5.03.11	A Course: I. 1b VIII. 44 B Course: II. 6c III. 12, 13 VIII. 37, 40

For more details and correlations to other state standards, go to: www.cambridge.org/ventures/correlations

NRS Educational Functioning Level Descriptors	English Language Proficiency and College and Career Readiness Standards
Interpretive ■ Determine the main idea and key details in a conversation about personal strengths. ■ Determine the main idea and key details in a reading about multiple intelligences. ■ Use *prefixes* and *roots* to determine the meaning of vocabulary related to personality types. ■ Determine the main idea and key details in a diagram about left-brain and right-brain functions. **Productive** ■ Deliver a short oral presentation that describes classmates. ■ Compose a paragraph about and provide examples for one personality type. ■ Report on an Internet research project to find careers that match a given personality type. **Interactive** ■ Participate in conversations about aptitudes and intelligent types. ■ Discuss men's and women's aptitudes in different areas of intelligence.	ELP Standards 1–10 Reading Anchors 1, 2, 4, 5, 6, 7, 8, 9, 10 Speaking & Listening Anchors 1, 2, 3, 4, 6
Interpretive ■ Determine the main topic and key details in a conversation about future educational plans. ■ Determine the main topic and key details in a written text about an immigrant family's success story. ■ Use a dictionary or thesaurus to determine the meaning of vocabulary about planning for success. ■ State an opinion and cite evidence to support it. **Productive** ■ Write a paragraph that has a topic sentence, examples, and a concluding sentence about someone you know who is successful. ■ Deliver a short oral presentation about a classmate's course registration. ■ Report on a short research project about a class from an adult school or community college. ■ Identify and use academic words in a reading about planning for success. **Interactive** ■ Participate in conversations about planning for success. ■ Discuss with a partner each other's writing about a person you know who is successful.	ELP Standards 1–10 Reading Anchors 1, 2, 4, 5, 6, 7, 8, 9, 10 Speaking & Listening Anchors 1, 2, 3, 4, 6
Interpretive ■ Determine the main topic and key details in a conversation about a student's absence. ■ Determine the main topic and key details in a written text about immigrant families. ■ Use context clues to determine the meaning of vocabulary about friends and family. ■ State an opinion and cite evidence to support it. **Productive** ■ Write a paragraph about differences between you and your parents or you and your children that has a transition between the two parts of your paragraph. ■ Deliver a short oral presentation about a classmate's life as a teenager. ■ Report on a short research project about rules that children should follow at home. ■ Identify and use academic words in a reading about parents and children. **Interactive** ■ Participate in conversations about the teenage years. ■ Discuss with a partner each other's writing about parents and children.	ELP Standards 1–10 Reading Anchors 1, 2, 4, 5, 6, 7, 8, 9, 10 Speaking & Listening Anchors 1, 2, 3, 4, 6
Interpretive ■ Determine the main topic and key details in a conversation about advice for coping with stress. ■ Determine the main topic and key details in a written text about stress. ■ Use *suffixes* to determine the meaning of vocabulary about stressful situations. ■ State an opinion and cite evidence to support it. **Productive** ■ Write a paragraph about how you cope with stress giving three examples and details for each example. ■ Deliver a short oral presentation about a classmate's situation that didn't go as planned. ■ Report on a short Internet research project about how to cope with anxiety before and during a test. ■ Identify and use academic words in a reading about stressful situations. **Interpretive** ■ Participate in conversations about a situation that didn't go as planned. ■ Discuss with a partner each other's writing about how to cope with stress.	ELP Standards 1–10 Reading Anchors 1, 2, 4, 5, 6, 7, 8, 9, 10 Speaking & Listening Anchors 1, 2, 3, 4, 6
Interpretive ■ Determine the main topic and key details in a conversation about responsibilities for volunteer jobs. ■ Determine the main topic and key details in a written text about a volunteer program for the blind. ■ Use context clues to determine the meaning of vocabulary about community involvement. ■ State an opinion and cite evidence to support it. **Productive** ■ Write a paragraph about someone you know who made a difference in your life or someone else's life that includes specific details that answer *wh-* questions. ■ Deliver a short oral presentation about a classmate's volunteer experiences. ■ Report on a short research project about ways that people have helped you. ■ Identify and use academic words in a reading about community involvement. **Interactive** ■ Participate in conversations about volunteer experiences. ■ Discuss with a partner each other's writing about someone who made a difference in your life.	ELP Standards 1–10 Reading Anchors 1, 2, 4, 5, 6, 7, 8, 9, 10 Speaking & Listening Anchors 1, 2, 3, 4, 6

UNIT	CASAS Competencies	Florida Adult ESOL Low Beginning	LAUSD ESL Beginning Low Competencies
Unit 6 **Time** Pages 70–81	0.1.2, 0.1.5, 0.1.6, 0.2.4, 1.1.3, 1.3.1, 1.4.1, 1.7.4, 2.1.1, 2.2.3, 4.5.1, 4.5.2, 4.5.5, 4.8.1, 6.0.1, 7.1.1, 7.1.4, 7.2.1, 7.2.3, 7.2.4, 7.2.5, 7.4.1, 7.4.2, 7.4.8, 7.5.1, 7.7.1	5.01.01, 5.01.02, 5.01.03, 5.03.02, 5.03.06, 5.03.11, 5.03.15	A Course: II. 5a B Course: II. 6a, 6b VIII. 37, 38
Unit 7 **Shopping** Pages 84–95	0.1.2, 0.1.3, 0.1.5, 0.1.6, 1.2.2, 1.3.1, 1.3.3, 1.4.1, 1.6.3, 1.7.1, 4.8.1, 6.0.1, 7.1.1, 7.1.4, 7.2.1, 7.2.3, 7.2.5, 7.4.2, 7.4.3, 7.4.8, 7.5.1	5.01.01, 5.03.02, 5.03.06, 5.03.11, 5.04.02, 5.04.09	A Course: IV. 21a B Course: VIII. 37
Unit 8 **Work** Pages 96–107	0.1.2, 0.1.3, 0.1.5, 0.1.7, 0.2.4, 2.3.1, 2.3.2, 2.4.1, 4.1.2, 4.1.6, 4.1.7, 4.1.8, 4.4.1, 4.4.2, 4.4.3, 4.4.4, 4.5.2, 4.5.5, 4.6.2, 4.7.3, 4.8.1, 4.8.2, 6.0.1, 7.1.1, 7.1.4, 7.2.1, 7.2.3, 7.2.7, 7.3.1, 7.3.2, 7.4.1, 7.4.2, 7.4.5, 7.5.1, 7.5.2, 7.5.6	5.01.01, 5.01.03, 5.03.02, 5.03.03, 5.03.06, 5.03.07, 5.03.11, 5.03.13	A Course: I. 4b VII. 34, 38a, 38b, 38c, 41 B Course: VIII. 37, 38, 41
Unit 9 **Daily living** Pages 110–121	0.1.2, 0.1.5, 1.4.1, 2.2.3, 2.3.3, 2.7.3, 4.8.1, 5.6.1, 5.7.1, 7.1.1, 7.2.1, 7.2.2, 7.2.6, 7.3.1, 7.3.2, 7.3.4, 7.4.2, 7.4.3, 7.5.1, 7.5.4, 8.3.1	5.01.01, 5.01.03, 5.02.02, 5.03.06, 5.03.11	B Course: II. 7 VIII. 37, 38
Unit 10 **Free time** Pages 122–133	0.1.1, 0.1.2, 0.1.5, 0.1.6, 0.2.4, 1.1.1, 1.1.5, 2.3.2, 2.5.7, 2.7.1, 2.7.2, 2.7.4, 4.5.2, 4.5.5, 4.8.1, 6.0.1, 7.1.1, 7.1.4, 7.2.1, 7.2.3, 7.2.4, 7.2.6, 7.4.1, 7.4.2, 7.4.4, 7.4.5, 7.5.1, 7.5.6	5.01.01, 5.01.03, 5.02.03, 5.03.06, 5.03.11	A Course: II. 5b B Course: II. 6b, 7, 9 VIII. 37, 38, 40

For more details and correlations to other state standards, go to: www.cambridge.org/ventures/correlations

NRS Educational Functioning Level Descriptors	English Language Proficiency and College and Career Readiness Standards
Interpretive ■ Determine the main topic and key details in a conversation about people's opinions about technology. ■ Determine the main topic and key details in a written text about the impact of technology. ■ Use context clues and parts of speech to determine the meaning of vocabulary about time and technology. ■ State an opinion and cite evidence to support it. **Productive** ■ Write a paragraph about a time-saving device that includes both advantages and disadvantages. ■ Deliver a short oral presentation about a classmate's time-saving device. ■ Report on a short Internet research project about a time-saving device you have or would like to have. ■ Identify and use academic words in a reading about time and technology. **Interactive** ■ Participate in conversations about time saving tools and devices. ■ Discuss with a partner each other's writing about a time-saving device.	ELP Standards 1–10 Reading Anchors 1, 2, 4, 5, 6, 7, 8, 9, 10 Speaking & Listening Anchors 1, 2, 3, 4, 6
Interpretive ■ Determine the main topic and key details in a conversation about returning merchandise. ■ Determine the main topic and key details in a written text about being a smart shopper. ■ Use *compound nouns* to determine the meaning of vocabulary about buying and returning merchandise. ■ State an opinion and cite evidence to support it. **Productive** ■ Write a paragraph that has transitions words to signal your list of reasons about why you should shop online. ■ Deliver a short oral presentation about a classmate's purchase. ■ Report on a short research project about the return policy for three stores. ■ Identify and use academic words in a reading about shopping. **Interactive** ■ Participate in conversations about a purchase you made. ■ Discuss with a partner each other's writing about shopping online.	ELP Standards 1–10 Reading Anchors 1, 2, 4, 5, 6, 7, 8, 9, 10 Speaking & Listening Anchors 1, 2, 3, 4, 6
Interpretive ■ Determine the main topic and key details in a conversation about a work problem and solution. ■ Determine the main topic and key details in a written text about job skills. ■ Use *prefixes* and *roots* to determine the meaning of vocabulary about success at work. ■ State an opinion and cite evidence to support it. **Productive** ■ Write a cover letter for a real or imaginary job that you are interested in that has at least two examples of your skills and experiences. ■ Deliver a short oral presentation about a classmate's experiences. ■ Report on a short Internet research project about how to write a good cover letter. ■ Identify and use academic words in a reading about success at work. **Interactive** ■ Participate in conversations about experiences. ■ Discuss with a partner each other's writing about their skills and experiences.	ELP Standards 1–10 Reading Anchors 1, 2, 4, 5, 6, 7, 8, 9, 10 Speaking & Listening Anchors 1, 2, 3, 4, 6
Interpretive ■ Determine the main topic and key details in a conversation about environmental problems and solutions. ■ Determine the main topic and key details in a written text about how all things are connected. ■ Use *antonyms* to determine the meaning of vocabulary about living green. ■ State an opinion and cite evidence to support it. **Productive** ■ Write a paragraph about an environmental problem in your city or community explaining the causes and their effects. ■ Deliver a short oral presentation about cause and effect relationships. ■ Report on a short research project about ways your school could be green. ■ Identify and use academic words in a reading about living green. **Interactive** ■ Participate in conversations about cause and effect relationships. ■ Discuss with a partner each other's writing about environmental problems.	ELP Standards 1–10 Reading Anchors 1, 2, 4, 5, 6, 7, 8, 9, 10 Speaking & Listening Anchors 1, 2, 3, 4, 6
Interpretive ■ Determine the main topic and key details in a conversation about differences in customs. ■ Determine the main topic and key details in a written text about special birthdays around the world. ■ Use context clues to determine the meaning of vocabulary about celebrations. ■ State an opinion and cite evidence to support it. **Productive** ■ Write a paragraph about your favorite holiday or celebration that has a conclusion that relates the celebration to your personal life. ■ Deliver a short oral presentation about a classmate's hopes for you. ■ Report on a short Internet research project about a holiday or celebration in another country. ■ Identify and use academic words in a reading about celebrations. **Interactive** ■ Participate in conversations about hopes and wishes. ■ Discuss with a partner each other's writing about favorite holidays and celebrations.	ELP Standards 1–10 Reading Anchors 1, 2, 4, 5, 6, 7, 8, 9, 10 Speaking & Listening Anchors 1, 2, 3, 4, 6

MEET THE **VENTURES** AUTHOR TEAM

(Top row) Dennis Johnson, K. Lynn Savage; (bottom row) Gretchen Bitterlin, Donna Price, and Sylvia G. Ramirez. Together, the *Ventures* author team has more than 200 years teaching ESL as well as other roles that support adult immigrants and refugees, from teacher's aide to dean.

Gretchen Bitterlin has taught Citizenship, ESL, and family literacy through the San Diego Community College District and served as coordinator of the non-credit Continuing Education ESL program. She was an item writer for CASAS tests and chaired the task force that developed the TESOL Adult Education Program Standards. She is recipient of The President's Distinguished Leadership Award from her district and co-author of *English for Adult Competency*. Gretchen holds an MA in TESOL from the University of Arizona.

Dennis Johnson had his first language-teaching experience as a Peace Corps volunteer in South Korea. Following that teaching experience, he became an in-country ESL trainer. After returning to the United States, he began teaching credit and non-credit ESL at City College of San Francisco. As ESL site coordinator, he has provided guidance to faculty in selecting textbooks. He is the author of *Get Up and Go* and co-author of *The Immigrant Experience*. Dennis is the demonstration teacher on the *Ventures Professional Development DVD*. Dennis holds an MA in music from Stanford University.

Donna Price began her ESL career teaching EFL in Madagascar. She is currently associate professor of ESL and vocational ESL / technology resource instructor for the Continuing Education Program, San Diego Community College District. She has served as an author and a trainer for CALPRO, the California Adult Literacy Professional Development Project, co-authoring training modules on contextualizing and integrating workforce skills into the ESL classroom. She is a recipient of the TESOL Newbury House Award for Excellence in Teaching, and she is author of *Skills for Success*. Donna holds an MA in linguistics from San Diego State University.

Sylvia G. Ramirez is a Professor Emeritus at MiraCosta College, a teacher educator, writer, consultant, and a recipient of the California Hayward award for excellence in education, honoring her teaching and professional activities. She is an online instructor for the TESOL Core Certificate. Her MA is in education / counseling from Point Loma University, and she has certificates in ESOL and in online teaching.

K. Lynn Savage first taught English in Japan. She began teaching ESL at City College of San Francisco in 1974, where she has taught all levels of non-credit ESL and has served as Vocational ESL Resource Teacher. She has trained teachers for adult education programs around the country as well as abroad. She chaired the committee that developed *ESL Model Standards for Adult Education Programs* (California, 1992) and is the author, co-author, and editor of many ESL materials including *Crossroads Café*, *Teacher Training through Video*, *Parenting for Academic Success*, *Building Life Skills*, *Picture Stories*, *May I Help You?*, and *English That Works*. Lynn holds an MA in TESOL from Teachers College, Columbia University.

TO THE STUDENT

Welcome to ***Ventures***! The dictionary says that "venture" means a risky or daring journey. Its meaning is similar to the word "adventure." Learning English is certainly a journey and an adventure. We hope that this book helps you in your journey of learning English to fulfill your goals. We believe that this book will prepare you for academic and career courses and give you the English skills you need to get a job or promotion, go to college, or communicate better in your community. The audio, grammar presentations, workbooks, and free Internet practice on the Arcade will help you improve your English outside class. Setting your personal goals will also help. Take a few minutes and write your goals below.

Good luck in your studies!

The Author Team
Gretchen Bitterlin
Dennis Johnson
Donna Price
Sylvia Ramirez
K. Lynn Savage

My goals for studying English

1. My first goal for studying English:	Date: ______
2. My second goal for studying English:	Date: ______
3. My third goal for studying English:	Date: ______

WELCOME

1 Meet your classmates

A Look at the picture. What do you see?

B What are the people doing?

1

2

3

4

2 Study habits and strategies

A **Listen.** Check (✓) the adjectives, study habits, and strategies you hear.

☐ active	☐ creative	☐ outgoing	☐ study in a group
☐ artistic	☐ fun-loving	☐ patient	☐ study while moving
☐ confident	☑ make vocabulary cards	☐ reliable	☐ use a dictionary

CD1, Track 2

Listen again. Check your answers.

B **Read** the list of study habits and strategies. Which ones have you tried? Check (✓) your answers on the chart. Then tell a partner about your answers.

Do you ever . . .?	Yes, I do.	No, I don't.
1. make vocabulary cards		
2. use a dictionary to learn new words		
3. ask a stranger a question in English		
4. study English with a friend		
5. use a to-do list to organize your time		
6. try to guess the meaning of new words		

C **Talk** with your classmates. Complete the chart.

A Song-mi, do you watch TV in English every day?
B Yes, I do.

Find a classmate who . . .	Name
1. watches TV in English every day	
2. asks questions when he or she doesn't understand something	
3. underlines important information in textbooks	
4. likes to sing songs	
5. speaks English at work	
6. sets goals for learning English	

Talk with your class. Ask and answer questions.

Who watches TV in English every day?

Song Mi does.

Manny does, too.

3 Verb tense review (past continuous and simple past)

A **Listen** to each sentence. Circle the verb form you hear.

1. listened	was listening	5. played	was playing
2. heard	was hearing	6. did	were doing
3. watched	was watching	7. drove	were driving
4. woke	were waking	8. vacuumed	were vacuuming

CD1, Track 3

Listen again. Check your answers.

Use the simple past to talk about an activity that began and ended at a particular time in the past: *yesterday, last night, a few days ago, in 2016.*
Use the past continuous to talk about an activity that was happening, but not completed, at a point of time in the past. Example: *I went to bed at 10:00. The phone rang at 10:30. I was sleeping when the phone rang.*

B **Read.** Complete the story. Use the correct verb form.

Last summer, my sister and I *drove* (1. drive) from Tucson to Phoenix. On our way, it ______ (2. be) very windy, and there ______ (3. be) dark clouds in the sky. We ______ (4. travel) slowly when suddenly we ______ (5. see) huge clouds of dust in the air. The sky ______ (6. turn) brown, and we couldn't see anything. It ______ (7. be) very scary.

While we ______ (8. drive), we ______ (9. look) for a place to turn off the road. Finally we ______ (10. come) to an exit and ______ (11. get) off the main road. We ______ (12. go) into a restaurant. The dust finally ______ (13. go) away while we ______ (14. wait) at the restaurant.

Listen and check your answers.

CD1, Track 4

C **Talk** with a partner. Ask and answer questions.

1. Talk about a time you were in bad weather. Describe the weather. Explain what happened.
2. What were you doing before the bad weather started?
3. What did you do while the bad weather was happening?

4 Verb tense review (3 uses of the present perfect)

A Listen and write the words you hear. Use the words from the word bank.

a few times | already | lately | ~~recently~~ | several times | since | yet

CD1, Track 5

1. recently
2. ______
3. ______
4. ______
5. ______
6. ______
7. ______
8. ______
9. ______
10. ______

Use	Example	Clue words
Events that began in the past and are still happening now	Jaime has studied for two years.	for, since
Events that have happened before now but the time is not clear	Sara has already seen that movie.	already, yet, recently, lately
Events that were repeated before now	Boun has flown on a plane many times.	many times, a few times, several times

Listen and check your answers.

B Read. Complete the conversations. Use the present perfect form of the verb in parentheses.

1. **A** Have you practiced English outside of class lately? (practice)
   B No, I haven't. I'm too shy.
2. **A** How many times ______ you ______ your friends today? (text)
   B I ______ my friends at least seven times so far today.
3. **A** How many times ______ you ______ Mexican food? (eat)
   B I ______ Mexican food many times. I love it!
4. **A** ______ Daniel ______ his homework yet? (do)
   B No, he ______. He needs to finish it before tomorrow.
5. **A** How long ______ you ______ at this school? (study)
   B I ______ at this school for three months.

Listen and check your answers.

CD1, Track 6

C Talk with your classmates. Ask and answer the questions.

1. Have you ever volunteered? What did you do?
2. Have you gone dancing recently? If yes, where did you go dancing?
3. Have you ever asked a stranger a question in English? What did you ask?
4. How long have you been a student at this school?
5. How many times have you flown in an airplane?

UNIT 1 PERSONAL INFORMATION

Lesson A Listening

1 Before you listen

A What do you see?

B What is happening?

2 Listen

A Listen and answer the questions.

1. Who are the speakers?
2. What are they talking about?

CD1, Track 7

B Listen again. Complete the chart.

CD1, Track 7

Family member	Good at	Example
1. Brenda	*math*	*got first place in a math contest*
2. Gerry		
3. Danny		
4. Nina		

3 After you listen

A Read. Complete the story.

aptitude	bright	fixing	mathematical	musical
brain	contest	gifted in	mechanical	well

Emily stops by Nina's house on her way home from jogging. They talk about Nina's three children. Brenda is very *mathematical* (1). She's just won a math ______ (2) at school. When Emily calls Brenda a ______ (3), Nina says that all her children are ______ (4), but in different ways. Gerry isn't ______ (5) math, but he's very ______ (6). He plays and sings very ______ (7) and even writes music. Danny is the ______ (8) one in the family. He's good at ______ (9) old cars. Emily thinks that Nina is also smart because she is such a good cook. Emily has no ______ (10) for cooking.

Listen and check your answers.

CD1, Track 8

B Discuss. Talk with your classmates.

1. How are the three children different?
2. Do you think that one child is more intelligent than the others? Why or why not?
3. Do you think that Nina is a good parent? Why or why not?

Lesson B Parts of speech

1 Grammar focus: nouns, verbs, adjectives, and adverbs

Adjectives describe nouns and answer the question *What kind of?* (*What kind of driver is he?*). Adverbs describe verbs and answer the question *How?* (*How does he drive?*). Most adverbs end in *-ly*, but some adverbs are irregular.

Watch

ADJECTIVE + NOUN			VERB + ADVERB		
Bill is a	**slow**	**driver.**	He	**drives**	**slowly**.
Helen is an	**intelligent**	**girl.**	She	**talks**	**intelligently**.
It was a very	**easy**	**game.**	I	**won**	very **easily**.
You're a	**good**	**dancer.**	You	**dance**	**well**.

Regular

Adjective	Adverb
bad	badly
easy	easily
intelligent	intelligently

Irregular

Adjective	Adverb
fast	fast
good	well
hard	hard

2 Practice

A **Write.** Complete the sentences with adjectives or adverbs. Underline the nouns and verbs that they describe.

1. Carol speaks very _intelligently_ (intelligent). She's a _bright_ (bright) girl.
2. That isn't a ______ (bad) guitar, but he's playing it ______ (bad).
3. Benny is an ______ (excellent) cook. His dinner last night was ______ (fantastic).
4. The mechanic did a ______ (good) job on my car. Now it runs ______ (perfect).
5. You danced very ______ (skillful) in the dance contest. You're a ______ (wonderful) dancer!
6. I don't type very ______ (fast). I can't move my fingers very ______ (quick).
7. That writing test was ______ (hard). Writing isn't an ______ (easy) subject for me.
8. You sang that song ______ (beautiful)! I didn't know you could sing so ______ (good)!
9. Your report is ______ (great). You wrote it very ______ (clear).
10. I work ______ (slow). I'm a ______ (careful) worker.

Listen and check your answers.

CD1, Track 9

B **Talk** with a partner. Ask and answer questions about the pictures. Use the adjective or adverb form of the words in the box.

> **A** What kind of artist is he?
> **B** He's a skillful artist.

> **A** How does he paint?
> **B** He paints beautifully.

beautiful	effective	fast	professional	terrible
careful	excellent	good	skillful	wonderful

1. artist / paint

2. seamstress / sew

3. driver / drive

4. swimmer / swim

5. carpenter / work

6. singer / sing

7. dancers / dance

8. speaker / speak

Write sentences about the people.

He's a skillful artist. He paints beautifully.

3 Communicate

A **Work** in a small group. Ask and answer the questions.

1. What kind of student are you?
2. How do you speak English?
3. What can you do very well?
4. What is something you do badly?
5. What kind of worker are you?
6. What can you do perfectly?
7. What do you do very fast?
8. What kind of shopper are you?

B **Share** information about your classmates.

> Armando says he's an excellent student.

Lesson C Noun clauses

1 Grammar focus: *that* clauses as objects

A clause is a group of words that has a subject and a verb. Sometimes a noun clause is used as the object of a sentence. It is called an *object clause*. An object clause follows an introductory clause and has the form *that* + subject + verb.

INTRODUCTORY CLAUSE	OBJECT CLAUSE
Emily realizes	**that Brenda has a good brain.**
People say	**that Gerry plays the guitar very well.**
Do you think	**that people are smart in different ways**?
Do you feel	**that you're smart**?

Introductory clauses

I think . . .	Do you think . . . ?	I feel . . .	Do you feel . . . ?
He realizes . . .	Does he realize . . . ?	People believe . . .	Do people believe . . . ?

Watch

USEFUL LANGUAGE

When speaking, we frequently omit *that* before a noun clause.

People think that she's smart.

People think she's smart.

2 Practice

A Write. Write the words in the correct order. Make a sentence with an object clause. Circle the object clause in your sentence.

1. there/ intelligence / that / are / Do / many / you / of / kinds / believe / ?

   Do you believe (that there are many kinds of intelligence)?
2. think / interesting / has / I / an / Nina / family / .

   ____
3. that / teachers / she / very / Brenda's / gifted / agree / is / .

   ____
4. Do / Nina / think / very / cooks / you / that / well / ?

   ____
5. become / Gerry / Many / famous / believe / a / will / people / musician /.

   ____
6. didn't / Danny / for / has / that / I / aptitude / cars / fixing / an / realize / .

   ____
7. are / you / Do / that / very / skills / feel / important / mechanical / ?

   ____
8. her / that / Nina / very / children / are / knows / different / .

   ____

Listen and check your answers.

CD1, Track 10

B **Talk** with a partner. Look at the picture. Answer the questions. Use introductory clauses from the box.

I believe . . . I suppose . . . I think . . . I'd say . . . I'm sure . . .

A I think (that) Robert is about 26 years old.

B I'd say (that) Robert is only 20.

1. How old are they?
2. Where are they going?
3. Where are they coming from?
4. What do they do for a living?
5. What do they like to do?
6. What are they thinking about?
7. What are they good at?
8. What aren't they good at?

Write sentences about your opinions.

I think that Robert is about 26 years old.

3 Communicate

A **Work** in a small group. Give your opinions. Use *I believe*, *I think*, *I'd say*, *I don't believe*, and other introductory clauses.

1. Are women more talkative than men?
2. Are boys better at math and science than girls?
3. Are men more mechanical than women?
4. Are women more musical than men?
5. Are men more interested in sports than women?
6. Can women do the same jobs as men?

USEFUL LANGUAGE
I (totally) agree with you.
I (strongly) disagree.

CULTURE NOTE
Studies have shown that girls and boys in the United States have a similar aptitude for math and science when they start elementary school.

B **Share** your classmates' opinions.

Marta thinks that women are more talkative than men.

Use *that* clauses as objects.

Lesson D Reading

1 Before you read

Talk with a partner. Look at the reading tip. Answer the questions.

1. What is this article about?
2. According to the article, how many ways are there to be smart?

> Before you begin reading, **skim**. Look at the title, headings, pictures, and boldfaced words to get a general idea of what the reading is about.

2 Read

Read the magazine article. Listen and read again.

CD1, Track 11

Many Ways to be SMART

Josh is a star on the school baseball team. He gets Ds and Fs on all his math tests. His brother Frank can't catch, throw, or hit a baseball, but he easily gets As in math. Which boy do you think is more intelligent? Howard Gardner, a professor of education at Harvard University, would say that Josh and Frank are both smart, but in different ways. His theory of multiple intelligences identifies nine different "intelligences" to explain the way people understand, experience, and learn about the world around them.

Verbal / Linguistic

Some people are good with words. They prefer to learn by reading, listening, and speaking.

Visual / Spatial

These "picture people" are often good at drawing or painting. They are sensitive to colors and designs.

Intrapersonal

Some people are "self smart." They can understand their own feelings and emotions. They often enjoy spending time alone.

Logical / Mathematical

These people have an aptitude for math. They like solving logic problems and puzzles.

Bodily / Kinesthetic

Some people are "body smart." They are often athletic. Kinesthetic learners learn best when they are moving.

Naturalist

These people are skilled in working with plants and animals in the natural world.

Musical / Rhythmical

These people are sensitive to sound, melodies, and rhythms. They are gifted in singing, playing instruments, or composing music.

Interpersonal

Certain people are "group smart." They easily understand other people. They are good at communicating and interacting with others.

Existential

Certain people are gifted in exploring deep questions about the meaning of life and death and ways to find inner peace.

According to Gardner, many people have several or even all of these intelligences, but most of us have one or two intelligences that are primary, or strongest.

3 After you read

A **Check** your understanding.

1. What is the main idea of this article?
2. Who is Howard Gardner and what is the name of his theory?
3. What are the nine intelligences that Professor Gardner identifies?
4. Explain how the illustrations in the article help the reader to understand each intelligence.
5. Susana is a vocational counselor at a community college. She volunteers at a senior center every Saturday. What do you think is her primary intelligence? Cite evidence in the reading to support your answer.
6. What words in the article help you to understand the meaning of *kinesthetic*?

B **Build** your vocabulary.

Understanding prefixes and roots of words will help you learn new words.

1. Find an example of each prefix or root in the reading. Write it on the chart.
2. Use a dictionary. Write the meaning of the words.
3. Guess the meaning of the prefixes and roots on the chart.

Prefixes	**Example from reading**	**Meaning of word**	**Meaning of prefix**
1. *intra-*	*intrapersonal*	*inside a person's mind or self*	*in, inside*
2. *inter-*			
3. *multi-*			
Roots			**Meaning of root**
4. *kine*			
5. *log*			
6. *prim*			
7. *vis*			

C **Talk** with a partner.

1. What is your primary intelligence?
2. What are good jobs for people with each of the following intelligences: intrapersonal, interpersonal, kinesthetic, logical, and visual?
3. In your opinion, are some intelligences more important than others? Explain your answer.
4. Which intelligence would you like to develop more in yourself?

For college and career readiness practice, see pages 136–138.

Evaluate content presented in diverse formats; use prefixes and roots to find the meaning of words

Lesson E Writing

1 Before you write

A **Write** *1* through *4* next to your strongest intelligences. (Your primary intelligence should be number 1.) Compare with your classmates.

_____ Verbal / Linguistic	_____ Visual / Spatial	_____ Intrapersonal
_____ Logical / Mathematical	_____ Bodily / Kinesthetic	_____ Naturalist
_____ Musical / Rhythmical	_____ Interpersonal	_____ Existential

B **Read** the writing tip. Then read the two paragraphs below. Circle the topic sentence and the concluding sentence in each paragraph.

> The topic sentence tells what the paragraph is about. A good paragraph has a topic sentence, supporting sentences and a concluding sentence.

1.

My strongest intelligence is mathematical. My parents say that I started counting before I was two years old. I've always liked to play games with numbers. I never forget my friends' birthdays or telephone numbers. I like to keep track of my monthly expenses so that I stay within my budget. Other people complain that balancing their checkbooks is hard, but I enjoy it. My aptitude for mathematics helps me in every part of my life.

2.

My strongest intelligence is kinesthetic. Since I was a child, I have loved to move my body. I've taken many types of dance classes, including ballet, modern, jazz, swing, salsa, and African. I can dance to any kind of music that I hear. My friends say that I'm a great dancer. I think I was born to move.

C **Work** with a partner. Complete the outlines of the two model paragraphs on page 14.

1. **Topic sentence** of 1st paragraph: ____________________

   Supporting details:

   - *started counting before age 2*
   - *like games with numbers*
   - *don't forget birthdays or phone numbers*
   - *keep track of expenses*
   - *enjoy balancing checkbook*

   Concluding sentence of 1st paragraph: ____________________

2. **Topic sentence** of 2nd paragraph: ____________________

   Supporting details:

   - ____________________
   - ____________________
   - ____________________
   - ____________________

   Concluding sentence of 2nd paragraph: ____________________

D **Plan** a paragraph about your primary intelligence. Make an outline like the ones in Exercise 1C to make notes on your ideas.

2 Write

Write a paragraph about your primary intelligence. Include a topic sentence, specific details to support it, and a concluding sentence. Use the paragraphs in Exercise 1B and the outlines in Exercise 1C and 1D to help you.

3 After you write

A **Check** your writing.

	Yes	No
1. My topic sentence tells what my paragraph is about.	☐	☐
2. I gave specific details to support my topic sentence.	☐	☐
3. My paragraph has a concluding sentence.	☐	☐

B **Share** your writing with a partner.

1. Take turns. Read your paragraph to a partner.
2. Comment on your partner's paragraph. Ask your partner a question about the paragraph. Tell your partner one thing you learned.

Lesson F Another view

1 Life-skills reading

Left-brain functions **Right-brain functions**

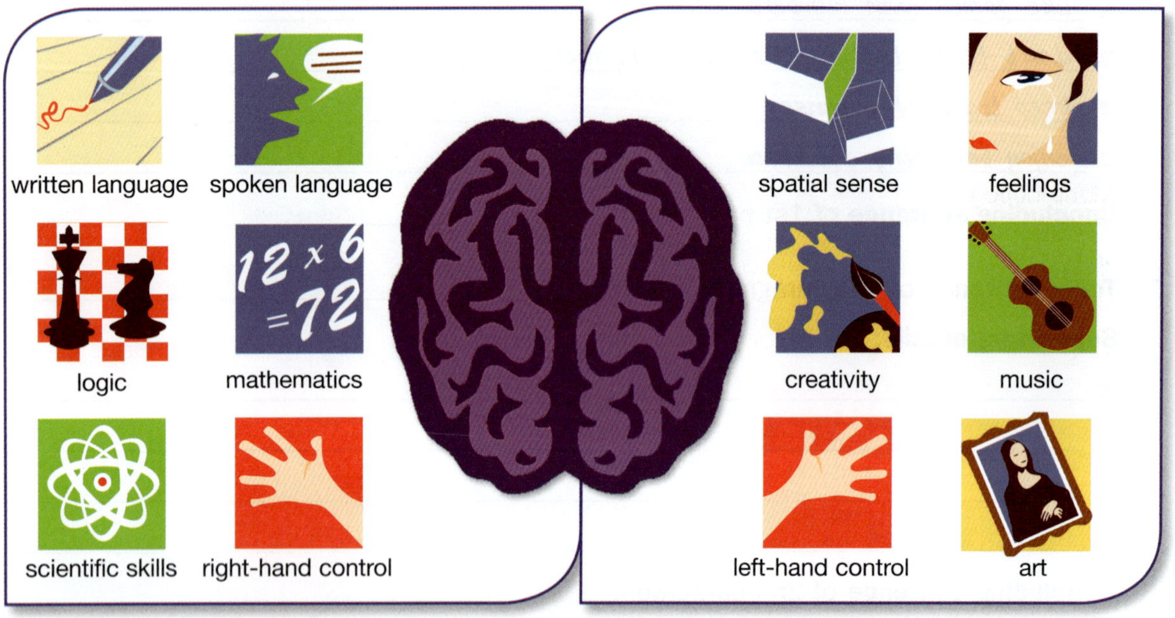

A **Read** the questions. Look at the diagram. Fill in the answer.

1. Which side of the brain controls verbal ability?
   - (●) left side
   - (B) right side
   - (C) both sides
   - (D) none of the above

2. What can you say about *left-brained* people?
   - (A) They are left-handed.
   - (B) They are very musical.
   - (C) They are artistic.
   - (D) They are logical.

3. Which abilities are right-brain functions?
   - (A) art
   - (B) music
   - (C) creativity
   - (D) all of the above

4. Which sentence is true?
   - (A) The left brain controls the left hand.
   - (B) The right brain controls the right hand.
   - (C) The left brain controls the right hand.
   - (D) none of the above

B **Solve** the problem. Give your opinion.

Jason is 17. He plays three musical instruments and is in a band with his friends. He wants to study music in college. His parents want him to be an engineer or a doctor. What should he do?

Grammar connections: *so* and *that*

Use *so* after certain verbs (*think, hope, believe, guess*) when you don't want to repeat the object clause.

	Yes answer	*No* answer
Do you think **that** math is essential to succeed at school?	Yes, I think **so**. (I think **that** math is essential to succeed at school.)	No, I don't think **so**. (I don't think **that** math is essential to succeed at school.)
Does Maria hope **that** robots will do most of the work in the future?	Yes, she hopes **so**. (She hopes **that** robots will do most of the work in the future.)	No, she hopes **not**. (She hopes **that** robots won't do most of the work in the future.)

Watch

A **Work** in a small group. Ask and answer the questions. Give reasons. Then complete the chart with your classmates' answers.

> **A** Do you think that there will be only one world language in the future?
>
> **B** No, I don't think so. There are too many people in small villages around the world. It would be difficult to get everyone to learn the same language.
>
> **C** Yes, I hope so . . .

Do you think that . . .	Lina (name)	(name)	(name)	(name)
1. it's easy to find a job?	No			
2. people waste too much time on the Internet?	Yes			
3. there will be only one world language in the future?	No			
4. more women will study science in the future?	Yes			
5. most people will live to be 100 in the future?	Yes			
6. smartphones will get cheaper?	No			

B **Talk** with a new partner. Ask and answer questions about your classmates.

> **A** Does Lina think that there will be only one world language?
>
> **B** No, she doesn't think so.

Scan a diagram for key details about brain function; use so in answers to replace object clauses

UNIT 2 AT SCHOOL

Lesson A Listening

1 Before you listen

A What do you see?

B What is happening?

1

2

La Costa Community College Course Schedule
Hospitality and Tourism Certificate Program

HOSP 100: Introduction to Hospitality and Tourism	**BUS 137:** Customer Service
Requirement: Pass English placement test.	**Requirement:** Pass HOSP 100.
Fall and spring T / Th 10:00–11:30 a.m. M / W 6:00–7:30 p.m.	Spring T / Th 8:00–9:30 a.m. (Online course also available.)
Room: T130	**Room:** B480

3

4

UNIT GOALS
Make educational plans **Write** a descriptive paragraph about a successful person
Scan a chart for the location of classes

2 Listen

A **Listen** and answer the questions.

1. Who are the speakers?
2. What are they talking about?

CD1, Track 12

B **Listen again.** Complete the chart.

1. Type of certificate	*Hospitality and Tourism*
2. Places of employment	
3. Number of required classes	
4. Time to complete the program	
5. Cost per unit	
6. Estimated cost to earn the certificate	

CD1, Track 12

3 After you listen

A **Read.** Complete the story.

bilingual	**deadline**	**industry**	**internship**	**qualify**
business	**high-paying**	**interpersonal**	**motivated**	**requirements**

Vasili hears a radio ad about the Hospitality and Tourism Certificate Program at La Costa Community College. The ad says graduates can find *high-paying* (1) jobs in the tourism ______ (2). Vasili goes to see his ESL counselor, Mrs. Ochoa. She tells him about the program ______ (3), which include an ______ (4) in a local tourism ______ (5). She also tells him about the ______ (6) for registration, and she says there is financial aid for students who ______ (7). Vasili is concerned about his English, but Mrs. Ochoa tells him not to worry. Vasili is ______ (8), he's very ______ (9), and he has good ______ (10) skills.

Listen and check your answers.

CD1, Track 13

B **Discuss.** Talk with your classmates. Is hospitality and tourism a good industry for Vasili? Would you like this type of career? Why or why not?

Lesson B The passive

1 Grammar focus: present passive

Use the passive voice to change the focus from *who* is doing something to *what* is being done. If the person or thing doing the action is important, use a *by* phrase.

ACTIVE	PRESENT PASSIVE
The college **gives** a placement test.	A placement test **is given** (by the college).
The college **offers** online classes every semester.	Online classes **are offered** (by the college) every semester.
Does the college **offer** financial aid?	**Is** financial aid **offered** (by the college)?
When **does** the college **arrange** internships?	When **are** internships **arranged** (by the college)?

Watch

2 Practice

A **Write.** Complete the sentences. Use the present passive.

1. **A** When ___is___ the English placement test ___given___ (give) to new students?
   B The English placement test ______________ (administer) a week before the first day of class.
2. **A** ______________ a math placement test also ______________ (require)?
   B No, a math placement test ______________ not ______________ (need).
3. **A** Where ______________ the financial aid office ______________ (locate)?
   B It ______________ (locate) next to the admissions office.
4. **A** Where ______________ the classes ______________ (hold)?
   B Most of the classes ______________ (hold) in the business building.
5. **A** ______________ classes ______________ (offer) at different times?
   B Yes. Both day and evening classes ______________ (offer).
6. **A** ______________ job placement services ______________ (provide) to graduates?
   B Yes. Job help ______________ (offer) to students who qualify.

Listen and check your answers. Then practice with a partner.

CD1, Track 14

B **Talk** with a partner. Ask and answer questions about the two courses on the flyer. Use the sentence prompts.

La Costa Community College Course Schedule
Hospitality and Tourism Certificate Program

HOSP 100: Introduction to Hospitality and Tourism	**BUS 137:** Customer Service
Requirement: Pass English placement test.	**Requirement:** Pass HOSP 100.
Fall and spring T / Th 10:00–11:30 a.m. M / W 6:00–7:30 p.m.	Spring T / Th 8:00–9:30 a.m. (Online course also available.)
Room: T130	**Room:** B480

Wh questions
Where / held

A Where is Hospitality 100 held?
B It's held in room T130.
B Where Is Business 137 held?
A It's held in room B480.

Yes / No questions
placement test / required

A Is a placement test required for Hospitality 100?
B Yes, a placement test is required.
B Is a placement test required for Business 137?
A No, a placement test is not required for Business 137.

1. Where / hold
2. Which days / give
3. What time / schedule
4. When /offer
5. What /require
6. placement test / require
7. online course / offer
8. spring classes / hold
9. evening classes /give
10. prerequisite / require

3 Communicate

A **Work** with a partner. Role-play a conversation between a counselor and a student who wants to enroll in a certificate program at your school. Ask and answer questions about the topics below. Predict the answers a counselor would give.

- online courses
- required courses
- English or math placement tests
- location of classes
- internships
- financial aid
- job counseling

Student Are online courses offered in the certificate program?
Counselor No. Online courses are not offered in that program.
Student What about internships?
Counselor Internships are arranged for each student in the program.

B **Perform** your role play for the class.

Lesson C The passive

1 Grammar focus: infinitives after the passive

Some passive verbs are followed by infinitives.
Students **are told to arrive** early on the first day of class.
Everyone **is encouraged to attend** class regularly.
Are students **required to do** homework every night?
How often **are** students **expected to meet** with their counselors?

Verbs often followed by infinitives

advise	expect
allow	require
encourage	tell

Watch

2 Practice

A **Write** complete statements or questions. Use the present passive with infinitives.

1. applicants / expect / meet / all application deadlines.
   Applicants are expected to meet all application deadlines.
2. new students / tell / come early / for registration.
   ____
3. all new students / require / take / a writing test?
   ____
4. some students / advise / enroll / in an English composition class.
   ____
5. students / expect / attend / every class?
   ____
6. students / encourage / meet / with a counselor regularly.
   ____
7. when / participants / expect / complete / their internships?
   ____
8. students / require / earn / a grade of C or better in each course.
   ____
9. students / tell / study / with a partner and to go to tutoring often.
   ____
10. students / allow / retake / course / if they don't pass?
   ____

Listen and check your answers.

CD1, Track 15

B **Talk** with a partner. Read the flyer. One student asks a question in the passive about the flyer. Another answers in the passive.

Work Experience Program at La Costa Community College

Earn up to 4 units of college credit by participating in the program.

The program:

- requires you to attend an orientation session.
- allows you to work and get college credit at the same time.
- expects you to work at least 75 paid hours or 60 volunteer hours.
- encourages you to visit the website for more information.
- tells students to consider this opportunity.
- advises you to call the Career Center at 777-555-2222
- permits you to enroll at the orientation session.
- reminds you to call to reserve a spot at the orientation.
- asks you to tell other students about this opportunity.

CULTURE NOTE
Work experience programs exist in many U.S. colleges to help adult students get credit for past and present work experience.

USEFUL LANGUAGE
One meaning of *you* is *people in general.*

What are you required to attend?

You are required to attend an orientation session.

1. What / require / attend
2. What / allow / do
3. How long / expect / work
4. What / encourage / visit
5. What / tell / consider
6. Who / advise / call
7. What / permit / do
8. What / remind / do
9. Who / ask / tell

3 Communicate

A **Work** with a partner. Read the announcement below. Ask and answer questions about the enrollment information.

A Are students required to register early?

B No, but students are encouraged to register early.

Do you want to enroll this fall?

You must:	It's a good idea to:
• Meet with a counselor	• Register early (space is limited)
• Sign up for a placement test	• Find out about tutoring support
• Choose courses	• Inquire about financial aid
• Buy books	

B **Share** information with your classmates.

Lesson D Reading

1 Before you read

Talk with a partner. Look at the reading tip. Answer the questions.

1. Who is the newspaper article about?
2. What places are mentioned in the newspaper article?
3. How old is their son now?

Scan a reading to find specific information such as names, places, and key words.

2 Read

Read the newspaper article. Listen and read again.

CD1, Track 16

www.newyorknews.com

New York News

An Immigrant Family's Success Story

Choi and Lili Wei left China with their baby boy in the early 1990s. They were poor field workers in their native country, and they wanted their child to have the opportunities they lacked. They arrived in New York and found a one-bedroom apartment in a poor, unstable area. They could only afford a bicycle for transportation, yet they felt fortunate to have the chance to begin a new life in the United States.

Choi and Lili faced many obstacles because they couldn't speak English and had no skills. They found night work cleaning businesses and restaurants. They saved every penny, and after six years, they were able to buy a small restaurant of their own.

They were determined to learn English, get an education, and make a good life for their son. The couple sacrificed a great deal. They never went to the movies, never ate out, and hardly ever bought anything extra. In their free time, they attended English and citizenship classes. Both of them eventually earned their GED certificates. Choi then enrolled in college while Lili worked in the restaurant.

This past spring, Choi fulfilled a lifelong dream of graduating from college. Now he is registered in a master's degree program in business beginning this fall. And what about their "baby" boy? Their son, Peter, now 21, received a scholarship to a private university, where he is working on his own dream to become an architect.

Choi and Lili are proud to be models of the "American dream." Choi has this advice for other new immigrants: "Find your passion, make a plan to succeed, and don't ever give up."

3 After you read

A **Check** your understanding.

1. What is the main idea of this newspaper article? Support your choice with two examples from the text.
2. What obstacles did Choi and Lili face in the United States?
3. Explain the expression *saved every penny* as it is used in paragraph 2.
4. What were five specific things the Wei family did to make a better life for their son?
5. Read Choi's advice for new immigrants. How do you think his advice influenced his son?

B **Build** your vocabulary.

USEFUL LANGUAGE
A synonym is a word that has the same meaning.
big - large
nice - kind
job - occupation

1. In the reading passage, underline the words from the chart.
2. Use a dictionary or a thesaurus. Write the part of speech. Write a synonym for each word.

Word	Part of speech	Synonym
lacked	*verb*	*missed; didn't have*
unstable		
fortunate		
faced		
obstacles		
determined		
passion		

3. Work in a small group. Write sentences with the synonyms.

- ____________________
- ____________________
- ____________________
- ____________________
- ____________________
- ____________________
- ____________________

C **Talk** with a partner.

1. What is your definition of the "American Dream"?
2. Do you know a family like the Wei family? What is their success story?
3. What is your passion? What is your plan for success?

For college and career readiness practice, see pages 139–141.

Read closely to determine what the text says explicitly and to make logical inferences from the text; use a dictionary or thesaurus to identify synonyms

Lesson E Writing

1 Before you write

A **Talk** with your classmates. Answer the questions.

1. What is success? Is it only money?
2. Do you know a successful person?
3. What did the person do to become successful?
4. What was one obstacle to this person's success?

B **Read** the paragraph.

My Successful Cousin

My cousin, Daniel, is the most successful person I know, even though he has had many obstacles on his road to success. First of all, his parents died in an automobile accident when he was 17 years old. Daniel needed to take care of his two younger brothers, so he quit school and found a job at a local supermarket. When his brothers were in school, he worked. At night, he helped them with homework and did all the chores. Even with all his responsibilities, Daniel was a very reliable worker. His boss decided to help him go to college. It took Daniel eight years, but finally he graduated. Now Daniel plans to enroll in a business management course. If he is accepted, he hopes to open his own business someday. Daniel has a dream, and he is working hard to achieve his dream. He is my hero!

C **Talk** with a partner.

1. What are two facts given in the paragraph?
2. What are two examples given in the paragraph?
3. What is Daniel's dream?

Use specific details such as facts, examples, and reasons to support your topic sentence.

D **Complete** the chart with Daniel's obstacles and successes.

Topic sentence: *My cousin, Daniel, is the most successful person I know, even though he has had many obstacles on his road to success.*

Daniel's obstacles	Daniel's successes
His parents died.	*He found a job in a local supermarket.*

Concluding sentence: ______________________________

E **Plan** a paragraph about a successful person you know. Use the chart to make notes on your own ideas.

Topic sentence: ______________________________

____________'s obstacles	____________'s successes

Concluding sentence: ______________________________

2 Write

Write a paragraph about someone you know who is successful. Include a topic sentence, examples of obstacles and successes, and a concluding sentence. Use the paragraph in Exercise 1B and the charts in Exercises 1D and 1E to help you.

3 After you write

A **Check** your writing.

	Yes	No
1. My topic sentence identifies a successful person.	☐	☐
2. I included examples of obstacles and successes.	☐	☐
3. I wrote a concluding sentence.	☐	☐

B **Share** your writing with a partner.

1. Take turns. Read your paragraph to a partner.
2. Comment on your partner's paragraph. Ask your partner a question about the paragraph. Tell your partner one thing you learned.

Lesson F Another view

1 Life-skills reading

Location of Career Technical Education (CTE) Classes	North Center	South Center	West Center	Downtown Center	East Center
Auto Technician	■	■	■		
Certified Nursing Assistant	■	■	■	■	■
Food Service Worker	■	■	■	■	■
Hospitality and Tourism	■				
Information Technology	■	■	■		■
Customer Service		■			
Welding	■		■		
Workplace Readiness	■	■	■	■	■

A **Read** the questions. Look at the chart. Fill in the answer.

1. Which program is *not* offered at all five centers?
   - (A) Certified Nursing Assistant
   - (B) Workplace Readiness
   - (C) Food Service Worker
   - (D) Information Technology

2. Which centers offer fewer than five programs?
   - (A) South Center and Downtown Center
   - (B) North Center and East Center
   - (C) Downtown Center and East Center
   - (D) none of the above

3. Which center offers more than six programs?
   - (A) West Center
   - (B) East Center
   - (C) North Center
   - (D) South Center

4. Which programs are offered at only one center?
   - (A) Hospitality and Tourism and Customer Service
   - (B) Welding and Customer Service
   - (C) Auto Technician and Information Technology
   - (D) Hospitality and Tourism and Welding

B **Solve** the problem Give your opinion.

Ahmed works 4 days and 2 nights at a computer store. He wants to study Information Technology. The closest class is at the East Center. However, the class meets on the same two nights he works. What should he do?

2 Grammar connections: *be + supposed to* and *be + not supposed to*

Be + supposed to **and** ***be + not supposed to*** **can show expectations about behavior.**

You'**re supposed to come** early to register for the class.	You'**re not supposed to miss** class without an appropriate excuse.

Watch

A **Talk** with a partner. Choose one of the places in the box. Describe expectations about behavior there. Your partner guesses the place. Take turns.

the bookstore	the classroom	the counseling office	the library
the cafeteria	the computer lab	the gymnasium	the tutoring office

A You're supposed to be quiet in this place. You're not supposed to eat here.
B Is it the computer lab?
A No, it isn't. You're supposed to do research and borrow books here.
B Is it the library?
A Yes, it is.

A You're supposed to use cash or credit cards here. You're not supposed to use personal checks.
B Is it the cafeteria?
A No, it isn't. You're not supposed to eat here. You're supposed to buy materials for your class here.
B Is it the bookstore?
A Yes, it is.

B **Share** information with the class.

You're supposed to be quiet in a library. You're not supposed to use your cell phones, and you're supposed to return books on time.

Scan a chart listing class locations to locate key details; contrast *be supposed to* and *be not supposed to* to show expectations about behavior

REVIEW

1 Listening

Listen. Take notes on the conversation.

CD1, Track 17

1. Type of certificate	*Automotive Technology*
2. Number of required classes	
3. Total number of courses	
4. Time to complete the program	
5. Cost per course	

Talk with a partner. Check your answers.

2 Grammar

A **Write.** Complete the story.

A Famous Athlete

Albert Pujols *is considered* (1. considers / is considered) one of the world's great baseball players. Raised in the Dominican Republic, he immigrated to the United States in 1996. He demonstrated his hitting skills __________ (2. quick / quickly) by batting over .500 in his first season of baseball in high school. By 2001, he was playing in the major leagues for the St. Louis Cardinals. He played so __________ (3. good / well) that in 2006 he became the fastest player in history to reach 19 home runs in a season. On June 3, 2017, playing for the Los Angeles Angels, he became the 9th player to hit at least 600 home runs. In 2007 he became a citizen of the United States, getting a __________ (4. perfect / perfectly) score on his citizenship test. Pujols __________ (5. admires / is admired) for his support of people with Down syndrome and other disabilities. A center for adults with Down syndrome, opened in 2009, __________ (6. names / is named) for Pujols.

B **Write.** Look at the words that are underlined in the answers. Write the questions.

1. **A** __________
   B Albert Pujols grew up in the Dominican Republic.
2. **A** __________
   B He became a citizen of the United States in 2007.
3. **A** __________
   B He is admired for his support of people with Down syndrome.

Talk with a partner. Ask and answer the questions.

3 Pronunciation: *-ed* verb endings

A **Listen** to the *-ed* verb endings in these sentences.

/t/

1. He has always **liked** playing number games.
2. She has **worked** as an accountant for ten years.

/d/

3. Emily has **realized** that Brenda has a good brain.
4. Naturalists are **skilled** in working with plants.

/ɪd/

5. The little boy **started** counting when he was two.
6. She is **gifted** in singing and dancing.

Listen again and repeat. Pay attention to the *-ed* verb endings.

CD1, Track 18

B **Listen and repeat.** Then check (✓) the correct pronunciation for each *-ed* verb ending.

CD1, Track 19

	/t/	/d/	/ɪd/
1. Classes are **located** at various elementary schools.			✓
2. All students are **advised** of the school rules.		✓	
3. An application is **required** for admission.		✓	
4. A math test is **needed** as well.			✓
5. The test is **administered** once a week.		✓	
6. The students are **expected** to pay their fees soon.			✓
7. Lucas hasn't **talked** with a counselor yet.	✓		
8. But he is **finished** with all his tests.	✓		

Talk with a partner. Compare your answers.

C **Talk** with a partner. Practice the conversations. Pay attention to the pronunciation of the *-ed* verb endings: /t/, /d/, or /ɪd/.

1. **A** Are classes offered on Saturday?
   B Yes, they are offered from 9:00 to 12:00.

2. **A** What are we expected to bring to class?
   B We are expected to bring a notebook, the textbook, and a pen.

3. **A** How did she cook?
   B She cooked very well.

4. **A** How did he paint?
   B He painted skillfully.

D **Write** five past tense questions. Use the following words: *administer, expect, finish, locate, provide, require* and *talk*. Then talk with a partner. Ask and answer your questions.

UNIT 3 FRIENDS AND FAMILY

Lesson A Listening

1 Before you listen

A What do you see?

B What is happening?

2 Listen

A **Listen** and answer the questions.

1. Who are the speakers?
2. What are they talking about?

CD1, Track 20

B **Listen again.** Take notes.

CD1, Track 20

Part 1	Part 2	Part 3
Reason for call: Lan absent from class	Mother's rules: ______	Reason mother is upset: ______
Action mother should take: ______	______	Lan's punishment: ______

3 After you listen

CULTURE NOTE
When a child gets into trouble at school, the school staff calls the parents to help enforce the school rules.

A **Read.** Complete the story.

argument	broke (the) rules	missed	permitted	strict
bring (someone) up	chaperone	on restriction	raised	trust

Mrs. Lee received a phone message from her daughter's school saying Lan ______(1) her 7th period class. Lan left school early to go to the mall with her friend Mary. At the mall, Lan tells Mary that her mother is too strict(2). Lan thinks it's because her mother wants to ______(3) her ______(3) the same way she was ______(4) in China. That's why Lan needs a ______(5) to go out on a date. At home, Lan and her mother have an ______(6). Lan is angry because she's not ______(7) to go to the mall alone. She thinks her mother doesn't ______(8) her. Mrs. Lee is upset because Lan ______(9) the ______(9). As a punishment, she says Lan is ______(10) for two weeks.

Listen and check your answers.

CD1, Track 21

B **Discuss.** Talk with your classmates.

Do you think Lan's mother is too strict? Give reasons for your opinion.

Lesson B Indirect questions

1 Grammar focus: indirect *Wh-* questions

An indirect question is a question inside a statement or another question. Indirect *Wh-* questions begin with a question word (*who, what, when*) and use subject-verb word order (*why she is so strict*). We do not use the auxiliary *do, does* or *did* with indirect questions.

DIRECT *WH-* QUESTIONS	INDIRECT *WH-* QUESTIONS
Why is she so strict?	I wonder **why she is** so strict.
How is everything at home?	I'd like to know **how everything is** at home.
Where did you **go**?	Can you tell me **where** you **went**?
When did they **leave**?	Do you know **when** they **left**?
What did they **do**?	I don't know **what they did**.

Watch

Introductory clauses

I'd like to know . . .	Could you tell me . . . ?	Can you tell me . . . ?
I don't know . . .	I wonder . . .	Do you know . . . ?

CULTURE NOTE
Indirect questions are often more polite than direct questions. Add "please" to make the questions even more polite.

2 Practice

A Write. Change the direct questions to indirect *Wh-* questions. Circle the indirect *Wh-* questions.

1. What is the student's name?
   A Do you know *what the student's name is*?
   B Her name is Lan.

2. What class did she miss?
   A Can you please tell me ________________?
   B Mr. Latham's 7th period English class.

3. Who did Lan go to the mall with?
   A I wonder ________________.
   B She went to the mall with Mary.

4. Why did she break the rules?
   A I would like to know ________________.
   B I don't know why. Perhaps she was bored in class.

5. When did she and her friend leave the school?
   A Can you tell me ________________?
   B They left after 6th period.

6. What did they do at the mall?
   A I want to know ________________.
   B They talked and went window-shopping.

7. When did they come home from the mall?
   A Do you know ________________?
   B I don't know when they came home.

8. What was Lan's punishment?
   A Could you please tell me ________________?
   B Her mother put her on restriction for two weeks.

CD1, Track 22

Listen and check your answers. Then practice with a partner.

B **Talk** with a partner about Lan's report card. Ask indirect questions.

A Do you know what grade Lan got in World History?

B She got a B.

School Report Card – First Semester		
Student's name: Lan Suzi Lee		**Advisor:** Mr. Green
Subject	Grade	Teacher
World History	B	Lopez
Advanced English	A	Latham
Algebra	B+	Smith
P.E.	C	Chin
Chemistry	C	Hogan
Ceramics	A	Azari

Write indirect questions about Lan's report card.

Do you know what grade Lan got in World History?

3 Communicate

A **Work** with a partner. Role-play conversations between a parent and a teenager. Use indirect questions with *who*, *what*, *where*, *when*, and *why*.

Parent I'd like to know why you're late.

Teenager I stayed after class to talk to my math teacher.

Parent OK. But next time, call me if you're going to be late. All right?

Situation 1: The teenager is two hours late coming home from school. The parent is worried.

Situation 2: The teenager's teacher called to say the teenager was cheating on a test. The parent is shocked.

Situation 3: The teenager's report card arrived in the mail. He or she got one A, two Bs, two Cs, and a D. Normally, the teenager gets all As and Bs. The parent is angry.

Situation 4: The parent received a $70 ticket in the mail for parking in a "no parking" area. The teenager got the ticket when she parked her parent's car, but she forgot to tell her parents about it. The parent is angry.

Situation 5: Make up your own conversation between a parent and a teenager.

B **Perform** your role play for the class.

Lesson C Indirect questions

1 Grammar focus: indirect *Yes / No* questions

An indirect *Yes / No* question is a question inside a statement or another question. Indirect *Yes / No* questions begin with *if* or *whether* and use subject-verb word order (*if you finished your homework.*) *If* is more common and *whether* is more formal. We do not use the auxiliary *do, does* or *did* with indirect questions.

Watch

DIRECT *YES / NO* QUESTIONS	INDIRECT *YES / NO* QUESTIONS
Did you finish your homework?	I'd like to know **if you finished** your homework.
Is her mother strict?	I wonder **if her mother is** strict.
Will they go to college?	Could you tell me **if they will go** to college?

2 Practice

A **Write.** Complete the conversation. Use indirect *Yes / No* questions with *if*.

Son Can I go to a party at Joe's house?

Father Maybe. First I need to know *if you finished your homework*.
1. Did you finish your homework?

Son Yes, I finished it an hour ago.

Father Do you know ______________________________?
2. Does the party start at 5:00 or 6:00?

Son It starts at 6:00.

Father OK. Can you tell me ______________________________?
3. Will his parents be home?

Son Yes, his parents will be there.

Father That's good. I wonder ______________________________.
4. Do you need to take a birthday gift?

Son No, I don't. It's not a birthday party.

Father I wonder ______________________________.
5. Are they going to serve dinner?

Son Yes. They're going to grill chicken for us.

Father What about your friend John?

Do you know ______________________________?
6. Is he invited to the party?

Son Yes, I think so.

Father Do you know ______________________________?
7. Can John's parents bring you home?

Son I'll ask them.

Father I am wondering ______________________________.
8. Can you text us when you are on the way home?

Son Sure. I'll do that.

Listen and check your answers. Then practice with a partner.

CD1, Track 23

B **Talk** with a partner. Imagine you are a parent. Read the information you want to ask your daughter about her new friend from school. Make indirect questions using *if* or *whether*. Use a variety of introductory clauses.

Can you tell me if she's a good student?

I'd like to know whether she lives at home.

- is a good student
- has a job
- has nice friends
- has a good relationship with her parents
- lives alone or at home
- is polite
- drives carefully
- has brothers or sisters

USEFUL LANGUAGE
In indirect *Yes / No* questions, *whether* = *if*.

Write the parents' indirect questions.

Can you tell me if she's a good student?

3 Communicate

A **Work** in a small group. Ask and answer questions about your lives when you were teenagers. Use indirect *Yes / No* questions. Discuss the items listed below.

- relationship with parents
- grades in school
- school activities
- things you were required to do at home
- things you were permitted to do
- things you weren't permitted to do

A I'd like to know if you got along well with your parents.
B Yes, I did. But sometimes I argued with them.
C I argued with my parents a lot.

B **Share** information about your classmates.

Elena sometimes argued with her parents.
Manny argued with his parents a lot.

Lesson D Reading

1 Before you read

Talk with your classmates. Answer the questions.

1. How many generations of your family are living in the United States? Which generation are you?
2. What are some of the differences between you and the other generations in your family?
3. Look at the reading tip. Look up the meaning of *barrier*, and predict what the story will be about.

Pay attention to words that repeat in a reading. They often give you an idea of what the reading is about.

2 Read

Read the magazine article. Listen and read again.

CD1, Track 24

BARRIERS between GENERATIONS

In immigrant families, language differences and work schedules often create barriers to communication between the generations. Dolores Suarez, 42, and her son Diego, 16, face both kinds of barriers every day. Dolores is an immigrant from Mexico who works seven days a week as a housekeeper in a big hotel. She doesn't use much English in her job, and she has never had time to study it. Consequently, her English is limited. Her son, on the other hand, was raised in the United States. He understands Spanish, but he prefers to speak English. When his friends come over to visit, they speak only English. "They talk so fast, I can't understand what they are saying," says Dolores. To make the situation more complicated, Diego and Dolores live with Dolores's father, who speaks Nahuatl, a native language spoken in Mexico. Diego can't understand anything his grandfather says.

Dolores's work schedule is the second barrier to communication with Diego. Because she rarely has a day off, Dolores isn't able to spend much time with him. She doesn't have time to help him with his homework or attend parent-teacher conferences at his school. In 1995, when Dolores immigrated to the United States, her goal was to bring up her son with enough money to avoid the hardships her family suffered in Mexico. Her hard work has permitted Diego to have a comfortable life and a good education. But she has paid a price for this success. "Sometimes I feel like I don't know my own son," she says.

3 After you read

A **Check** your understanding.

1. What is the main idea of this article?
2. What are the two barriers to communication between Dolores and her son?
3. Why is Dolores's English limited?
4. According to the author, why does Diego prefer to speak English instead of Spanish?
5. Why can't Diego communicate with his grandfather?
6. What was Dolores's goal when she came to the United States?
7. Explain the expression *paid a price* as it is used in paragraph 2.

B **Build** your vocabulary.

1. In the reading passage, underline the words from the chart.
2. Use a dictionary. Fill in the chart with the missing word forms.

Noun	Verb	Adjective
immigrant	*immigrate*	*immigrant*
differences		
	create	
communication		
education		
success		

3. Complete the sentences. Write the correct form of the word from Exercise B2.
   a. My family decided to ______________ to the United States because there was a war in my country.
   b. Parents and teenagers almost always ______________ in the kind of music they prefer.
   c. Shosha paints beautiful and unusual oil paintings. She's very ______________.
   d. Debra's son isn't very ______________. It's hard to know what he's thinking.
   e. It's a parent's responsibility to ______________ children about right and wrong behavior.
   f. You need two things to be ______________ in life: motivation and luck.

C **Talk** with a partner.

1. What are some ways that you and your parents are different?
2. How can people communicate if they don't speak the same language?
3. Is it necessary to go to school to be an educated person? Explain your answer.

For college and career readiness practice, see pages 142–144.

Read closely to determine what the text says explicitly and to make logical inferences from the text; use a dictionary to find related word forms

Lesson E Writing

1 Before you write

A **Talk** with a partner. What are some differences between you and your parents or you and your children? Write your information on the charts.

Me	My parents
like salads and sandwiches	like lamb and rice

Me	My children
play cards	play video games

B **Read** the paragraph.

Transitions like *for example* and *on the other hand* show the relationship between sentences or ideas in a paragraph. Underline the transition words in the paragraph that separate the different eating habits.

www.myblog.com

Different Eating Habits

One difference between my parents and me is that we don't have the same eating habits. My family is Iranian, but I was brought up in the United States. Since most of my friends are American, I enjoy eating "American style." For example, I like to eat salads and sandwiches instead of meat and rice. Because of my job, I don't have time to cook, so I like fast food. I also love to eat in restaurants. On the other hand, my parents still eat like they did back home. They eat rice with every meal, and they eat a lot of lamb and vegetables. They don't like to eat in restaurants because my father thinks my mother is the best cook in the world. Actually, I agree with him. I still love my mother's cooking even though our eating habits are different.

C **Work** with a partner. Complete the outline of the model paragraph.

Topic sentence: *One difference between my parents and me is that we don't have the same eating habits.*

1 Me: *I enjoy eating "American style."*

a. Example: *I like to eat salads and sandwiches.*

b. Example: *I don't eat a lot of meat and rice.*

c. Example: *I like fast food.*

Transition: *On the other hand*

2 My parents: ______________________________

a. Example: ______________________________

b. Example: ______________________________

c. Example: ______________________________

D **Plan** a paragraph about a difference between you and your parents or you and your children. Include at least three examples to support your main idea. Make an outline. Use your own paper.

2 Write

Write a paragraph about a difference between you and your parents or you and your children. Include a topic sentence that identifies the difference. Give examples to support the main idea, and use a transition between the two parts of your paragraph. Use the paragraph in Exercise 1B and the outlines in Exercises 1C and 1D to help you.

3 After you write

A **Check** your writing.

	Yes	No
1. My topic sentence states the difference between my parents and me or my children and me.	☐	☐
2. I gave examples to support the main idea.	☐	☐
3. I used a transition between the two parts of my paragraph.	☐	☐

B **Share** your writing with a partner.

1. Take turns. Read your paragraph to a partner.
2. Comment on your partner's paragraph. Ask your partner a question about the paragraph. Tell your partner one thing you learned.

Lesson F Another view

1 Life-skills reading

U.S. Census Bureau

2015 American Community Survey – 1 year estimates | Total number of households: 118,208,250

Subject	Married couple family households	Female householder, no spouse present	Male householder, no spouse present	Non-family household
Total number of households	56,715,795 48%	15,083,980 13%	5,730,981 5%	40,677,494 34%
Average family size	3.26	3.33	3.10	X
Households with one or more children under 18	42.1%	63.9%	56.1%	.9%
Households with one or more people 60+ years old	38.3%	27.2 %	27.8%	43.1%

source: U.S. Census Bureau - Households and Families

A **Read** the questions. Look at the survey results. Fill in the answer.

1. Which of the four types of households is the least common?
   - (A) married couple households
   - (B) female householder, no spouse
   - (C) male householder, no spouse
   - (D) a non-family household

2. In a 2010 study, the percent of married couple households with one or more people 60+ years old was 34.1%. Compare this to the 2015 study. What can you conclude?
   - (A) The percent of older people in married couple households is growing.
   - (B) Married couples are staying married longer.
   - (C) The percent of older people in married couple households is decreasing.
   - (D) The United States population is getting younger.

3. What percentage of households are non-family households?
   - (A) 5%
   - (B) 34%
   - (C) 13%
   - (D) 48%

4. What is true about households led by females with no spouse present?
   - (A) They have a higher percentage of children than married couple households.
   - (B) There are over 15,000,000 of these households.
   - (C) More than 1/4 of them have one or more people 60+ years old
   - (D) all of the above

B **Solve** the problem. Give your opinion.

Emma has 2 daughters. Last month her two nephews moved in with them. The Census Bureau is coming soon to survey Emma's household. She is afraid to say 5 people are in her house because she doesn't want her landlord to know. What should she do?

2 Grammar connections: *say* and *tell* with reported speech

Use *say* or *tell* to report what someone said. Use *tell* with an object (*He told me...*). Use *say* when there is no object. We don't say ~~*He said me...*~~. Change the pronoun in the reported speech from the first person (*I* or *we*) to the 3rd person (*he, she or they*).

Watch

DIRECT SPEECH	REPORTED SPEECH
	Tatiana **said (that)** she has a cat.
"I have a cat."	She **told me (that)** she has a cat.
	She **told Andrew (that)** she has a cat.

A **Work** in a small group. One person asks a question from the list. One person answers. One person reports the answer with *say*. One person reports the answer with *tell*. Take turns.

A Who do you live with?
B I live with my cousin.
C She said that she lives with her cousin.
D She told him that she lives with her cousin.

Questions:

1. Who do you live with?
2. Where do you live?
3. What language do you speak at home?
4. What kind of car do you drive?
5. How many brothers and sisters do you have?
6. Do you have children? How many?
7. What kinds of foods does your family eat?
8. What is your favorite food?
9. What do you do for fun?
10. Why do you study English?
11. How often are you absent from class?
12. How often are you late to class?
13. What school subjects do you like?
14. Do you have a job? Where do you work?

B **Share** information about your classmates.

Laura told Andrew that she lives with her cousin. She told him she lives downtown. She said that she speaks Spanish at home.

UNIT 4 HEALTH

Lesson A Listening

1 Before you listen

A What do you see?

B What is happening?

1

2

3

4

5

2 Listen

CD1, Track 25

A Listen and answer the questions.

1. Who are the speakers?
2. What are they talking about?

B Listen again. Complete the chart.

CD1, Track 25

Sara's symptoms	Mike's advice
1. *can't sleep*	4. ______
2. ______	5. ______
3. ______	6. ______

3 After you listen

A Read. Complete the story.

anxiety	calm down	cope with	positive	techniques
breathing	concentrate	meditation	stressed out	tense

Mike is driving Sara to the Department of Motor Vehicles (DMV) to take her driving test. He notices that she's very ___*tense*___ (1). Sara says she's ______ (2) because she was late to work again. She's worried that her boss will fire her if she's late one more time. She's so afraid of losing her job that she can't eat, she can't sleep, and she can't ______ (3). Mike says that she has to ______ (4) if she wants to pass her driving test. He suggests three ______ (5) to help her ______ (6) her ______ (7). One is deep ______ (8). The second one is thinking ______ (9) thoughts, and the third one is ______ (10).

Listen and check your answers.

CD1, Track 26

B Discuss. Talk with your classmates.

1. Do you ever feel stressed out? What makes you feel stressed out?
2. What helps you when you feel stressed out?

Lesson B Modals

1 Grammar focus: *should*, *shouldn't*, *have to*, *don't have to*

Use *should* / *shouldn't* to give advice. Use *have to* / *has to* to indicate it is necessary to do something. Use *don't have to* / *doesn't have to* to indicate it is not necessary to do something.

ADVISABLE = GOOD IDEA	NOT ADVISABLE = BAD IDEA
Sara **should learn** how to meditate.	She **shouldn't get** stressed out.
NECESSARY	**NOT NECESSARY**
Sara **has to take** public transportation because she doesn't have a car.	She **doesn't have to take** her driving test today. She can take it next week.

Watch

2 Practice

A **Write.** Complete the story. Use *should*, *shouldn't*, *have to*, and *don't have to*.

Ana and Bill just got engaged, and they are planning to get married in four weeks. Because the wedding is so soon, they are feeling a lot of pressure. Ana's mother wants a big wedding, but Ana and Bill don't. Because they are paying for the wedding themselves, they believe they ___should___ (1) do what they want. Another pressure is all the things Ana and Bill ______________ (2) do before the wedding. For example, Ana ______________ (3) buy a dress, choose her bridesmaids, and send out the invitations. Bill ______________ (4) plan the reception and order the food. Most importantly, they ______________ (5) decide where the wedding will be. Ana wants to get married outdoors, but Bill thinks they ______________ (6) plan an outdoor wedding because it might rain. Now Bill has a different idea. He realizes that they ______________ (7) get married so soon. Maybe they ______________ (8) postpone the wedding by a few months. That way, they ______________ (9) feel so much pressure.

Listen and check your answers.

CD1, Track 27

B **Talk** with a partner. Make sentences about the people in the pictures. Use *should*, *shouldn't*, *ought to*, *have to*, and *don't have to*. Use the items from the box in your sentences.

Carmela and Hugo ought to try to meet new people.

Chul and Sun-mi have to find a new place to live.

USEFUL LANGUAGE
ought to = should

Carmela and Hugo
- just got married
- just moved to a new town

Chul and Sun-mi
- just had a baby
- live in a studio apartment

Kevin
- just started his first job
- still lives with his parents

try to meet new people	ask lots of questions
call parents about every problem	find a new place to live
learn how to manage money	follow their (his) parents' advice
try to do everything perfectly	make decisions by themselves (himself)
buy baby furniture	be responsible
meet the neighbors	volunteer at a local organization

Write sentences about the people in the pictures.

Carmela and Hugo ought to try to meet new people.

3 Communicate

A **Work** in a small group. Discuss the following situations, and give advice. Use *should*, *shouldn't*, *ought to*, *have to*, and *don't have to*.

They have to buy furniture.

They should check the newspaper for furniture sales.

1. The Wong family just bought a house. The house has no furniture at all. Also, it is far from Mr. Wong's job, and the family doesn't have a car.
2. Etsuko and Hiro immigrated to the United States. They are anxious because there are so many things to do. They don't have a big enough place to live, they aren't enrolled in English classes, and their children aren't registered for school.
3. Boris just started a new job. He hasn't met his coworkers. He also has duties that he hasn't done before, and he doesn't know the company's policies and procedures.

B **Share** your group's advice with your classmates.

Lesson C Past modals

1 Grammar focus: *should have* and *shouldn't have*

Use past modals *should have / shouldn't have* for regrets or advice about something that happened in the past. Use the past participle form of a verb after *should have / shouldn't have.*

REGRET IN THE PAST	ADVICE IN THE PAST
I don't like my new job.	Robert is late to work.
I **should have kept** my old job.	He **should have left** the house earlier.
I **shouldn't have changed** jobs.	He **shouldn't have read** the newspaper before work.

Past Participles

regular	irregular
called	eat / ate
stayed	go / went
studied	make / made
talked	sleep / slept

Watch

2 Practice

A Write. Read about Imelda. Write sentences with *should have* and *shouldn't have*.

Imelda left the Philippines last year and immigrated to the United States. None of her family came with her. She got homesick and depressed.

1. She didn't talk to anyone about her problems.
   She should have talked to someone about her problems.
2. She didn't go out with friends.
   ______
3. She stayed home alone all the time.
   ______
4. She didn't make new friends.
   ______
5. She didn't exercise.
   ______
6. She didn't eat regular, balanced meals.
   ______
7. She ate lots of junk food.
   ______
8. She slept so much.
   ______
9. She didn't call her family.
   ______

Listen and check your answers.

CD1, Track 28

B **Talk** with a partner. Look at the pictures. What should Nikolai and his boss have done differently? Use *shouldn't have*.

Nikolai shouldn't have overslept.

1.

stay up late

2.

oversleep

3.

forget (his) briefcase

4.

miss (his) bus

5.

arrive late

6.

criticize (someone) in public

7.

leave the meeting

8.

lose (their) temper

Write sentences about what Nikolai and his boss should have done instead.

Nikolai should have gotten up on time.

3 Communicate

A **Work** in a small group. Think about a past situation in your life that didn't go well. Take turns asking and answering questions about it.

1. What was the situation?
2. What did you do that you shouldn't have?
3. What didn't you do that you should have?

B **Share** information about your classmates.

Lesson D Reading

1 Before you read

Talk with your classmates. Answer the questions.

1. When you are in a stressful situation, what happens to your body?
2. Read the **boldfaced** questions (section heads) in the article. Talk with a partner. Share your answers to these questions before you read the article.

Before you read an article, read the title and section heads. Relate them to your own background and experience.

2 Read

Read the magazine article. Listen and read again.

CD1, Track 29

STRESS: What You Ought to Know

What is stress?

Stress is our reaction to changing events in our lives. The reactions can be mental – what we think or feel about the changes – and physical – how our body reacts to the changes.

What causes stress?

Stress often comes when there are too many changes in our lives. The changes can be positive, like having a baby or getting a better job, or they can be negative, such as an illness or a divorce. Some stress is healthy. It motivates us to push forward. But too much stress over time can make us sick.

What are the signs of stress?

There are both physical and emotional signs of stress. Physical signs may include tight muscles, elevated blood pressure, grinding your teeth, trouble sleeping, an upset stomach, and back pain. Common emotional symptoms are anxiety, nervousness, depression, trouble concentrating, and nightmares.

How can you manage stress?

To prevent stress, you should eat right and exercise regularly. When you know there will be a stressful event in your day – such as a test, a business meeting, or an encounter with someone you don't get along with – it is really important to eat a healthy breakfast and to limit coffee and sugar.

When you find yourself in a stressful situation, stay calm. Take a few deep breaths to help you relax. Roll your shoulders or stretch to loosen any tight muscles. And take time to think before you speak. You don't want to say something you will regret later!

We all have some stress in our lives. It's important for us to use strategies for handling it, so that the stress doesn't overwhelm us.

3 After you read

A **Check** your understanding.

1. In the third paragraph, find the word *symptoms* and underline it. What other word do you find in the paragraph that is a synonym for *symptom*?
2. What examples does the author give of both positive and negative experiences that can cause stress?
3. According to the article, there can be physical and emotional reactions to stress. What examples does the article give?
4. The article says that some stress can be healthy. What example does it give to support that statement?
5. The article says that an encounter with someone you don't get along with can be stressful. What advice in the fifth paragraph may help you?
6. If you eat healthy and exercise regularly, can you expect that you will never have problems with stress? Cite evidence from the article to support your answer.

B **Build** your vocabulary.

1. English uses suffixes to change the part of speech of a word. Underline words in the reading that end with the suffixes in the left column.
2. Complete the chart. Use a dictionary if necessary.

Suffix	Example	Part of speech	Main word	Part of speech
-ful	*stressful*	*adj*	*stress*	*noun*
-en				
-ly				
-ness				
-ion				

C **Talk** with a partner.

1. Think of a time when there were many changes in your life. Were the changes positive or negative? How did you feel? How did your body react?
2. What's a stressful situation you've been in recently?
3. Do you have a favorite exercise that you do to reduce stress? If so what is it?
4. After reading this article, is there something you would do differently to handle stress? If so, what?

For college and career readiness practice, see pages 145–147.

Read closely to determine what the text says explicitly and to make logical inferences from the text; recognize suffixes that change part of speech

Lesson E Writing

1 Before you write

A **Talk** with a partner. Look at the pictures. Answer the questions.

1. How do the people in the pictures cope with stress?
2. What are some healthy ways of coping with stress?
3. What are some unhealthy ways of coping with stress?
4. What makes you feel stressed?

B **Read** the paragraph.

How I Cope with Stress

When I feel stressed on a warm summer day, I like to work in the community garden in my neighborhood. The sun on my back as I pull weeds provides relief from hunching over a computer and lessens the muscle tension. The birds, sucking nectar from the flowers and splashing in the birdbath, relax me. Talking with the other volunteers makes me forget my troubles.

When I feel stressed on a cold winter day, I like to curl up with my cat, listen to classical music, and read an interesting book. Stroking my cat's soft fur helps my body relax, and soon I feel less tense. The sound of classical music with piano and string instruments shuts out the noises around me and reduces my anxiety. I like to listen with my eyes closed until my muscles start to relax. Then I open my eyes and pick up a book. I usually choose stories about people and the difficult events in their lives because they help me forget about all the stressful things I have to do in my own life.

One way to organize details in a paragraph is to write about cause and effect.
I like to listen with my eyes closed (cause) *until my muscles start to relax* (effect).

C **Work** with a partner. Complete the two outlines, one for each of the two model paragraphs.

Topic sentence for the first paragraph: When I feel stressed on a warm summer day,

____

____.

Ways of reducing stress:

cause: *sun on my back* → effect: *lessens muscle tension*

cause: ______________ → effect: ______________

cause: ______________ → effect: ______________

Topic sentence for the second paragraph: When I feel stressed on a cold winter day,

____

____.

Ways of reducing stress:

cause: ______________ → effect: ______________

cause: ______________ → effect: ______________

cause: ______________ → effect: ______________

D **Plan** a paragraph about how you cope with stress. Make an outline like the ones in Exercise 1C to make notes on your ideas.

2 Write

Write a paragraph about how you cope with stress. Identify at least three ways you reduce stress (causes) and the effect of each. Use details to describe each effect. Use the paragraphs in Exercise 1B and the outlines in Exercises 1C and 1D to help you.

3 After you write

A **Check** your writing.

	Yes	No
1. My topic sentence identifies three ways of reducing stress.	☐	☐
2. For each cause, I described an effect.	☐	☐
3. I used details to describe each effect.	☐	☐

B **Share** your writing with a partner.

1. Take turns. Read your paragraph to a partner.
2. Comment on your partner's paragraph. Ask your partner a question about the paragraph. Tell your partner one thing you learned.

Lesson F Another view

1 Life-skills reading

Many companies today recognize that stressed employees can impact the company's profit. Some hire consulting firms to survey employees about their stress and determine its effect on the company. Here is the report on one such survey.

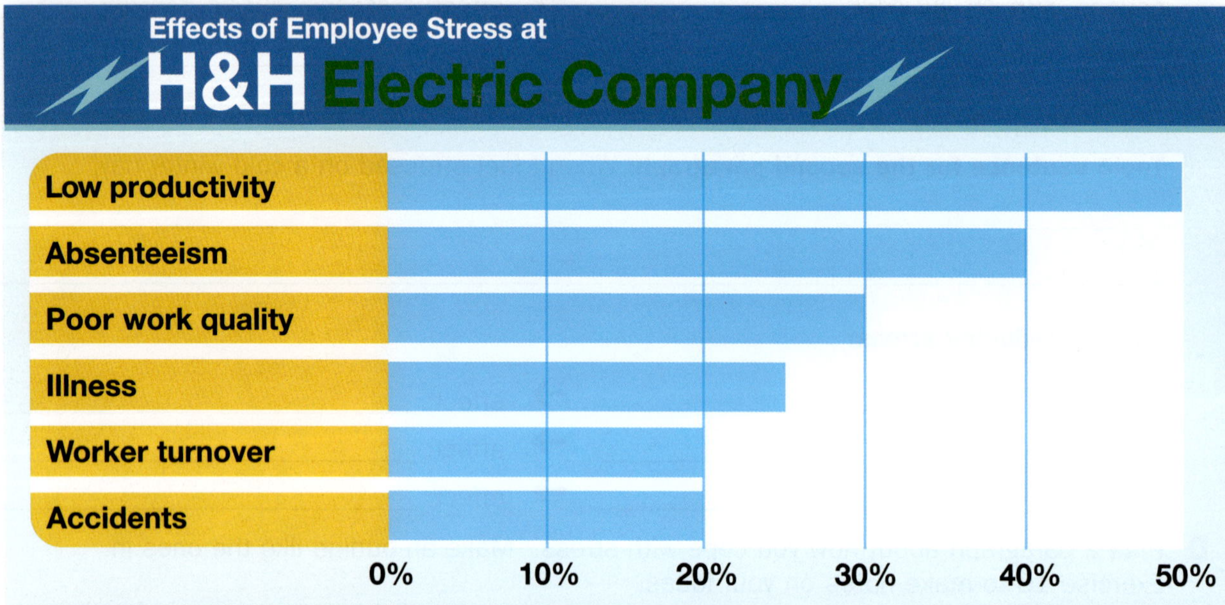

A **Read** the questions. Look at the bar graph. Fill in the answer.

1. This chart is about ____.
   - (A) how stress affects employees
   - (B) how stress affects a business
   - (C) both *a* and *b*
   - (D) neither *a* nor *b*

2. Employee stress is the cause of ____.
   - (A) 30 percent of poor quality work
   - (B) 20 percent of worker turnover
   - (C) both *a* and *b*
   - (D) neither *a* nor *b*

3. Employee stress contributes to worker turnover less than it contributes to ____.
   - (A) low productivity
   - (B) poor work quality
   - (C) illness
   - (D) all of the above

4. The chart does not show how stress affects ____.
   - (A) absenteeism
   - (B) illness
   - (C) tardiness
   - (D) accidents

B **Solve** the problem. Give your opinion.

You work in the accounting department of a medium-sized company. The quality of one of your coworkers has gone down. She has also called in sick quite a lot recently, which means you end up doing more work. What should you do?

2 Grammar connections: *must* and *may / might*

Use *must* and *must not* to make conclusions on the facts you know.
Use *may* and *might* when something is a possibility, but not for sure.

Watch

Situation: Sergio works 60 hours a week

Conclusions	Possibilities
He **must be** tired	He **might be** tired, but he **may enjoy** the work.
He **must get** paid overtime.	He **may get** overtime, but I don't know.
He **must need** the money.	He **might need** the money. He just bought a new house!

After *must, must not, may,* and *might*, use the base form of a verb.

A **Work** in a small group. Look at the results of the stress test. Say what you think about the people. Use *may*, *might*, and *must* in your answers.

A Tina eats only one meal a day.
B She must be on a diet.
C She may snack during the day.
D She might want to save money.

Stress Test

Name	Tina	Sergio	Larisa
1. How many meals do you eat a day?	One	Five	Three
2. Do you eat balanced meals?	No	No	Yes
3. How many cups of coffee do you drink a day?	Five	Two	None
4. How many hours do you sleep at night?	Five	Six	Nine
5. How often do you exercise?	Once a day	Never	Once a week
6. Do you worry about other people?	Yes	No	Yes
7. How often do you get angry?	Never	Every day	Rarely
8. Do you take time each day for yourself?	No	No	Yes
9. How often do you do fun things with friends or family?	Rarely	Once a week	Every day
10. How many hours a week are you at work or school?	45	60	25

B **Share** your group's ideas with the class.

Most of us think that Tina is on a diet although some of us think she may snack during the day or she might want to save money.

REVIEW

1 Listening

Listen to the phone conversation. Take notes.

CD1, Track 30

Yesenia's symptoms	Sue's suggestions
1. *tense*	4.
2.	5.
3.	6.

Talk with a partner. Check your answers.

2 Grammar

A **Write.** Complete the story. Use indirect questions.

Ann's Night Out

Ann is 16 years old. It's midnight, and she isn't home yet. She went out with her friend Liz. Ann's mom doesn't know *where they went* (1. Where did they go?). She wonders ______ (2. Are Ann and Liz safe?). Ann's mother wants to call Liz's house, but she doesn't know ______ (3. What is the phone number?). Ann's father is worried, too. He wonders ______ (4. Can he find them?). Then he hears a sound downstairs. For a minute, he doesn't know ______ (5. Who is it?). It's Ann! Her father says, "We had no idea ______ (6. Where were you?), but we're glad you're home."

B **Write.** Look at the words that are underlined in the answers. Write the questions.

1. **A** ______
   B Ann should have been home at 11:00.
2. **A** ______
   B She should have called her parents.
3. **A** ______
   B Ann's parents should put her on restriction.

Talk with a partner. Ask and answer the questions.

3 Pronunciation: intonation in *Wh-* questions

A **Listen** to the intonation in these *Wh-* questions.

Direct question	Indirect question
Where did he go?	Can you tell me where he went?

CD1, Track 31

Listen again and repeat. Pay attention to the intonation.

B **Listen and repeat.** Then draw arrows to show rising or falling intonation in the questions.

CD1, Track 32

1. **A** What does Ann do to reduce stress?
   B She listens to music.
2. **A** Why are you so tense?
   B I have my driver's test today.
3. **A** Do you know what Rodolfo does to calm down?
   B He walks or jogs.
4. **A** When did Ivan miss his class?
   B He missed his class on Tuesday.
5. **A** Can you tell me where Andy lives?
   B He lives on East Fifth Street.
6. **A** Do you know why they're always late?
   B No, I don't know.

Talk with a partner. Compare your answers.

C **Talk** with a partner. Ask and answer the questions. Use the correct intonation.

1. What is one thing you should have done today or yesterday?
2. What is a common punishment for teenagers when they come home late?
3. What were your favorite things to do when you were growing up?
4. Can you tell me what you do to reduce stress?
5. Do you know why it's important to exercise regularly?
6. Do you know if meditation is difficult to do?

D **Write** five questions. Make at least three indirect questions. Ask your partner.

Can you tell me how you cope with stressful situations?

1. ______________________________
2. ______________________________
3. ______________________________
4. ______________________________
5. ______________________________

Talk with a partner. Ask and answer the questions.

UNIT 5 AROUND TOWN

Lesson A Listening

1 Before you listen

A What do you see?

B What is happening?

1

2

3

4

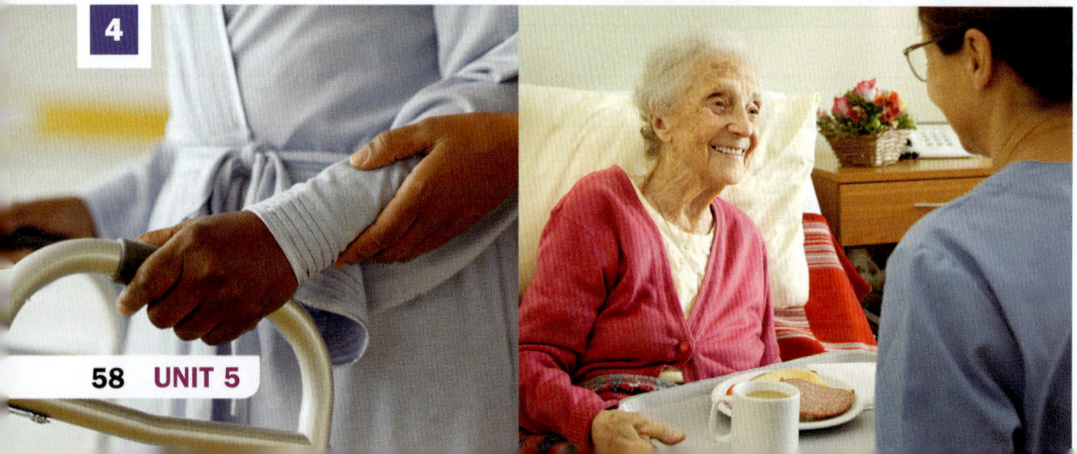

5

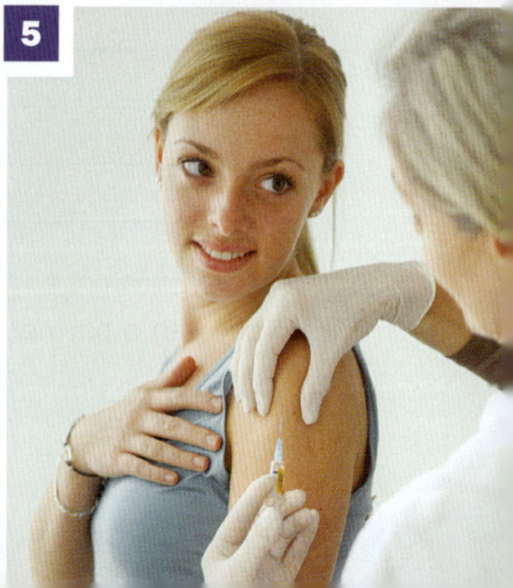

UNIT GOALS

Describe benefits of volunteering **Describe** someone who made a difference
Identify information in advertisements for volunteer positions

2 Listen

A **Listen** and answer the questions.

1. Who are the speakers?
2. What are they talking about?

CD1, Track 33

B **Listen again.** Complete the chart.

CD1, Track 33

Almaz's responsibilities at the library	Volunteer responsibilities at Quiet Palms
1. worked with adults learning to read	4.
2.	5.
3.	6.

3 After you listen

A **Read.** Complete the story.

can't wait	**compassionate**	**orientation**	**residents**	**volunteer**
commitment	**coordinator**	**patient**	**responsibilities**	**worthwhile**

Last summer, Almaz volunteered at the public library downtown. She liked working with the older people because she felt that she was doing something worthwhile (1). Today, she is meeting with Steve, the volunteer ______ (2) at Quiet Palms, a nursing home. She wants to ______ (3) there to find out if she likes working in the health-care field. Steve tells her about some of her ______ (4) at Quiet Palms. He says it's very important for volunteers to be ______ (5) and ______ (6) when they are working with the ______ (7). He asks Almaz to make a ______ (8) to volunteer at least three hours per week. Almaz agrees to attend an ______ (9). She says she ______ (10) to start volunteering.

CULTURE NOTE

A *nursing home* is a place where elderly people live when their families can't take care of them.

CD1, Track 34

Listen and check your answers.

B **Talk** with your classmates.

What are some places in your community to volunteer? What are some benefits of volunteering?

Lesson B Time clauses

1 Grammar focus: clauses with *until* and *as soon as*

Dependent time clauses with *as soon as* and *until* can come at the beginning or end of a sentence. *As soon as* and *until* can be about the present, the past or the future.

AS SOON AS = RIGHT AFTER	*UNTIL* = UP TO A PARTICULAR TIME
Present: **As soon as** Mr. Shamash **finishes** his lunch, Almaz **leaves** Quiet Palms.	**Present:** Almaz **stays** with Mr. Shamash **until** he **finishes** lunch.
Past: **As soon as** Mr. Shamash **finished** his lunch, Almaz **left** Quiet Palms.	**Past:** Almaz **stayed** with Mr. Shamash **until** he **finished** his lunch.
Future: **As soon as** Mr. Shamash **finishes** his lunch, Almaz **will leave** Quiet Palms.	**Future:** Almaz **will stay** with Mr. Shamash **until** he **finishes** his lunch.

Watch

2 Practice

A **Write.** Complete the sentences with *until* or *as soon as*. Circle the time clause.

1. **A** Mr. Shamash is in pain. When will he start to feel better?
   B He'll feel better *as soon as* he takes his medication.
2. **A** How long will Mr. Shamash stay at Quiet Palms?
   B He'll stay ____________ his broken hip heals.
3. **A** When can Mr. Shamash begin exercising again?
   B ____________ Mr. Shamash feels stronger, he can start doing moderate exercise.
4. **A** When does Mr. Shamash get ready for his walk?
   B He gets ready ____________ Almaz arrives.
5. **A** How long will Mr. Shamash and Almaz play cards?
   B They'll play cards ____________ it is time for lunch.
6. **A** How long did Mr. Shamash nap yesterday?
   B He napped ____________ Almaz came to visit him.
7. **A** When is Mr. Shamash going to go to sleep?
   B ____________ his visitors leave, he'll take his medicine and go to sleep.
8. **A** When did the nurse assistant help Mr. Shamash with his shower?
   B ____________ Mr. Shamash woke up, the nurse assistant helped him with his shower.

Listen and check your answers. Then practice with a partner.

CD1, Track 35

B **Talk** with a partner. Discuss Charles's volunteer activities at a nursing home. Use *as soon as* or *until*. Use the present tense.

> As soon as Charles arrives at work, he puts on his name tag.

> Charles doesn't put on his name tag until he arrives at work.

USEFUL LANGUAGE
In speaking and informal writing, you may use *'til* for *until*.

1. arrive / put on name tag

2. get his assignment/ go to Mrs. Halliday's room

3. walk with Mrs. Halliday / feel tired

4. read to Mrs. Halliday / lunchtime

5. stop reading / lunch is delivered

6. stay with Mrs. Halliday / finish eating

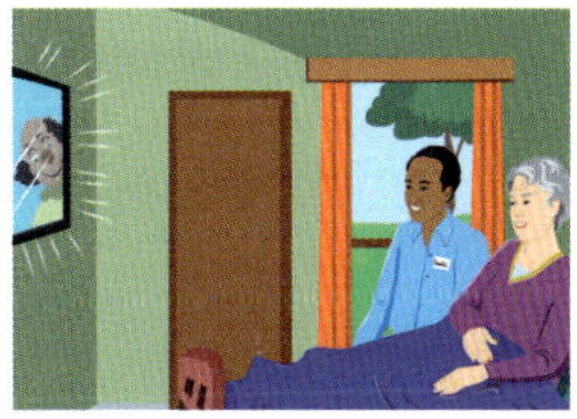
7. watch TV with Mrs. Halliday / time to rest

8. go home / finish playing a game with Mrs. Halliday

Write sentences about Charles's volunteer activities.

As soon as Charles arrives at work, he puts on his name tag.

CULTURE NOTE
Volunteering is a popular activity among Americans of all ages, from children to senior citizens.

3 Communicate

A **Choose** one time when you helped someone or volunteered. Make a list of your activities. Use Exercise 2B to help you.

B **Work** with a partner. Ask questions about each other's activities. Use *as soon as* and *until*. Use the past tense.

A I volunteered at an animal shelter.
B What did you do as soon as you arrived?
A I checked the board for my duties.
B How late did you stay?
A I stayed until the shelter closed for the day.

C **Share** information about your partner.

Lesson C Verb tense contrast

1 Grammar focus: repeated actions in the present and past

In sentences that talk about repeated actions, the correct word order is subject + verb + number of times + time expression. The number of times answers the question *How often?* The time expression answers the question *When?*

Watch

		NUMBER OF TIMES	TIME EXPRESSIONS
PRESENT	This year, Sana **volunteers** at the homeless shelter	once twice three times several times many times	a week. each month.
	This year, Sana **is volunteering** at the homeless shelter		
PAST	Sana **volunteered** at the homeless shelter		last year. two years ago. when she was 12.
PRESENT PERFECT	Sana **has volunteered** at the homeless shelter		so far. recently. in her life.

2 Practice

A Write. Complete the story with the present, present perfect, or past forms of the verbs.

Sharing with Sally

Sally Sutherland created "Sharing with Sally," a volunteer organization that helps seniors stay connected with the outside world. The organization *has delivered* (1. deliver) over 5,000 dinners to seniors so far. Sharing with Sally ____________ (2. begin) six years ago. Several times a week, Sally and her volunteers ____________ (3. deliver) meals, ____________ (4. talk) to seniors on the phone, and ____________ (5. visit) the ones who can't leave their homes. Over 200 people volunteer at Sharing with Sally. Jake, a college student, ____________ (6. volunteer) all last year. He ____________ (7. call) elderly people on the phone once a week and ____________ (8. talk) to each person. He said it was a very valuable experience. Betsy, a 35-year-old mother of two, ____________ (9. volunteer) for two years so far and loves it.

Listen and check your answers.

CD1, Track 36

B **Talk** with a partner. Make sentences about Betsy's volunteer experience. Include the number of times and time expressions.

USEFUL LANGUAGE
she's visited = she has visited

A Betsy visited seniors at their homes 30 times last year.
B She's also visited them 15 times so far this year.

Activity	Number of times last year	Number of times this year
Visit seniors at their homes	30	15
Call seniors on the phone	45	25
Help Sally put meals in the truck	5	1
Deliver meals	25	10
Return equipment to the truck	20	5
Take her children with her to the seniors' homes	10	3
Volunteer to read to seniors	5	2
Clean the truck	10	4

Write sentences about Betsy's activities.

Betsy visited seniors at their homes 30 times last year.

3 Communicate

A **Make** a list of your experiences volunteering or helping people.

Last year	This year
took my grandmother to the hairdresser	*volunteer at a homeless shelter*

B **Work** with a partner. Share your lists. Ask questions about your partner's activities. Use *How often . . . ?* or *How many times . . . ?*

How often did you take your grandmother to the hairdresser last year?
Every week.

How often do you volunteer at a homeless shelter?
Several times a year.

How many times have you volunteered at the homeless shelter so far this year?
Three times.

C **Share** information about your partner.

Lesson D Reading

1 Before you read

Talk with your classmates. Answer the questions.

1. Look at the picture. What is unusual about it?
2. Read the title. What do you think the story will be about?

Use titles and pictures to help predict what a reading is about.

2 Read

Read the newspaper article. Listen and read again.

CD1, Track 37

RUNNING WITH ROPES

Imagine running with your eyes closed. How do you feel? Insecure? Afraid? Justin Andrews knows these feelings very well. Justin is a former long-distance runner who lost his vision because of a grave illness. For the past six months, he has been running twice a week with the help of volunteer runners at Running with Ropes, an organization that assists blind and visually impaired runners. "Running with Ropes has changed my life," Justin says. "Until I heard about it, I thought I'd never run outside again."

Volunteers at Running with Ropes make a commitment to volunteer two to four hours a week. Scott Liponi, one of the running volunteers, explains what they do. "We use ropes to join ourselves to the blind runners and guide them around and over obstacles, such as holes in the road and other runners." Scott has learned how to keep the rope loose so the blind runner has more freedom. He deeply respects the blind runners' tenacity. "They are incredibly determined," he says. "It doesn't matter if it's hot, raining, or snowing – they are going to run." Scott says it is gratifying to share in the joy of the runners and to feel that they trust him. "The four hours I spend at Running with Ropes are the most rewarding part of my week," he says. "It's really a worthwhile commitment."

3 After you read

> When you see a new word, look at the words around it to guess if the meaning is positive or negative.
>
> *He lost his vision because of a **grave** illness.*
>
> You can guess that *grave* has a negative meaning because loss of vision and illness are both negative events.

A **Check** your understanding.

1. According to the author, why is *Running with Ropes* a worthwhile organization?
2. Who is Justin Andrews? What happened to him?
3. How is Justin able to run?
4. Compare what Justin says in paragraph 1 and what Scott says in the last paragraph about *Running with Ropes*. How are the statements similar?
5. Based on Justin and Scott's statements about their experiences, do you think they will continue to participate in the program? Why or why not?

B **Build** your vocabulary.

1. Look at the reading tip above. Then, in the reading passage, underline the words from the chart. Decide if their meanings are positive or negative. Fill in the clues that helped you guess.

Word	Positive	Negative	Clue
1. grave		✓	*He lost his vision because of an illness.*
2. insecure			
3. impaired			
4. freedom			
5. tenacity			
6. gratifying			
7. rewarding			

2. Work with your classmates. Write four more words from the reading that have positive or negative meanings. Indicate if their meanings are positive or negative. Fill in the clues that helped you guess.

Word	Positive	Negative	Clue
a.			
b.			
c.			
d.			

C **Talk** with a partner.

1. When do you feel most insecure?
2. Tell about something that takes tenacity.
3. Describe a gratifying experience.
4. What is a commitment you have made in your life?

For college and career readiness practice, see pages 148–150.

Determine a central idea of a text and how it is conveyed through key details; use context clues to decide if a word has a positive or negative meaning

Lesson E Writing

1 Before you write

A **Talk** with your classmates. Look at the picture. Answer the questions.

1. Who are the people in the picture? Where are they? What are they doing?
2. Do you think the young woman is doing something important? Why or why not?

B **Read** the paragraph.

Story Lady

My friend Vivianne is one of the most compassionate people I have ever met. After college, she wanted to do something truly worthwhile, so she spent a year working as a literacy volunteer in northeastern Brazil. At the time, this area didn't have any libraries, so Vivianne traveled to different schools in a mobile library van. As soon as she arrived at a school, the children would run outside and shout, "Story Lady! Story Lady!" Then everyone went inside, sat down, and listened quietly while she read them a story. Vivianne made a huge difference in these children's lives. She introduced them to literature and taught them to love reading. Today, she still gets letters from children who remember her generosity and kindness.

Make your writing more interesting by including specific details that answer the questions *who, what, where, when, why,* and *how*.

C **Work** with a partner. Write the words *who, what, where, when, why,* or *how* next to the details from the paragraph.

1. ___who___ my friend Vivianne
2. __________ after college
3. __________ a literacy volunteer
4. __________ northeastern Brazil
5. __________ because the area didn't have any libraries
6. __________ in a mobile library van
7. __________ read stories to the children
8. __________ taught the children to love reading

D **Plan** a paragraph about someone you know who made a difference. Use the chart to make notes.

Who made a difference?	
What did he or she do?	
Where did it happen?	
When did it happen?	
Why did this person do it?	

2 Write

Write a paragraph about someone you know who made a difference in your life or someone else's life. Include specific details that answer *Wh-* questions. Use the paragraph in Exercise 1B and the chart in Exercise 1D to help you.

3 After you write

A **Check** your writing.

	Yes	No
1. My topic sentence names the person who made a difference.	☐	☐
2. I included specic details in my paragraph.	☐	☐
3. The details in my paragraph answer *Wh-* questions.	☐	☐

B **Share** your writing with a partner.

1. Take turns. Read your paragraph to a partner.
2. Comment on your partner's paragraph. Ask your partner a question about the paragraph. Tell your partner one thing you learned.

Lesson F Another view

1 Life-skills reading

HOME ABOUT US CONTACT US

Want to get involved?

Volunteer opportunities are listed every Wednesday.

1. Health
Agency: San Antonio Meals for Seniors
Need: Volunteers to drive meals to seniors' homes
Contact: Jim Jefferies, 555-2324
Site: Downtown area
Time commitment: 3 hours per week

2. Literacy
Agency: San Antonio Literacy Foundation
Need: Volunteers to tutor basic reading, writing, and math skills to adults
Contact: 555-3131
Site: Around the city
Time commitment: 4 hours per week, 3-month commitment, plus 12 hours training

3. Animals
Agency: "Make People Smile" Animal Therapy
Need: Volunteers and their pets to visit hospitals and nursing homes
Contact: Judy, jsmith@mpsat.org
Site: Throughout the city
Time commitment: 4 hours per month

A **Read** the questions. Look at the advertisements for volunteer positions. Fill in the answer.

1. Which volunteer position requires the biggest time commitment?
   - (A) 1
   - (B) 2
   - (C) 3
   - (D) They are all the same.

2. Which position requires a driver's license?
   - (A) 1
   - (B) 2
   - (C) 3
   - (D) none of the above

3. Which word could replace *tutor* in the Literacy opportunity?
   - (A) know
   - (B) learn
   - (C) teach
   - (D) understand

4. Which statement is true?
   - (A) San Antonio Meals for Seniors has a bigger time commitment than the San Antonio Literacy Foundation.
   - (B) San Antonio Literacy Foundation requires more training than the other places.
   - (C) "Make People Smile" Animal Therapy has the biggest time commitment of the three places.
   - (D) San Antonio Meals for Seniors requires more training than the other places.

B **Solve** the problem. Give your opinion.

Ann volunteers at a day-care center. She thought she would be reading to the children and doing art projects with them, but the teachers ask her to organize the room and do clerical work for them. She doesn't spend very much time with the children. What should she do?

2 Grammar connections: *used to and be used to*

Use *used to* + base form of a verb for past situations that are not true now. Use *be used to* + gerund or noun for things a person is accustomed to.

I **used to eat** a lot of sandwiches as a child. I **didn't use to eat** meat.	I **am used to eating** fish for dinner. I **am not used to eating** dessert. Katia **is used to American food**.
What **did** you **use to eat** as a child?	What **are** you **used to eating** for dinner?

Watch

A **Work** in a small group. Play the game. Write your name on a small piece of paper. Flip a coin to move your paper. Then tell your group your answer to the question in the square. Use *used to* or *be used to* in your answer. Take turns.

= 1 space

= 2 spaces

This says, "What did you use to do for fun as a child?" Well, I used to play in the park with my sister. We had a lot of fun.

Start here →	What did you use to do for fun as a child? →	How often are you used to going to the supermarket? →	How did you use to get to school as a child?
Who are you used to helping in your family?	← What kind of weather are you used to?	← What did you use to do after school as a child?	← What noises are you used to hearing in your neighborhood?
What time are you used to going to school? →	What time did you use to go to school as a child? →	What is something you used to do, but don't do now? →	What are you used to eating in the morning?
Finish!	← What are you used to hearing (or seeing) in your neighborhood?	← What is something you didn't use to do, but do now?	← What kind of food did you use to eat as a child?

B **Share** information about your classmates.

Julia used to play in the park with her sister for fun.

Oswaldo is used to going to the supermarket once a week.

Scan an announcement about community events to locate key information; contrast *use to* and *be used to*

UNIT 6 TIME

Lesson A Listening

1 Before you listen

A What do you see?

B What is happening?

2 Listen

A **Listen** and answer the questions.

1. Who are the speakers?
2. What are they talking about?

CD2, Track 2

B **Listen again.** Complete the chart.

	Time-saving device	Opinion about time-saving device
1. Mrs. Rosen	*address stamper*	
2. Mr. Chung		
3. Ms. Morales		

CD2, Track 2

3 After you listen

A **Read.** Complete the story.

convenient	distracting	email	manual	technology
devices	electronic	innovative	spam	text message

Today, a reporter from KESL Radio asked three people about ___*technology*___ (1) and their favorite time-saving ________ (2). Mrs. Rosen's favorite device is ________ (3). She says it saves time, even though it isn't ________ (4). Mr. Chung isn't a fan of technology. In fact, he says technology *wastes* more time than it saves. For example, he says he doesn't like ________ (5) because he gets lots of ________ (6). He also finds email ________ (7). He doesn't think it is ________ (8). Ms. Morales loves technology. She uses the camera on her cell phone in a very ________ (9) way – to send her daughter pictures of clothes that are on sale. Her daughter sends a ________ (10) back: "Buy." or "Don't buy."

Listen and check your answers.

CD2, Track 3

B **Discuss.** Talk with your classmates.

1. Do you agree with the people interviewed? Why or why not?
2. In general, do you think technology saves time or wastes time? Give examples.

Lesson B Clauses of concession

1 Grammar focus: *although* clauses

Use *although* to connect two clauses that show a contrast. The information in one clause is surprising or unexpected because of the information in the other clause. *Although* goes with the information that is known or not surprising.

Watch

KNOWN INFORMATION	UNEXPECTED INFORMATION	EXAMPLE
It takes thirty hours to drive from Denver to Los Angeles.	William refuses to fly.	**Although** it takes thirty hours to drive from Denver to Los Angeles, William refuses to fly.
Jake sets his alarm clock every day.	Jake often wakes up late and misses his bus.	Jake often wakes up late and misses his bus **although** he sets his alarm clock every day.

2

A **Write.** Which sentence is surprising or unexpected? Circle it. Then combine the two sentences. Use *although* in front of the sentence that is not surprising or unexpected.

1. Mrs. Sanchez can't operate her digital camera. She read the directions many times.
   Mrs. Sanchez can't operate her digital camera although *she read the directions many times*.
2. Mrs. White's car has a GPS system. She gets lost all the time.
   Although *Mrs. White's car has a GPS system, she gets lost all the time.*
3. Mr. Green doesn't use his microwave. He paid a lot of money for it.
   __________, although __________.
4. Mr. Chung doesn't like to use it. Email is fast.
   Although __________, __________.
5. I prefer to read paperback and hardcover books. E-books are very popular.
   __________.
6. Ms. Kaye had urgent business 1000 miles away. She refused to travel by plane.
   __________.
7. I prefer to use a fan when it's hot. My house has central air-conditioning.
   __________.
8. Ben never sets his alarm clock. He still gets to work on time.
   __________.
9. I play my CDs on my CD player at home. All my music is available online.
   __________.

Listen and check your answers.

CD2, Track 4

B **Talk** with a partner. Choose pairs of pictures and make sentences about Mr. Chung. Use *although* and *even though* with verbs from the box.

clean **find information** **have** **listen** **use** **wash** **write**

Even though Mr. Chung has a computer, he prefers to write letters by hand.

USEFUL LANGUAGE
Even though is stronger than *although.*
Though is a less formal form of *although.*

1.

2.
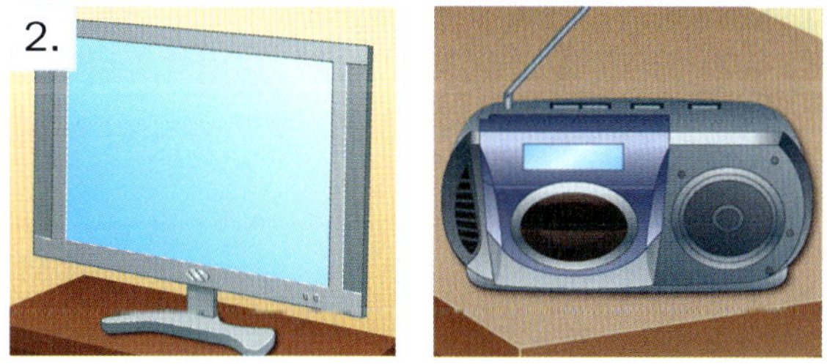

3.
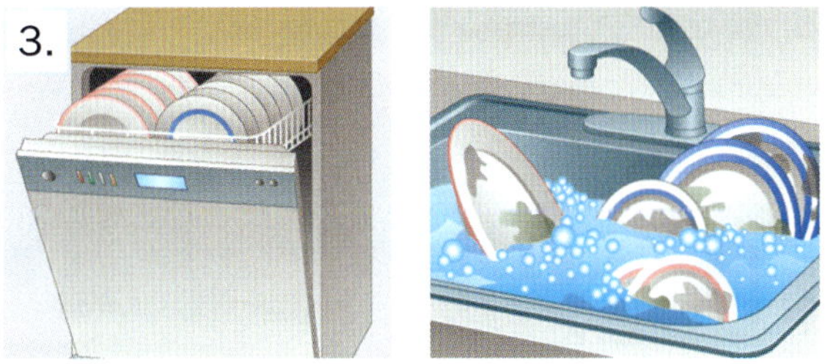

4.

5.

6.

Write sentences about Mr. Chung.

Although Mr. Chung has a computer, he prefers to write letters by hand.

3 Communicate

A **Work** in a small group. Talk about time-saving devices or tools that you own but don't use. Give reasons. Use *although* and *even though*.

A Although I have a food processor, I almost never use it.
B Why?
A It's too hard to clean.

CULTURE NOTE
In the United States, many people hold garage or yard sales to sell household items they no longer use.

B **Share** information about your classmates.

Lesson C Clauses of reason and concession

1 Grammar focus: contrasting *because* and *although*

Use *because* to join two clauses in which one gives a reason for the other. Use *although* to join two clauses that contrast with each other – one is surprising or unexpected based on the other.

Because cable Internet is fast, many people want it.

Although cable Internet is fast, many people cannot afford it.

Watch

2 Practice

A **Write.** Complete the story. Use *because* or *although*.

___Although___ (1) Pam and Beth are sisters, they are very different. Pam is very modern. She loves electrical appliances ______ (2) they are fast and convenient. For example, she loves her microwave ______ (3) she can use it to thaw meat quickly. She enjoys shopping for the latest kitchen devices ______ (4) some of them are very expensive. Beth has a different attitude about modern technology. She prefers not to use electrical appliances. For instance, she never uses a microwave ______ (5) she thinks the radiation is bad. She dries her clothes outside on a line ______ (6) she likes their smell after they've been in the fresh air. She washes her dishes by hand ______ (7) she says dishwashers waste energy. Pam doesn't understand why Beth is so old-fashioned. But ______ (8) the sisters have different lifestyles, they appreciate and enjoy one another very much.

Listen and check your answers.

OD2, Track 5

B **Talk** with a partner. Compare Mr. Techie and Mr. Nontech. Use *because* and *although*.

Mr. Techie uses a smartphone to calculate because it's convenient.

Mr. Nontech uses an adding machine to calculate although it isn't always convenient.

Mr. Techie	Mr. Nontech
uses a smartphone to calculate	uses an adding machine to calculate
shops online	shops in stores
texts his lunch order	brings lunch from home
travels by plane	travels by train
looks up phone numbers on the Internet	uses the phone book
has prepared dinners delievered	cooks his own dinners
uses a cell phone	uses a landline
corresponds by "email"	corresponds by "snail mail"

Write sentences about Mr. Techie and Mr. Nontech.

Mr. Techie uses a smartphone to calculate because it is convenient.

Mr. Nontech uses an adding machine to calculate although it isn't always convenient.

3 Communicate

A **Work** with a partner. Ask and answer questions about the activities in Exercise 2B. Give reasons for your answers.

A Do you drive to work or take public transportation?

B Well, although driving is faster, I take public transportation.

A Why?

B Because I don't have a car!

USEFUL LANGUAGE

Use *neither* when the answer to both choices in a question is negative.

A *Do you drive to work or take public transportation?*

B *Neither. I ride my bike.*

B **Share** information about your partner.

Lesson D Reading

1 Before you read

Talk with your classmates. Answer the questions.

1. How has technology changed transportation?
2. How has technology impacted the way we communicate with others?

The first paragraph usually identifies the topic and the last paragraph often repeats the main idea. The paragraphs between provide details about the main idea. Before you read the entire article, **skim**. Read the first and last paragraph and the first sentence of the paragraphs between. This will give you an overview, or general idea, of the article.

2 Read

Read the article. Listen and read again.

CD2, Track 6

The Impact of Technology

By Katelyn Houston

Changes in technology can change people's lives. The development of transportation — trains, cars, and planes — provides us with one example. Before the 19th century, most people lived within walking distance of work. In the 20th century many people began to commute between home and work because trains and cars connected cities with suburbs. Today, because of airplanes, many people travel great distances for their work. Some, because of the Internet, don't need to travel at all.

Technological changes have also impacted the media — for example, how we get the news. Newspapers were once people's primary source for the news: in 1965, 72% of Americans reported that they read a newspaper on an average day. By 2005, that number was down to 50%. In the past, a common way people got news was by listening to the radio. I suppose nearly everyone had a radio then. By the 1950s, television was overtaking radio. Now even the number of people watching the news on television has declined, dropping from 60% in 1993 to 28% in 2006. So what's the latest source for news? The web. The number of Americans who use the internet to get the news is increasing. Most people access the news on their smart phones.

Media has also changed the way people get jobs. People used to look for job openings in the classified ads of a newspaper. Then they would mail an application through the US Postal Service (now called snail mail by some). Finally, if someone was lucky enough to get an interview, that person would go to the job site. Today people can find notices for jobs online and then submit their applications over the Internet. The employer can even interview them over the internet using programs, such as Skype, that provide voice-over and video-over calls. These changes save time for both the employer and the applicant.

Another example of the impact of technology is how people pay for goods and services. Until the mid-1940s, people had to carry large amounts of cash in their purses and wallets. Then, one day in 1949, a man named Frank McNamara took some business associates to dinner, but he left his wallet at home. He had to call his wife to bring him money to pay the bill. Mr. McNamara vowed to find a way to avoid carrying cash. Although some stores already had their own charge cards, there was no single, multi-purpose credit card. A year later he returned to the same restaurant with the same people but paid with the credit card he had created, called "Diner's Club." Today, people don't even need to carry a credit card. They can pay with their smartphones.

In what other ways do you think technology may change people's lives in the future?

3 After you read

A **Check** your understanding.

1. In what four areas does the author provide examples for how technology has changed people's lives?
2. What statistics does the article give to support the statement that the number of people who get their news through the newspaper has declined?
3. According to the author, nearly everyone had a radio in the past. What phrase does the article use that tells you whether this is fact or opinion?
4. Sometimes text provides examples that help us understand the meaning of a word. What examples does this text give for *media*? For *transportation*?
5. The article says some people refer to the U.S. Postal Service as "snail mail." How are snails and the U.S. mail similar?
6. Do you think the author believes that changes in technology have a positive or a negative impact on people's lives? Cite evidence from the article to support your opinion.

B **Build** your vocabulary.

1. Read the dictionary entry. How many definitions are there?

   impact /n/ 1 force 2 effect

2. Find the words in the story. Underline the sentence. Determine the part of speech and write it next to the word. Use a dictionary to find the definition that fits the reading.

Vocabulary	Definition that fits context	One other definition
1. impact *(n)*	*effect*	*force*
2. commute		
3. source		
4. average		
5. classified		
6. application		

C **Talk** with a partner.

1. What technological change has most impacted your life? How has it affected you?
2. Do you think paying for goods and services with smart phones is a good idea? Why or why not?
3. Recently companies have been developing and testing driverless cars. If they become popular, how do you think that will impact jobs?

For college and career readiness practice, see pages 151–153.

Distinguish opinion and inference from explicit facts in a text; use a dictionary to find multiple meanings of words

Lesson E Writing

1 Before you write

A **Work** in a small group. Make a list of time-saving devices you and your classmates use. Write one advantage and one disadvantage of each.

Device	Advantage	Disadvantage
calculator	*does math quickly*	*breaks easily*
1.		
2.		
3.		
4.		
5.		
6.		
7.		
8.		

B **Read** the paragraph.

My Favorite Time-saving Device

My favorite time-saving device, voicemail, has many advantages, but it also has some disadvantages. Before I had voicemail, I used to answer my phone every time it rang, even if I was busy. But with voicemail, I don't have to interrupt my work. The caller can just leave a message, and I can get it later. Another benefit of voicemail is that it allows me to avoid talking to people I don't want to talk to. But, of course, that is also a disadvantage because they can avoid talking to me! Another problem is that not only friends leave messages. Sometimes there are voicemail messages from salespeople. So even though voicemail is very convenient, it has drawbacks as well.

One way of organizing a paragraph is by describing advantages and disadvantages.

C **Work** with a partner. Complete the diagram of the model paragraph.

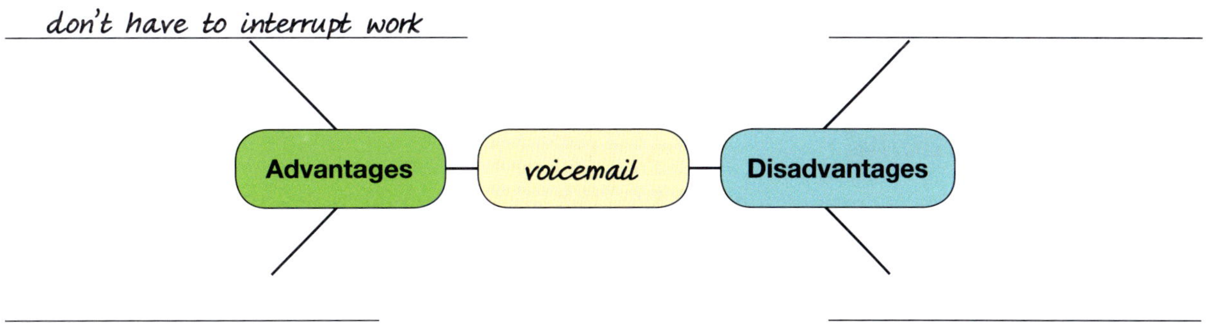

D **Plan** a paragraph that discusses the advantages and disadvantages of a time-saving device. Use the diagram to make notes on your ideas.

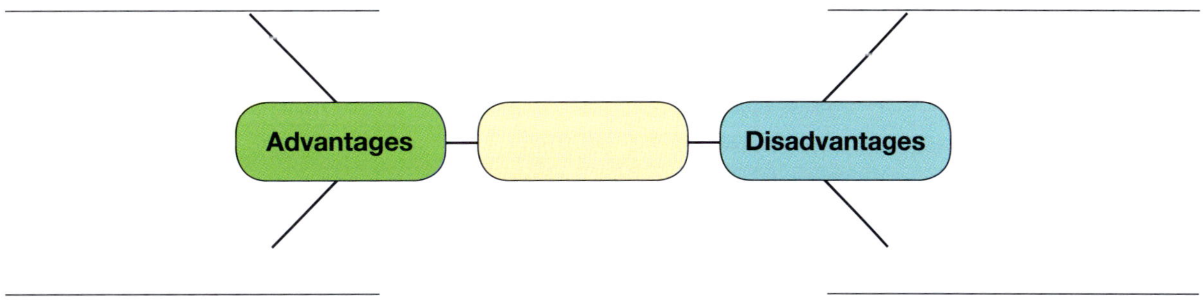

2 Write

Write a paragraph about a time-saving device. Give the paragraph a title, include a topic sentence, and describe at least two advantages and two disadvantages. Use the paragraph in Exercise 1B and the diagrams in Exercises 1C and 1D to help you.

3 After you write

A **Check** your writing.

	Yes	No
1. My paragraph has a title.	☐	☐
2. My topic sentence names the time-saving device.	☐	☐
3. I described at least two advantages and two disadvantages.	☐	☐

B **Share** your writing with a partner.

1. Take turns. Read your paragraph to a partner.
2. Comment on your partner's paragraph. Ask your partner a question about the paragraph. Tell your partner one thing you learned.

Lesson F Another view

1 Life-skills reading

Internet use has increased significantly since its beginnings in the 1960s. Reasons for using it have also increased. The following data show the results of one county's survey to compare its use by seniors with other adults.

Internet Activities of Adults* in Green County		
Activity	**18-64 years**	**65+ years (Seniors)**
Use the internet	97.50%	75.00%
Communication: e-mail, chats,	90.00%	72.25%
Social networks: share events, opinions	70.50%	45.75%
Consumer services: shop, make reservations, sell things	68.01%	64.00%
Financial services: bank, pay bills	64.00%	48.00%
Entertainment: stream / download music & videos; play games	53.40%	00.15%
Searches: information, people	48.00%	62.00%

*One hundred adults were interviewed. Twenty of those were seniors.

A **Read** the questions. Look at the chart. Fill in the answer.

1. How many seniors were interviewed?
   - (A) 100
   - (B) 75
   - (C) 20
   - (D) none of the above

2. Of those surveyed, how many were adults under 65?
   - (A) 97.5%
   - (B) 75%
   - (C) 100%
   - (D) 80%

3. Which internet activity is more popular with seniors than with other adults?
   - (A) Consumer services
   - (B) Searches
   - (C) Communication
   - (D) Social networks

4. In which area is there the biggest difference in how seniors and other adults use the internet?
   - (A) Social networks
   - (B) Consumer services
   - (C) Financial services
   - (D) Entertainment

B **Solve** the problem. Give your opinion.

Last year Juan gave his teenage son a computer for his birthday. It is in his bedroom. Now he spends a lot of time in his bedroom playing games online. His grades are not good, and his teachers report that he doesn't turn in his homework. What should Juan do?

2 Grammar connections: *so* and *such*

So and *such* make the meaning stronger. Use *so* before an adjective. Use *such (a)* before a noun.

SO + ADJECTIVE	*SUCH* + ADJECTIVE + NOUN	OPTIONAL *THAT* CLAUSE
That clock is **so small**	That's **such a small clock**	**that** it's hard to see the time
Those cars are **so nice**	Those are **such nice cars**	**that** I want to drive them

Watch

A **Talk** with a partner. Describe the pictures with *so* and *such*. Take turns.

A That watch is so old (that no one would use it).

B That is such an old watch (that no one would use it).

USEFUL LANGUAGE
In conversation people often omit the "that" clause. Formal writing usually includes the "that" clause.

B **Work** in a small group. Describe items in the word box with your own information. Use *so* and *such*. Take turns.

your Internet connection at home	your commute to work / school
your house / apartment / room	your cell phone
your television	your watch

A I have such a fast Internet connection at home that I can watch videos online easily.

B You're lucky! My Internet connection at home is so slow that I don't use it very often.

REVIEW

1 Listening

Listen. Take notes on a radio interview.

CD2, Track 7

Characteristics of tutors	Requirements to be a tutor
1. *compassionate – care about helping*	4.
2.	5.
3.	6.

Talk with a partner. Check your answers.

2 Grammar

A **Write.** Complete the story.

A Love of Technology

My friend Bob loves technology. *As soon as* (1. As soon as / Until) a new computer comes out, he buys it. The same is true with his cell phone. He doesn't wait ________ (2. as soon as / until) the end of his contract. ________ (3. Because / Even though) his cell phone is still good, he buys a new one. ________ (4. Because / Even though) he loves the latest technology, his house is filled with new devices. ________ (5. Although / Until) he has the newest devices, he keeps the old ones. His wife is unhappy. She has told him, "No more electronic gadgets ________ (6. as soon as / until) you get rid of the old ones." ________ (7. Although / Until) Don really wants a new phone, he can't bear to discard his older devices.

B **Write.** Look at the words that are underlined in the answers. Write the questions.

1. **A** ________
   B Bob loves technology.
2. **A** ________
   B He buys a new cell phone as soon as a new one comes out.
3. **A** ________
   B His house is filled with new devices.
4. **A** ________
   B Because of all the electronic gadgets, Bob's wife is unhappy.

Talk with a partner. Ask and answer the questions.

3 Pronunciation: stressed and unstressed words

Content words (nouns, main verbs, adverbs, adjectives, negatives, and question words) are usually stressed. Function words (pronouns, prepositions, conjunctions, articles, *be* verbs, and auxiliary verbs) are usually not stressed.

A **Listen** to the stressed and unstressed words in each sentence. The stressed words are underlined.

CD2, Track 8

1. Pam loves electrical appliances because they save her time.
2. She wants to volunteer in the health-care field.
3. Even though computers are time-savers, some people don't use them.
4. Will he go to sleep as soon as his visitors leave?

Listen again and repeat. Stress the underlined content words.

B **Listen and repeat.** Then underline the stressed content words.

CD2, Track 9

1. She delivers meals to seniors.
2. Volunteers should be patient and compassionate.
3. Do you walk to work or drive?
4. Mr. Chung isn't a fan of e-mail.

Read your sentences to a partner. Compare your answers.

C **Read** the paragraph. Underline the stressed words.

Ingrid worked with computers in her native country, so she wants a job working with computers in the U.S. She's been looking for several months, but she hasn't found a job yet. Finally, she decided to do some volunteer work until she could find a paying job. Ingrid volunteers at the local zoo. She does office work on the computer.

Talk with a partner. Compare your answers. Read the paragraph to your partner.

D **Write** five sentences from Units 5 and 6. Then work with a partner. Underline the stressed words in your partner's sentences.

1. ______________________________
2. ______________________________
3. ______________________________
4. ______________________________
5. ______________________________

UNIT 7 SHOPPING

Lesson A Listening

1 Before you listen

A What do you see?

B What is happening?

2 Listen

A **Listen** and answer the questions.

1. Who are the speakers?
2. What are they talking about?

CD2, Track 10

B **Listen again.** Complete the chart.

CD2, Track 10

1. kind of camera Rosa bought	*a digital camera*
2. problem	
3. date purchased	
4. today's date	
5. store policy for refunds	
6. store policy for exchanges	

3 After you listen

A **Read.** Complete the story.

camera	customer service	exchanges	policy	store credit
condition	defective	merchandise	refund	warranty

Rosa wants to return the ___*camera*___(1) that she bought and get a ________(2). She is told that she needs to speak with someone in ________(3). The clerk there asks Rosa if the camera is ________(4), and she says it isn't. The clerk tells her about the store ________(5) for returns and ________(6). It's too late for Rosa to return the camera, but she can exchange it if the ________(7) is in perfect ________(8). Rosa still has the camera box with the instruction book and the ________(9) card. Since Rosa is in a hurry, she decides to get a ________(10), and she will use it at a later time.

Listen and check your answers.

CD2, Track 11

B **Discuss.** Talk with your classmates.

1. What are some reasons that people may want to return merchandise to a store?
2. What are some situations where it may be impossible to return merchandise?
3. Do you think people should get a refund for something they have used? Why or why not?

Lesson B Subject-pattern adjective clauses

1 Grammar focus: *who, that* and *which*

Adjective clauses come after a noun and begin with a relative pronoun. *Who, that* and *which* are examples of relative pronouns. Use *who* with people, *which* with things, and *that* with people or things.

The camera costs only $99. (It) is on sale.	The clerk helped the customer. (She) lost her receipt.
The camera **which** is on sale costs only $99.	The clerk helped the customer **who** lost her receipt.
The camera **that** is on sale costs only $99.	The clerk helped the customer **that** lost her receipt.

Watch

2 Practice

A **Write**. Circle the subject in the second sentence. Then combine the sentences by making the second sentence into an adjective clause and replacing the subject with *which* or *who*.

1. I want to buy a camera. (It)'s not too expensive.
   I want to buy a camera which is not too expensive.
2. I'd like to get a good camera. It will last for many years.
   ____
3. Many people shop online. They are looking for cameras.
   ____
4. My friend told me about a camera store. It sells used merchandise.
   ____
5. Customers like to shop at Super Camera. They appreciate good service.
   ____
6. The clerk is very helpful. He works in customer service.
   ____
7. These days, many people want an expensive camera. It has separate lenses.
   ____
8. Sometimes people need to return merchandise. It is defective.
   ____
9. Buyers may be sorry later. They don't ask about a store's return policy.
   ____
10. Many people now have smart phones. The phones have excellent cameras.
   ____

Listen and check your answers.

CD2, Track 12

B **Talk** with a partner. Ask and answer questions to identify the following people in the picture: the cashier, the cleaning person, the customer, the greeter, the stock clerk, and the store manager. Use adjective clauses with *who, that* or *which*. Choose verbs from the box.

carry	**give**	**help**	**listen**	**smile**	**sweep**
clean	**have**	**hold**	**put**	**stand**	**wear**

A Which one is the cashier?

B He's the man who's putting the video camera into the bag.

A You mean the one that's standing behind the counter?

B Right.

Write **sentences about the people in the picture.**

The cashier is the man who's putting the video camera into the bag.

3 Communicate

A **Work** in a small group. Ask and answer questions about the topics. Use adjective clauses with *that*, *who*, or *which*.

A Nadia, what kinds of supermarkets do you like?

B I like supermarkets that are open 24 hours a day. What about you, Phuong?

C I like supermarkets that have lots of fresh fish.

- books
- clothing stores
- internet sites
- malls
- restaurants
- salesclerks
- supermarkets
- (your idea)

B **Share** information about your classmates.

Lesson C Object-pattern adjective clauses

1 Grammar focus: *that*

Adjective clauses come after a noun and begin with a relative pronoun. *That* is an example of a relative pronoun. Use *that* with people or things.

I like the car.	The mechanic has 20 years of experience.
You bought (it.)	I use (him.)
I like the car **(that)** you bought.	The mechanic **(that)** I use has 20 years of experience.

Watch

2 Practice

A **Write**. Circle the object in the second sentence. Then combine the sentences by changing the second sentence into an adjective clause with *that*.

1. A good friend needed a new car. I've known (her) for several years.
   A good friend that I've known for several years needed a new car.
2. She used to drive an old car. She got it from her father.
   ____
3. Last January, the old car stopped working. She was driving it.
   ____
4. The mechanic couldn't fix it. Her neighbor recommended the mechanic.
   ____
5. Finally, she decided to buy a used car from a man. She knew the man at work.
   ____
6. He's an honest person. She trusts him completely.
   ____
7. The price was really good. He named it.
   ____
8. The used car is only three years old. He sold her the car.
   ____
9. It's a reliable car. She can drive it for a long time.
   ____
10. Suzy is happy to have a vehicle. She doesn't have to worry about it.
   ____

Listen and check your answers.

CD2, Track 13

B **Talk** with a partner. Ted and Lisa got married recently. Unfortunately, they have had some bad luck. Look at the chart and make sentences by choosing an item from each column.

The dishes Ted and Lisa received from Aunt May were broken.

USEFUL LANGUAGE
In object-pattern adjective clauses, you can leave out *that*.

dishes	found on the Internet	the wrong size
computer	bought on sale	scratched
car	ordered from a catalog	broken
camera	got as a wedding present	damaged
rug	received from Aunt May	torn
lamps	picked up at a garage sale	the wrong color
coffee table	purchased from a friend	too slow

Write sentences about Ted and Lisa.

The dishes that they received from Aunt May were broken.

3 Communicate

A **Work** in a small group. Tell about a shopping "mistake." Include the information below.

- What was the item?
- Where did you buy it?
- What did you do about it?
- When did you buy it?
- What was wrong with it?

A The chicken I bought last week at Paglia's Meats was spoiled.

B What did you do about it?

A I took it back to the store and asked them to give me a fresh package.

USEFUL LANGUAGE
Use the following adjectives to say what is wrong with something you bought: *broken, defective, damaged, spoiled, torn, too big, too small.*

B **Share** information about your classmates.

Lesson D Reading

1 Before you read

Talk with your classmates. Answer the questions.

1. Have you ever tried to exchange an item or get a refund? Describe your experience.
2. In your native country, is it easy or difficult for people to get a refund for something that they purchased?

Sometimes an important word is replaced by a synonym. This makes the reading more interesting. For example, *seller* and *retailer* are two nouns that have the same meaning.

2 Read

Read the newspaper advice column. Listen and read again.

CD2, Track 14

The Smart Shopper

Dear Smart Shopper,

I'm a jewelry lover, and I enjoy shopping online. Unfortunately, I just bought a pair of gold earrings that I don't like. When I tried to return them, I learned that the seller has a no-return policy. Don't I have the right to get a refund?

Mad Madelyn

Dear Mad Madelyn,

If the merchandise is defective, the seller must return your money or make an exchange. However, if the merchandise was in good condition when you received it, and if the retailer has a no-return policy, there is nothing you can do. This is true for store purchases as well as Internet purchases. In the future, here are some questions you should ask before you buy anything:

- Does the seller say "satisfaction guaranteed or your money back"?
- Is there a time limit on returns, such as two weeks?
- Who pays the shipping costs on items that are returned?
- Do you need to return the merchandise in its original package?
- Is the original receipt required?
- Does the retailer give a store credit instead of a cash refund?
- If the retailer has a store in your area, can you return the merchandise to the store instead of shipping it?

Next time, find the return policy on the merchant's Web site and print it, or ask the merchant for the return policy in writing. It's important to get all the facts that you need before you buy!

Smart Shopper

3 After you read

A **Check** your understanding.

1. What is the purpose of *The Smart Shopper* newspaper column?
2. What problem does Madelyn write about?
3. According to the article, when must a retailer return a customer's money?
4. Do you believe that Madelyn is happy with the answer to her question? Why or why not?
5. What should Madelyn have done before she bought the earrings?
6. What is another word in the reading with the same meaning as *seller* and *retailer*?

B **Build** your vocabulary.

Compound nouns are noun + noun combinations that have special meanings. Sometimes you can explain compound nouns with adjective clauses. For example, a *jewelry lover* is a person who loves jewelry.

1. Find compound nouns in the reading that match the meanings. Write them on the chart.

Compound noun	Meaning
1. *jewelry lover*	a person who loves jewelry
2.	a limit that is related to time
3.	costs that are related to shipping
4.	a credit that is given by a store
5.	a refund that is made in cash
6.	a policy that is related to returns
7.	
8.	

2. Find two more compound nouns in the reading. Write them on the chart. Use adjective clauses to explain what they mean.
3. Work in a small group. Make a list of other compound nouns you know. Use adjective clauses to explain what they mean.

C **Talk** with a partner.

1. Are you a jewelry lover? What do you love to buy?
2. Are you a smart shopper? Explain your answer.
3. Have you ever gotten a cash refund? For what? Why?
4. What is something you wanted to return, but didn't?

For college and career readiness practice, see pages 154–156.

Determine the main idea of a text by analyzing key details; identify and explain the meanings of compound nouns

Lesson E Writing

1 Before you write

A **Talk** with a partner. List some reasons people should or shouldn't shop online.

Reasons people should shop online	Reasons people shouldn't shop online
It's convenient.	*It's hard to choose merchandise you can't touch.*

B **Read** the paragraph.

Reasons You Shouldn't Shop Online

There are some good reasons you shouldn't shop online. First, it's hard to choose merchandise that you can't touch. For example, a piece of jewelry might look very good on the computer screen, but after you buy it and look at it closely, you may find that it's very ugly and poorly made. Furthermore, shopping online is slow. It may take several days to receive the merchandise. If you are not satisfied, it may take weeks to exchange the merchandise or get your money back. Finally, shopping online can be dangerous. People can steal your credit card number and use it to buy expensive items. An irresponsible seller can take your money and never send you the merchandise. I'm going to do my shopping in stores!

Use transition words such as *first*, *second*, *next*, *furthermore*, *moreover*, and *finally* to signal a list of reasons in a paragraph.

C **Complete** the outline with information from the model paragraph.

Transition words		Reasons and supporting details
First	First reason:	hard to choose merchandise you can't touch
	Supporting detail:	
________	Second reason:	
	Supporting detail:	
	Supporting detail:	
________	Third reason:	
	Supporting detail:	
	Supporting detail:	

D **Plan** a paragraph about why you *should* shop online. Think of two or more reasons and one or more supporting details for each reason. Make notes about your ideas in an outline like the one in Exercise 1C. Use your own paper.

2 Write

Write a paragraph about why you should shop online. Give at least two reasons and one supporting detail for each reason. Use transition words to signal your list of reasons. Use the paragraph in Exercise 1B and the outlines in Exercises 1C and 1D to help you.

3 After you write

A **Check** your writing.

	Yes	No
1. I wrote two or more reasons to shop online.	☐	☐
2. I gave one or more supporting details for each reason.	☐	☐
3. I used transition words like *first*, *furthermore*, and *finally* to signal my list of reasons.	☐	☐

B **Share** your writing with a partner.

1. Take turns. Read your paragraph to a partner.
2. Comment on your partner's paragraph. Ask your partner a question about the paragraph. Tell your partner one thing you learned.

Lesson F Another view

1 Life-skills reading

JedsSports.com RETURNED-MERCHANDISE FORM

Please complete this form and send it with the returned merchandise within 21 days to JedsSports.com, 3209 W. Foster Ave., Chicago, IL 60625. Include a copy of the invoice and the original packaging. Call us for a Returned-Merchandise Authorization number (M–F, 8 a.m.–5 p.m., CST) at 800-555-4143.

Name: *Rita Miller* **RMA#:** *98704370*

Address *271 Dade Drive* **City** *Largo* **State** *FL* **Zip** *33771*

Check one:
☐ Store Credit
☑ Exchange

List items for return:

Item #	Description	Size	Color	Reason	Additional Comments
P4103	*sweatshirt*	*medium*	*red*	*wrong size*	*I ordered a large.*

List items to receive in exchange:

Item #	Description	Size	Color		
P4128	*sweatshirt*	*large*	*red*		

A **Read** the questions. Look at the returned-merchandise form. Fill in the answer.

1. Why is the buyer using this form?
   - (A) She wants her money back.
   - (B) She wants a store credit.
   - (C) She wants to exchange the merchandise.
   - (D) none of the above
2. What does the buyer need to include with this form?
   - (A) the invoice
   - (B) the item that she is returning
   - (C) the original packaging
   - (D) all of the above
3. Which statement is true?
   - (A) The buyer must return the items within 21 days.
   - (B) The buyer is satisfied with her purchase.
   - (C) The buyer needs a smaller sweatshirt.
   - (D) The buyer lives in New Jersey.
4. Which statement is not true?
   - (A) The buyer is returning one item.
   - (B) The buyer needs a different size.
   - (C) The merchandise was defective.
   - (D) The buyer wants the same color.

B **Solve** the problem. Give your opinion.

Catherine lives in an apartment building where all the mailboxes are just inside the main door. The mail carrier usually leaves packages on the floor beside the mailboxes. Recently Catherine ordered a soccer uniform from JedsSports.com. She never received her package even though the store says that the package was delivered a few days ago. What should she do?

2 Grammar connections: Clarifying questions

To ask for clarification of words not heard or understood, insert a question word into the statement.

Watch

STATEMENT	CLARIFYING QUESTIONS
I went to the mall.	You went **where**?
There was a sale last weekend.	There was a sale **when**?
I bought some shirts.	You bought some **what**?
They were $20 each.	They were **how much**?
I bought five of them.	You bought **how many**?
They're for my sister.	They're for **who**?

A **Complete** the paragraph to make a story. Then talk with a partner. Your partner will listen and ask a clarifying question after every sentence. Answer your partner's question.

A I needed to buy a laptop case.
B You needed to buy what?
A A laptop case.

I needed to buy ________(1). So I went to ________(2). I got there at ________(3) o'clock. I couldn't find any, so I talked to ________(4). That person told me to go ________(5). Finally I found one. It only cost $ ________(6). I didn't buy just one. I bought ________(7)! I took them home and showed them to ________(8). He / She / They said, "________(9)!"

B **Share** your partner's story with the class. The class will ask clarifying questions.

A Luis needed to buy a laptop case.
B Class He needed to buy what?
A A laptop case.

Scan a form for key details about returning merchandise; ask clarifying questions for words not heard or understood

UNIT 8 WORK

Lesson A Listening

1 Before you listen

A What do you see?

B What is happening?

1

2

3

4

5

6

UNIT GOALS

Identify problems at work and school **Describe** hard and soft skills
Provide solutions and identify consequences to those solutions

2 Listen

A **Listen** and answer the questions.

1. Who are the speakers?
2. What are they talking about?

CD2, Track 15

B **Listen again.** Complete the diagram.

CD2, Track 15

____
Yolanda's problem

Possible solutions

1. ________________
2. ________________
3. ________________
4. ________________

____
Yolanda's decision

3 After you listen

A **Read.** Complete the story.

advice	**close up**	**exhausted**	**negotiate**	**tasks**
chart	**deal with**	**initials**	**share**	**work (something) out**

Yolanda and David work at Daria's Donut Shop. Lately, David has been leaving work early, and Yolanda has to ___close up___ (1) the shop by herself. Tonight, Yolanda is having coffee with her friends. She is ________ (2). Her friends give her ________ (3). Teresa thinks she should talk to her boss, but Yolanda wants to try to ________ (4) things ________ (4) with David first. Julie thinks Yolanda should make a ________ (5) of their duties. Then she should ________ (6) with David and decide who is going to do which ________ (7). When they finish a task, they should write their ________ (8) on the chart. If David isn't doing his ________ (9) of the work, it will show in the chart. Then, Yolanda can show the chart to their boss and let her ________ (10) the situation.

Listen and check your answers.

CD2, Track 16

B **Discuss.** Talk with your classmates.

Lesson B Verb tense contrast

1 Grammar focus: present perfect and present perfect continuous

The present perfect is formed by *have / has* + past participle. One use of the present perfect is to talk about recently finished actions (often with the word *just*) with no specific time of completion of those actions.

The present perfect continuous is formed by *have / has* + *been* + present participle (*-ing*). Use the present perfect continuous to talk about actions that started in the past, continue to now, and will probably continue in the future.

Watch

PRESENT PERFECT (RECENTLY FINISHED ACTION)	PRESENT PERFECT CONTINUOUS (CONTINUING ACTION)
Yolanda **has (just) mopped** the floor. It's clean now.	Yolanda **has been mopping** the floor **for** 15 minutes.

2 Practice

A **Write**. Complete the sentences. Use the present perfect or present perfect continuous forms of the verbs. Use *just* where possible.

1. Daria Thompson is the owner of Daria's Donut Shop. She *has been selling* (sell) donuts at this location for more than 20 years.
2. It's 7:00 a.m. Daria ________ (make) donuts for three hours.
3. It's 7:30 a.m. Daria ________ (open) the shop for customers.
4. It's 10:30 a.m. Daria's son ________ (help) her all morning.
5. He ________ (finish) cleaning the counters and shelves. Everything is spotless.
6. Daria needs more help in the shop. She ________ (decide) to hire Yolanda.
7. Yolanda's shift begins at 6:00 a.m. today. She ________ (wait) for the bus for 30 minutes. She's worried that she's going to be late.
8. It's 6:05 a.m. Yolanda ________ (call) to say she will be late.
9. It's 6:30 a.m. Yolanda ________ (arrive) at the store. Daria is really glad to see her!
10. It's noon. Yolanda ________ (work) for several hours and she's ready to take a break.

Listen and check your answers.

CD2, Track 17

B **Talk** with a partner. Look at Yolanda's work schedule. Make sentences about the things she has just done and has been doing at the following times: 6:15, 6:30, 7:30, 11:00, 12:00, 2:00, and 4:00.

It's 6:15 a.m. Yolanda has just arrived.

It's 11:00 a.m. Yolanda has been serving customers for three and a half hours.

Yolanda's Schedule

6:15 a.m.	Arrive Turn off the security alarm
6:30 a.m.	Open the cash register Make coffee
7:30 a.m.	Open the shop for customers
7:30 a.m.–11:00 a.m.	Serve customers Take phone orders
11:00 a.m.–12:00 noon	Eat lunch Go to the bank
12:00 noon–4:00 p.m.	Serve customers Take phone orders
2:00 p.m.	Refill sugar containers Receive shipment of coffee
4:00 p.m.	Go home

Write sentences about Yolanda's schedule.

It's 6:15 a.m. Yolanda has just arrived.
It's 11:00 a.m. Yolanda has been serving customers for three and a half hours.

3 Communicate

A **Work** with a partner. Think about your own schedule. Your partner says a time. You say what you have been doing and what you have just done.

A Natalia, pretend it's 10:30 a.m.

B OK, it's 10:30 a.m. I've been working for two hours. I've just read my email.

B **Share** information about your partner.

It's 10:30 a.m. Natalia has been working for two hours. She has just read her email.

Lesson C Participles as adjectives

1 Grammar focus: adjectives ending in *-ed* and *-ing*

Participles are forms of verbs. They can end in *-ed* or *-ing*. Sometimes we use them as adjectives. Often the *-ing* form describes a thing or person and the *-ed* form describes the way someone feels.

Watch

-ed ADJECTIVES	*-ing* ADJECTIVES	
I'm **tired** of this job.	This is a **tiring** job.	This job is **tiring**.
He's **interested** in this task.	This is an **interesting** task.	This task is **interesting**.
They're **disappointed** about their grades.	These are **disappointing** grades.	These grades are **disappointing**.

2 Practice

A **Write**. Circle the correct adjective.

1. **A** I heard that Juan and his friends went to a party after work. How was the party?
   B It was really **exciting** / **excited**.
2. **A** What did Juan and his friends like the most about the party?
   B There was a lot of **interesting** / **interested** music from different countries.
3. **A** How did Juan feel the next day at work?
   B He was **exhausting** / **exhausted**.
4. **A** How long did he have to work?
   B He had to work from 9:30 to 6:30. It was a **tiring** / **tired** day.
5. **A** Does Juan usually start working at 9:30?
   B No, he overslept! He was **shocking** / **shocked** that he didn't hear the alarm clock.
6. **A** How did his boss react when he showed up late?
   B His boss was **irritating** / **irritated**.
7. **A** What did his boss say to him?
   B He told Juan that he was **disappointing** / **disappointed** in him.
8. **A** How did Juan feel after his boss told him that?
   B Juan felt **embarrassing** / **embarrassed**.
9. **A** Juan didn't have a good day, I guess. What did he do later that night?
   B He stayed home and had a **relaxing** / **relaxed** night in front of the TV.
10. **A** So, is Juan going to go out again on a weeknight?
    B I don't think so. He said it was an **exhausting** / **exhausted** experience.

Listen and check your answers. Then practice with a partner.

CD2, Track 18

B **Talk** with a partner. For each picture, describe the person and the activity. Choose participial adjectives from the boxes.

> The man is excited.

> Getting an award is exciting.

Positive	
amusing	amused
exciting	excited
interesting	interested
relaxing	relaxed

Negative	
annoying	annoyed
boring	bored
frightening	frightened
frustrating	frustrated

1. 

2. 

3. 

4. 

5. 

6. 

7. 

8. 

Write two sentences about each picture.

The man is excited.
Getting an award is exciting.

3 Communicate

A **Work** in a small group. Ask and answer questions about your experiences. Use the adjectives from Exercise 2B.

A What's an amusing experience that you have had at work?

B I was very amused when . . . it was amusing because . . .

B **Share** information about your classmates.

Lesson D Reading

1 Before you read

Talk with your classmates. Answer the questions.

1. What are some skills, such as following directions, that are necessary for most jobs?
2. What special skills do you have?

2 Read

Read the magazine article. Listen and read again.

CD2, Track 19

Hard and Soft Job Skills

Som Sarawong has been working as an automotive technician at George's Auto Repair for over five years. Today was a special day for Som, a 35-year-old Thai immigrant, because he received the Employee of the Year award. According to Ed Overton, Som's boss, Som received the award "because he's a great 'people person' and he has superb technical skills. I even have him work on my own car!"

Som has the two kinds of skills that are necessary to be successful and move up in his career: soft skills and hard skills. Soft skills are personal and social skills. Som gets along with his co-workers. He has a strong work ethic; in five years, he has never been late or absent from work. Customers trust him. Hard skills, on the other hand, are the technical skills a person needs to do a job. Som can repair cars, trucks, and motorcycles. He learned from his father, who was also a mechanic. Then he took classes and got a certificate as an auto technician.

Soft and hard skills are equally important, but hard skills are easier to teach and assess than soft skills. People can learn how to use a machine and then take a test on their knowledge. However, it's harder to teach people how to be cooperative and have a good work ethic. George Griffith, the owner of George's Auto Repair, explains, "I've been working in this business for over 30 years, and most of the time when I've needed to fire someone, it was because of weak people skills, not because they didn't have technical abilities." Soft skills and good technical knowledge are a winning combination, and today, Som Sarawong was the winner.

3 After you read

A **Check** your understanding.

1. What is the main idea of this article?
2. How does the quotation from Ed Overton support the main idea of the article?
3. What is the difference between a soft skill and a hard skill? Give examples from the article.
4. What are three examples of Som's soft skills?
5. According to the article, why are hard skills easier to evaluate than soft skills?
6. Which example shows that Som has a good work ethic?
7. According to George Griffith, do more workers lose their jobs because of weak soft skills or weak hard skills? Do you agree with George? Why or why not?

Quotations are used to explain or support a main idea. They also make a reading more interesting.

CULTURE NOTE
The expression *work ethic* is the belief that if you work hard in life you will get ahead and become successful.

B **Build** your vocabulary.

1. Find an example in the reading of each prefix and root. Write it in the chart.
2. Use a dictionary. Write the meaning of the words.
3. Guess the meaning of the prefixes and roots in the chart.

Prefixes	Example from reading	Meaning of word	Meaning of prefix
1. *re-*	*repair*	*to fix what is torn or broken*	*again*
2. *co-*			
3. *auto-*			
Roots			**Meaning of root**
4. *tech*			
5. *super*			
6. *equ*			

4. Work in a small group. Make a list of other words you know with the same prefixes and roots. Write a sentence for each new word.

C **Talk** with a partner.

1. What is something that you can do superbly?
2. What are some examples of technical skills?
3. What is a hobby or profession that requires good technical skills?
4. What are two hard skills and two soft skills that you have?

For college and career readiness practice, see pages 157–159.

Determine the main idea, facts and key details in a text; identify prefixes and roots

Lesson E Writing

1 Before you write

A **Talk** with a partner. Answer the questions.

1. What is a cover letter? What information does it include?
2. Have you ever written a cover letter? Tell your partner about your experience.
3. Today, most people write email cover letters. Why do you think this is true?

B **Read** the cover letter.

New Message

From: Ester Yitbarek <eyitbarek@youmail.com>

Subject: Teacher's assistant position

To: lynn.stevens@osbornk12.edu

Attachment: Resume_Ester Yitbarek

Dear Ms. Stevens:

I read your advertisement online for a position as a teacher's assistant. I am very interested in this position and have attached my résumé.

I have been working as a teacher's assistant at Hilltop Elementary School for three years. In this job, I have taught reading and math to students in small groups. I have also tutored individual students who were having problems with the lessons. I'm very interested in child development, and I love working with children. I get along very well with my co-workers, and I'm also skilled at dealing with parents.

I am planning to move to a new home in your district. I hope you will call me to schedule an interview. My phone number is 773-555-2673. I look forward to hearing from you.

Sincerely,

Ester Yitbarek

Ester Yitbarek
773-555-2673
eyitbarek@youmail.com

OBJECTIVE: To obtain a position as Teacher's Assistant

SUMMARY OF QUALIFICATIONS

- Teacher's assistant at Hilltop Elementary for three years
- Taught reading in small groups
- Tutored students who need extra help
- Bilingual English / Amharic

CULTURE NOTE
Applicants are usually expected to include a résumé — a written statement of their educational and work experience — with their cover letter.

D **Work** with a partner. Answer the questions.

1. Who wrote the email cover letter?
2. Who did she write it to?
3. What position is she applying for?
4. Where did she hear about the job?
5. How much experience does she have?
6. What are some of her skills?
7. What is the purpose of the last paragraph?

In the body of a cover letter, include:
- the title of the job you are applying for
- how you found out about the job
- information about your skills and experience
- how the employer can contact you

D **Plan** a cover letter for a real or an imaginary job. Complete the information.

Paragraph 1:

1. Title of the job you are applying for: ____________________
2. How you found out about it: ____________________

Paragraph 2:

3. Your skills and experience: ____________________

____

____

Paragraph 3:

4. How the employer can contact you: ____________________

2 Write

Write an email cover letter for a real or an imaginary job that you are interested in. Include the title of the job in the first sentence and say how you found out about it. Give at least two examples of your skills and experience. Use the cover letter in Exercise 1B and your outline in Exercise 1D to help you.

3 After you write

A **Check** your writing.

	Yes	No
1. My first sentence says the title of the job I am applying for.	☐	☐
2. I included how I found out about the job.	☐	☐
3. I gave two or more examples of my skills and experience.	☐	☐
4. I gave information about how to contact me.	☐	☐

B **Share** your writing with a partner.

1. Take turns. Read your letter to a partner.
2. Comment on your partner's letter. Ask your partner a question about the letter. Tell your partner one thing you learned.

Lesson F Another view

1 Life-skills reading

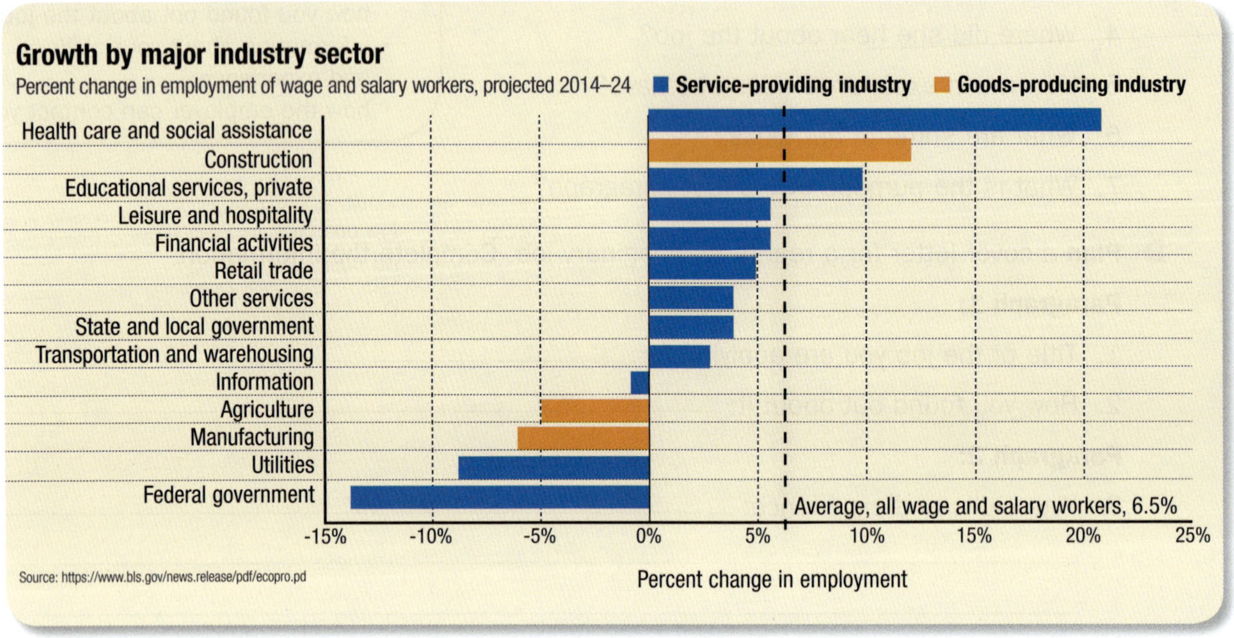

A Read the questions. Look at the chart. Fill in the answer.

1. Which service-providing industry will most likely have the largest increase in employment?
   - (A) Construction
   - (B) Federal government
   - (C) Health care and social assistance
   - (D) Manufacturing

2. What percent of job growth will there be for teachers?
   - (A) 5
   - (B) 10
   - (C) 15
   - (D) 20

3. What is *not* true about manufacturing?
   - (A) It's a goods-producing industry.
   - (B) An increase in the percentage of change in employment is expected.
   - (C) It will lose more jobs than Agriculture.
   - (D) It will decrease by more than 5% by 2024.

4. According to the chart, which of the major industries listed below project the least growth from 2014–2024?
   - (A) Agriculture
   - (B) Federal government
   - (C) Leisure and hospitality
   - (D) none of the above

B Solve the problem. Give your opinion.

Kumio is a 40-year old man who was working as an electronic assembler at a large manufacturing company for 12 years. Last month Kumio and a large number of assemblers were laid off. He's thinking about getting a job in health care. He heard about a private training program that costs $2,500. He also heard about a low-cost program at a community college, but it takes longer. What should he do?

2 Grammar connections: polite requests and offers

Polite requests ask someone to do something to help you. To make a polite request, use *Could you, Would you* or *Can you* with the base form of the verb. You can also use *Would you mind* with the gerund (verb + *-ing*) form of the verb.

Polite offers say you can do something to help someone. To make a polite offer, use *Could I, Can I, May I, Let me,* or *Why don't I* with the base form of the verb.

Watch

	QUESTIONS	ANSWERS
Polite requests	**Would / Will you move** your chair? **Could / Can you help** me with this box? **Would you mind helping** me?	Sure. No problem. I'd be glad to.
Offers	**Why don't I move** this box for you? **May / Can / Could I help** you with that? **Let me open** that for you.	OK, thanks. I'd appreciate it. That'd be great.

I'd = I would
that'd = that would

A **Talk** with a partner. Use the pictures to make and respond to requests for the situation. Then use the pictures to make and respond to offers for the situation. Take turns.

A Could you help me with this box?
B Sure.

A Let me move those books out of your way.
B Thanks! That'd be great!

1. 

2. 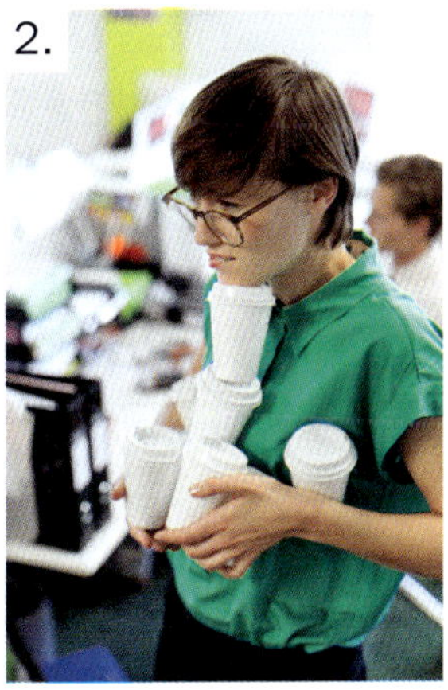

3. 

4. 

B **Talk** with a partner. Look at the places in the box. Have a conversation in each place. Make a request or offer in each conversation. Take turns.

a bus	a grocery store	an airplane
a dark movie theater	a post office	an office

A It's dark in here. Would you mind helping me find my seat?
B I'd be glad to. Follow me.
A OK, thanks.

Scan a chart to locate key information about job growth; make and respond to polite requests and offers

REVIEW

1 Listening

Listen. Take notes on a class lecture.

CD2, Track 20

Job skills for an electronics store	Job skills for a restaurant
1. *good communication skills*	4.
2.	5.
3.	6.

Talk with a partner. Check your answers.

2 Grammar

A **Write.** Complete the story.

Joanie's Problem

Joanie is at the electronics store. She *has been talking* (1. has talked / has been talking) with a clerk in customer service for the past 15 minutes. She wants to return a scanner. He told her she could exchange the scanner. However, Joanie ______ (2. has looked / has been looking) at scanners for several months, and she still ______ (3. hasn't found / hasn't been finding) another one she likes. She wants a refund. The clerk ______ (4. has just called / has been calling) his manager this minute to see if Joanie can get a refund, but the manager is not in his offi ce. This situation is very ______ (5. frustrating / frustrated) for Joanie. She's ______ (6. tiring / tired) and wants to go home.

B **Write.** Look at the words that are underlined in the answers. Write the questions.

1. **A** ______
   B Joanie wants to return her scanner.
2. **A** ______
   B Joanie has been talking to the clerk for 15 minutes.
3. **A** ______
   B The customer-service clerk says that she can exchange the scanner.
4. **A** ______
   B Joanie went to the store on Saturday afternoon.

Talk with a partner. Ask and answer the questions.

3 Pronunciation: stressing function words

Normally, function words such as pronouns, prepositions, conjunctions, articles, to *be* verbs, and auxiliary verbs are not stressed. However, when strong feelings or disagreements are expressed, function words can receive strong stress.

CD2, Track 21

A **Listen** to the stressed function words in each conversation.

1. **A** Is the camera defective?
   B It's defective and too small!
2. **A** Don't you usually finish at 5:00?
   B I do usually finish at 5:00, but not today.
3. **A** Why aren't you applying for that job?
   B I am. I'll go there tomorrow
4. **A** I don't trust the man who sold you this car.
   B Well, I do! It's my decision, not yours.
5. **A** Is he excited about his new job?
   B No, but his wife is.
6. **A** Did you put the returned merchandise on my desk?
   B No, I put it in your desk.

Listen again and repeat. Stress the underlined function words.

CD2, Track 22

B **Listen and repeat.** Then underline the stressed function words.

1. **A** I'd like to exchange this sweater.
   B Why?
   A It's too big, and it has a hole.
2. **A** You can't leave early again!
   B Yes, I can and I will.
3. **A** Why don't you clean the counters?
   B Why don't you?
4. **A** Let's talk about a raise after you've worked here for six months.
   B Can we talk before six months?

Talk with a partner. Compare your answers.

C **Talk** with a partner. Practice the conversations. Pay attention to the stressed function words.

1. **A** We don't give refunds or exchanges on watches.
   B My warranty says you can if the merchandise is defective.
   A So, is it defective?
   B Yes, it is.
   A Then I can give you a refund.
2. **A** Who just mopped the floors, you or Kevin?
   B I did. And I cleaned the tables.
   A Good work. I do enjoy seeing a clean bakery.
   A And I love working here.

D **Write** two new conversations using stressed function words. Practice with a partner.

A Does Karen need more help?
B No, but I do.

UNIT 9 DAILY LIVING

Lesson A Listening

1 Before you listen

A What do you see?

B What is happening?

1

2

3

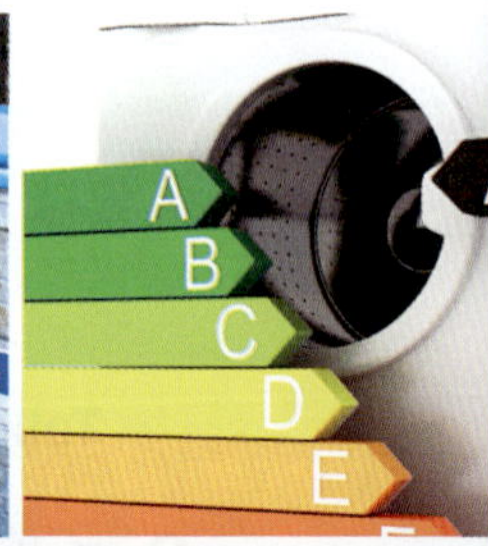

4

2 Listen

A **Listen** and answer the questions.

1. Who are the speakers?
2. What are they talking about?

CD2, Track 23

B **Listen again.** Complete the diagram.

CD2, Track 23

Ideas for saving our planet	Will the family try?
1. *cut down on driving*	*no*
2.	
3.	
4.	
5.	
6.	

3 After you listen

A **Read.** Complete the story.

appliances	carpool	energy-efficient	global warming	recycle
Biology	cut down on	environment	planet	responsibility

Mei was late to dinner because she was looking at a website about saving the ___*planet*___(1). She wants to take more ________(2) for saving the earth from ________(3). Mei tells her parents about the guest speaker who came to her ________(4) class. The speaker suggested simple things people could do to reduce their energy use and protect the ________(5). For example, they could ________(6) instead of driving alone, ________(7) their bottles and cans, and use ________(8) lightbulbs. Mei's parents agree that it is important to ________(9) energy use since it would also help them save money. However, they can't afford to buy new ________(10) right now.

Listen and check your answers.

CD2, Track 24

B **Discuss.** Talk with your classmates. Which of the speaker's suggestions can you try? Which are difficult for you? Why?

Lesson B Conditionals

1 Grammar focus: present unreal

Use the present unreal conditional to talk about what would happen in an imaginary (not real) situation. Use *if* with verb in past tense in the clause that describes the imaginary situation. Use *would* with the base form of the verb in the results clause.

If everybody **drove** smaller cars, we **would use** less gasoline.	**If** she **used** energy-efficient lightbulbs, she **would save** electricity
We **would use** less gasoline **if** everybody **drove** smaller cars.	She **would save** electricity **if** she **used** energy-efficient lightbulbs.

Watch

2 Practice

A **Write.** Complete the sentences. Use the present unreal conditional.

1. Many people put their newspapers in the trash can. If everybody ____recycled____ (recycle) newspapers, we ____would save____ (save) millions of trees.
2. Noah never takes his car in for a tune-up. Noah's car ____________ (use) less gas if he ____________ (tune up) his car regularly.
3. Mr. Brown drives his own car to his job downtown. Mr. Brown ____________ (save) money on gas if he ____________ (carpool) to work.
4. Many items in the supermarket are packaged in plastic. If you ____________ (buy) products that are packaged with recycled paper, you ____________ (help) to reduce global warming.
5. Jessica always stays in the shower for a very long time. If Jessica ____________ (take) shorter showers, she ____________ (save) water.
6. Some kinds of fish contain large amounts of lead, a poisonous metal. You ____________ (be) healthier if you ____________ (stop) eating fish that contains lead.
7. Energy efficient appliances use less electricity. If Mei's family ____________ (buy) a new washing machine, they ____________ (save) money on their electric bill.
8. Kristina never puts enough air in her tires. If Kristina ____________ (put) more air in her tires, she ____________ (buy) less gasoline.

Listen and check your answers.

CD2, Track 25

B **Talk** with a partner. Match each action with a result. Some items have more than one correct answer. Use the present unreal conditional.

If everybody bought energy-efficient appliances, we would save electricity.

Actions	Results
buy energy-efficient appliances	save gas
fix water leaks	cut down on energy use
replace lightbulbs with energy-efficient ones	save water
recycle cans, bottles, glass, and paper	reduce air-conditioning and heating use
put enough air in their tires	reduce the amount of trash in landfills
close off unused rooms	save electricity

Write sentences about the actions and results.

If everybody bought energy-efficient appliances, we would save electricity.

3 Communicate

A **Work** in a small group. Look at the picture of the beach. Talk about actions people could take to help the environment.

If more people picked up the trash on the beach, everyone would enjoy a clean beach.

B **Share** ideas with your classmates.

Lesson C Connectors

1 Grammar focus: *since* and *so*

Connectors are words at the beginning of a sentence or clause. Use the connector *since* to introduce a cause (reason) clause. Use the connector *so* to introduce an effect (result) clause.

CONNECTOR OF CAUSE
Since the earth is getting warmer, the polar ice caps are melting.
The polar ice caps are melting **since** the earth is getting warmer.

CONNECTOR OF EFFECT
The earth is getting warmer, **so** the polar ice caps are melting.
The earth is getting warmer, **so** the sea water is getting warmer.

Watch

2 Practice

A **Write**. Combine the sentences. Use the connectors in parentheses.

1. There is a buildup of harmful gases in the atmosphere. Global warming is increasing.
   (since) *Since there is a buildup of harmful gases in the atmosphere, global warming is increasing.*
2. Warm water is expanding in the oceans. The sea level is rising.
   (so) *Warm water is expanding in the oceans, so the sea level is rising.*
3. The sea level is rising. Towns near oceans are in danger of flooding.
   (since) ______________________
4. Global warming changes weather patterns. Many places will have less rainfall.
   (since) ______________________
5. The mosquito population will increase. There will be an increase in diseases like malaria.
   (so) ______________________
6. The ocean water is getting warmer. Typhoons and hurricanes are becoming more frequent.
   (since) ______________________
7. Cities are growing. Many plants and animals may lose their natural habitats.
   (so) ______________________
8. Summer temperatures will continue to rise. There will be longer periods of no rain and increased days of very high temperatures.
   (so) ______________________

Listen and check your answers.

CD2, Track 26

B **Talk** with a partner. Combine sentences in different ways using the connectors *since*, *because*, *therefore*, and *so*.

> **A** Since people are building homes in forests, animals are losing their natural habitats.
>
> **B** Animals are losing their natural habitats because people are building homes in forests.

USEFUL LANGUAGE

Because can replace *since*.

Therefore can replace *so*.

Use a semicolon before *therefore* and a comma after it.

The earth is getting warmer; therefore, the polar ice caps are melting.

Causes	Effects
1. People are building homes in forests.	Animals are losing their natural habitats.
2. There is habitat loss.	Animals are moving into towns and cities.
3. Animals are moving into towns and cities.	The animals are frightened.
4. The animals are frightened.	Sometimes they attack people.
5. Wild animals sometimes attack people.	People are afraid of them.
6. People are afraid of wild animals.	They kill the animals.

Write sentences about the causes and effects. Use the connectors *since, because, therefore* and *so*.

Since people are building homes in forests, animals are losing their natural habitats.

3 Communicate

A **Work** in a small group. Read the newspaper headlines. Discuss the possible causes and effects of each event. Think of other possible headlines to discuss.

> Coyotes are losing their natural habitats, so they're moving into towns.

> Coyotes are moving into towns because they're losing their natural habitats.

B **Share** information about your classmates.

Use the connectors *since* and *because* to show cause and the connectors so and *therefore* to show effect

Lesson D Reading

1 Before you read

Talk with your classmates. Answer the questions.

1. What is a *fable*?
2. Do you know any fables or folktales from your native country? Which ones?

Ask yourself questions when you read to identify a cause-and-effect relationship.
- To find an effect, ask, "What happened?"
- To find a cause, ask, "Why did it happen?"

2 Read

Read the fable. Listen and read again.

CD2, Track 27

All Things Are Connected

Long ago, there was a village chief who never allowed anyone to disagree with him. Whenever he wanted to do something, he asked the members of his court for their advice. But whether the chief's idea was wise or foolish, his advisors always said the same thing, "Indeed, it is wise." Only one old woman dared to give a different answer. Whenever the chief asked for her advice, she always replied, "All things are connected."

One night, the chief was awakened by the sound of frogs croaking in the swamp. It happened again the next night and the next and the next. The chief decided to kill all the frogs in the swamp. When he consulted the members of his court, they replied as usual, "Indeed, it is wise." But the old woman kept silent. "And you, old woman, what do you think?" the chief demanded. "All things are connected," she replied. The chief concluded that the old woman was a fool, and he ordered his servants to kill all the frogs. Therefore, the chief slept peacefully.

But soon the mosquitoes in the swamp began to multiply since there were no frogs to eat them. They came into the village and made everyone miserable. The chief ordered his servants to go into the swamp and kill the mosquitoes, but it was impossible. Furious, the chief summoned the members of his court and blamed them, saying, "Why didn't you tell me that killing the frogs would make the mosquitoes multiply and everyone would be miserable? I should have listened to the old woman."

Because the mosquitoes were there, all the people of the village were forced to go away. Finally, the chief and his family left, too. Until he died, the chief never forgot the old woman's words, "All things are connected."

3 After you read

A Check your understanding.

1. What is the overall meaning (moral) of this fable?
2. What was the chief's main problem?
3. When the chief wanted advice, what did almost all his advisors say? Why did they say that?
4. Why did the chief assume the old woman was a fool?
5. What two things were connected in this fable?
6. In paragraph 2, what does *croaking* mean? What words provide clues to the meaning?
7. Read the last paragraph. Do you think the chief understood the old woman's words? Why or why not?

USEFUL LANGUAGE
an **antonym** is a word that has the opposite meaning.
good – bad
hard – easy
tall – short

B Build your vocabulary.

1. In the reading passage, underline the words from the chart.
2. Use a dictionary or a thesaurus. Write the part of speech. Write an antonym for each word.

Word	Part of speech	Antonym
wise	*adjective*	*foolish*
connected		
peacefully		
multiply		
miserable		
furious		
summoned		
blamed		
swamp		

3. Work in a small group. Write sentences with the words in the chart.

■ ______________________________

■ ______________________________

■ ______________________________

C Talk with a partner.

1. How can people who disagree solve their conflicts peacefully?
2. What do you do when you have a problem and you can't find a solution?
3. Do you think it is wise to follow other people's advice? Why or why not?

For college and career readiness practice, see pages 160–162.

Analyze how the text makes connections among individuals, ideas and events; use a dictionary to identify antonyms

Lesson E Writing

1 Before you write

A **Talk** with a partner. Answer the questions.

1. What is the environmental problem in this photo?
2. Why is it a problem? (causes)
3. How does this problem hurt people and the environment? (effects)

B **Read** the paragraph.

The Causes and Effects of Smog

Smog is a serious environmental problem in my city. One cause is that there are too many cars on the roads and highways. Most of the cars have only one person – the driver. People seem to take a lot of unnecessary trips. They drive to the drugstore instead of walking two blocks. Another cause of smog in my city is that we use too much electricity. Since many homes are not energy-efficient, our city's power plant has to produce more electricity. The burning coal from the power plant produces more air pollution. The smog is thick, so the air is hard to breathe. Consequently, on many days it is unsafe for children and senior citizens to be outside. Smog also kills many trees and plants that produce oxygen and clean the air. If people drove less and used less electricity, I am sure our air quality would improve.

One way to organize a paragraph is to discuss the causes and effects of a problem.

C **Work** with a partner. Complete the graphic organizer with information from the model paragraph.

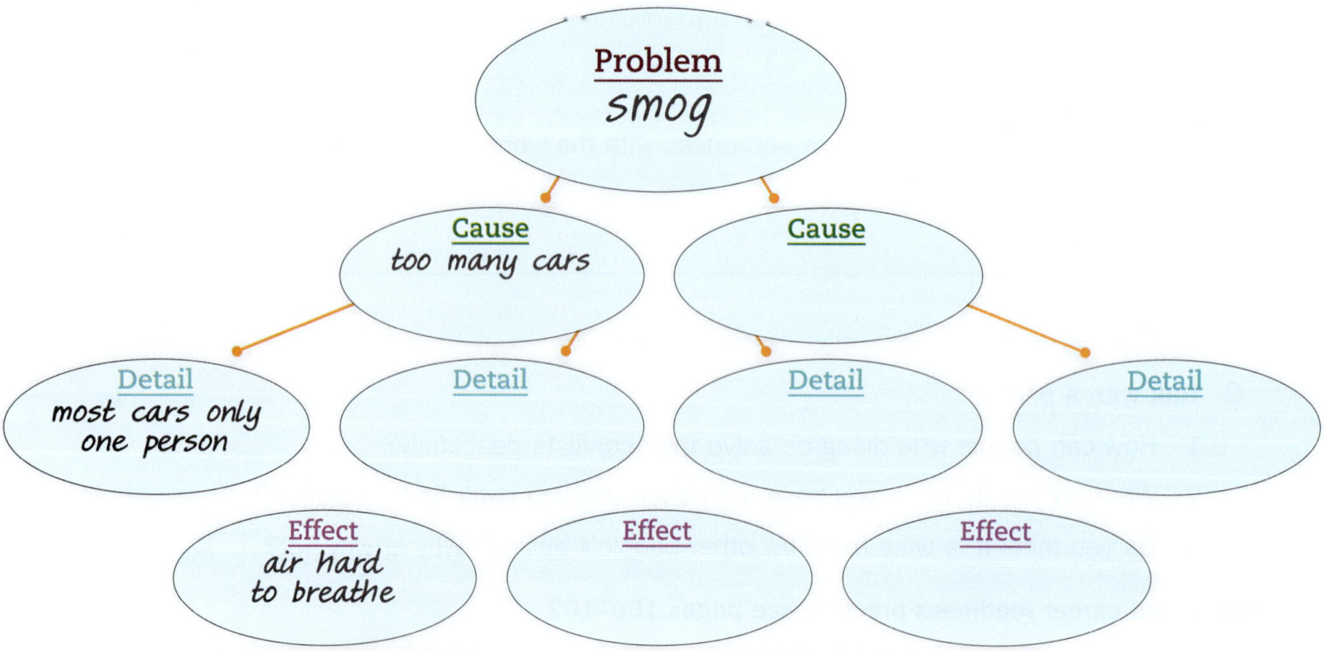

D **Plan** a paragraph about an environmental problem in your city or community. Include the causes and effects of the problem. Use the graphic organizer to make notes on your ideas.

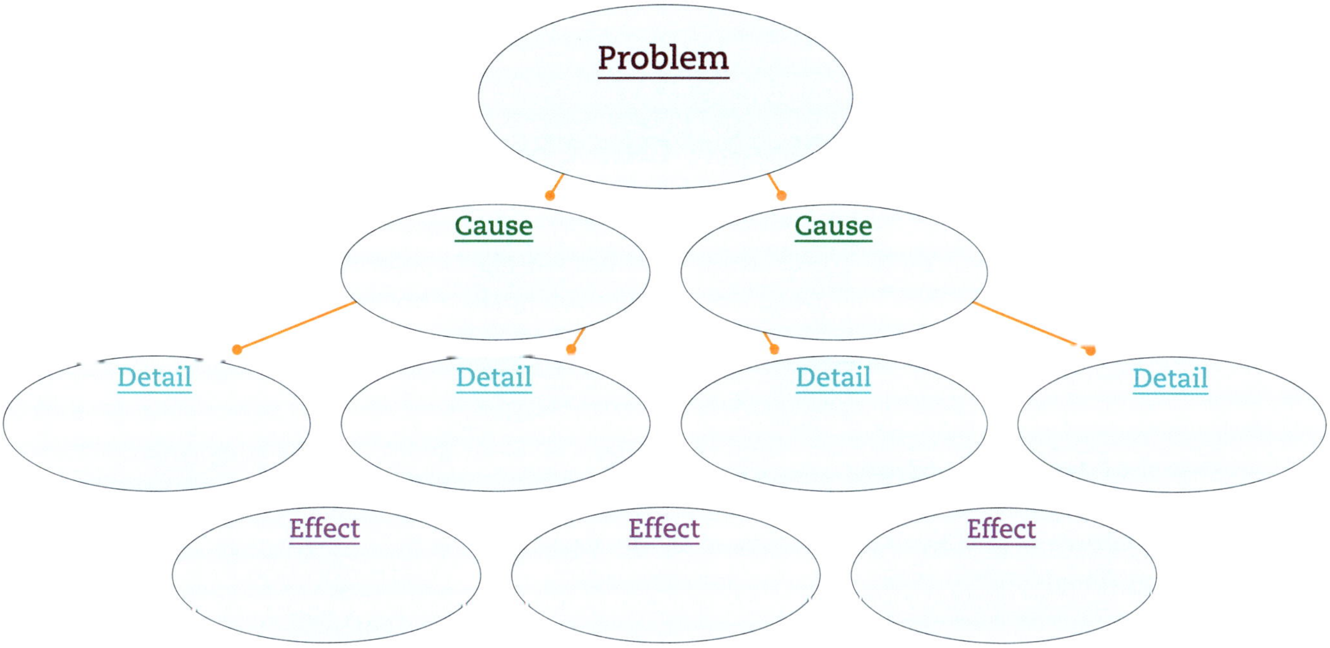

2 Write

Write a paragraph about an environmental problem in your city or community. Identify the problem in your topic sentence. Explain the causes and their effects and provide supporting details for each cause. Use the paragraph in exercise 1B and the graphic organizers in exercises 1C and 1D to help you.

3 After you write

A **Check** your writing.

	Yes	No
1. My topic sentence identifies an environmental problem.	☐	☐
2. I clearly explained the causes and effects.	☐	☐
3. I provided supporting details for the causes of the environmental problem.	☐	☐

B **Share** your writing with a partner.

1. Take turns. Read your paragraph to a partner.
2. Comment on your partner's paragraph. Ask your partner a question about the paragraph. Tell your partner one thing you learned.

Lesson F Another view

1 Life-skills reading

Save our Planet: Our Choices Matter

150 percent more energy is used by regular lightbulbs than energy-efficient (compact fluorescent) bulbs.	**400** gallons of water are wasted every month when you have a leaky faucet.	**1,000** years is how long plastic bottles take to decompose in landfills.
1,200 pounds of organic garbage are thrown out by the average American in a year.	**95,000** pounds of pollution are produced by driving a car for one year.	**14,000,000** trees are cut down to produce the 10,000,000,000 paper bags that Americans use every year.

A Read the questions. Look at the handout. Fill in the answer.

1. What does the number 95,000 represent?
   - (A) pounds of organic garbage thrown out
   - (B) pounds of smog from factories
   - (C) pounds of pollution from a car in one year
   - (D) none of the above

2. According to the handout, why are plastic bottles bad?
   - (A) require a lot of energy to make
   - (B) take a long time to decompose
   - (C) expensive to make
   - (D) none of the above

3. In the sentence *400 gallons of water are wasted every month when you have a leaky faucet*, what does *wasted* mean?
   - (A) used carefully
   - (B) used carelessly
   - (C) used wisely
   - (D) used on purpose

4. The handout does not discuss _____.
   - (A) plastic bottles in landfills
   - (B) pollution from cars
   - (C) pollution from airplanes
   - (D) cutting down trees to make bags

B Solve the problem. Give your opinion.

Joshua rents an apartment. He has a leaky faucet in the bathroom sink. He hates to waste water, and he is worried the leak will get worse. He tried to fix it, but he couldn't stop the leak. He called the landlord, but the landlord hasn't returned his call. What should he do?

2 Grammar connections: present real conditional vs. present unreal conditional

Use present real conditional when something is possible or always true.
Use present unreal conditional when something is not possible or not likely.

PRESENT REAL	PRESENT UNREAL
If I **have** time, I **walk** to school.	**If** I **found** a large bag of money, I **would give** it to charity.
If you **heat** water to 212° F, it **boils**.	**If** I **were** a bird, I'**d fly** all over the world.

Watch

A **Work** in a small group. Play the game. Write your name on a small piece of paper. Flip a coin to move your paper. Then tell your group about the topic in the square. Use the present real or present unreal conditional to finish the sentence. Take turns.

If I'm late to English class, I come in quietly.

Start here →	If I'm late to English class . . . →	If I went on my dream vacation . . . →	If I didn't need to sleep . . . ↓
If I won the lottery . . . ↓	← If I'm thirsty . . .	← If I bought all new appliances . . .	← If the weather is nice . . .
If I only rode my bicycle . . . →	If I don't understand something . . . →	If I were the leader of my country . . . →	If I stay up too late . . . ↓
Finish!	← If I were invisible . . .	← If I could do one thing to save our planet . . .	← If I don't eat breakfast . . .

B **Share** information about your classmates.

If Pedro is late to English class, he comes in quietly.

If Sally went on her dream vacation, it would be in a warm and sunny place.

Scan a lecture handout to identify information about key environmental problems; contrast present real and present unreal conditionals

UNIT 10 FREE TIME

Lesson A Listening

1 Before you listen

A What do you see?

B What is happening?

1

2

3

4

2 Listen

A **Listen** and answer the questions.

1. Who are the speakers?
2. What are they talking about?

CD2, Track 28

B **Listen again.** Complete the chart.

CD2, Track 28

	American customs	Vietnamese customs
1. gifts	*register in a store*	
2. use of rice		
3. dress color		

3 After you listen

A **Read.** Complete the story.

acquaintances	courses	fortune	reception	symbolizes
bride	customs	looking forward	registered	tradition

Cathy and Thanh are talking about wedding ___*customs*___ (1). Cathy is invited to a Vietnamese wedding, and she is surprised that the bride and groom are not ________ (2) for gifts at any stores. In contrast, Thanh is surprised by the American ________ (3) of throwing rice at the bride and groom. Next, they talk about clothes. Thanh says a Vietnamese ________ (4) wears a red dress because the color red ________ (5) good ________ (6). Then Cathy asks why she was invited only to the wedding ________ (7), not the ceremony. Thanh explains that traditionally the ceremony is only for the family. The couple's friends and ________ (8) are invited to the evening reception. In fact, Thanh says the evening party will include seven or eight ________ (9) of food. Cathy says she is ________ (10) to the wedding.

Listen and check your answers.

CD2, Track 28

B **Discuss.** Talk with your classmates. Share some special wedding customs from your culture.

Lesson B Conditionals

1 Grammar focus: future real and future unreal

Use the future real conditional to talk about a result that will likely happen if a certain condition is true. Use the future unreal conditional to talk about a future result that is unlikely to happen because the condition is not true or possible at this time.

FUTURE REAL (POSSIBLE)	FUTURE UNREAL (NOT POSSIBLE)
If I **go** to the wedding, I **will wear** my new shoes.	**If** I **went** to the wedding, I **would wear** my new shoes. (But I'm not going.)
If Jane **isn't working** on Saturday, she **will go** to the wedding.	**If** Jane **weren't working** on Saturday, she **would go** to the wedding. (But Jane will be working on Saturday.)

Watch

USEFUL LANGUAGE
The future unreal conditional form of the verb *be* is *were*.

2 Practice

A Write. Complete the sentences. Use the future real or future unreal conditional.

1. The Patels are from India, but they live in the United States now. They are planning a wedding for their daughter, Parveen. If they ___lived___ (live) in India, the groom's family ___would pay___ (pay) for the wedding.
2. The wedding will be in the United States. If the Patels __________ (have) the wedding in India, the wedding celebration __________ (last) three days. Here it will last for one day.
3. The Patels don't have a lot of money. If they __________ (be) rich, they __________ (invite) 300 people; instead, they will invite about 150.
4. The Patels are planning to have music for the reception. If a band __________ (not / charge) too much, they __________ (have) live music.
5. It's possible that the weather will be nice on the day of the wedding. If the weather __________ (be) nice, they __________ (have) the ceremony outside.
6. It is possible Parveen and her husband will get some vacation time from work. If Parveen and her husband __________ (get) enough time off from work, they __________ (take) a trip to Hawaii for their honeymoon.
7. They don't have a lot of time off from work. If they __________ (have) more time, they __________ (go) to India for their honeymoon.
8. Parveen and her new husband will live in their own apartment. If they __________ (be) in India, they __________ (live) with the groom's parents.

Listen and check your answers.

CD2, Track 30

B **Talk** with a partner. Take turns making sentences about Victor's real and unreal plans for New Year's Eve.

> **A** If Victor stays home on New Year's Eve, he will have a party with his friends.
> **B** But if he traveled to Florida, he would spend New Year's Eve near the beach.

Future real (possible)	Future unreal (not possible)
stay home / have a party with his friends	travel to Florida / spend New Year's Eve near the beach
have a party at his house / cook for his friends	have a lot of money / take his friends to a nice restaurant in Florida
go to his parents' house / have a quiet celebration with family	be in Mexico / eat 12 grapes at midnight
travel to New York / celebrate New Year's Eve in Times Square	travel to Brazil / watch fireworks on the beach at midnight
go to a club / dance all night	be in France / have a special dinner

Write sentences about Victor's real and unreal plans.

If Victor stays home on New Year's Eve, he will have a party with his friends.
If he traveled to Florida, he would spend New Year's Eve near the beach.

3 Communicate

A **Work** with a partner. Complete the chart with your real and unreal plans for some future holidays or special events.

Holiday or event	Real	Unreal
New Year's Eve	*stay home*	*be in my native country*
birthday		
(your idea)		
(your idea)		

B **Work** in a small group. Share your charts. Ask and answer questions about each other's plans.

> **A** If you stay home on New Year's Eve, how will you celebrate?
> **B** If I stay home, i'll invite my friends to come over and celebrate with me.

> **A** If you were in your native country on New Year's Eve, how would you celebrate?
> **B** If I were in my native country, I would watch fireworks at midnight.

B **Share** information about your classmates.

Lesson C *Hope and wish*

1 Grammar focus: possible and impossible

Use *hope* to talk about something you want that is possible in the present or future. Use *wish* to talk about situations that are not possible in the present or future.

Possible situations	Situations that are not possible
Samira **hopes** her cousin **will come** to her wedding.	Samira **wishes** her cousin **would come** to her wedding.
Samira **hopes** her cousin **comes** to her wedding.	Samira **wishes** she had more money.
Nick and Mia **hope** they **can go** to the party.	Nick and Mia **wish** they **could go** to the party.

Watch

2 Practice

A **Write.** Complete the sentences. Use *hope* or *wish* and the correct form of the verb or modal.

1. Paul's high school graduation is tomorrow. His friend Luis has to work. Luis *wishes* he *could go* (can go) to Paul's graduation.
2. Paul's father has asked for the day off so that he can attend his son's graduation. He ________ he ________ (get) the day off.
3. Paul's grandfather has been sick. He's not sure if he will attend the graduation. Paul ________ his grandfather ________ (will attend) the ceremony.
4. Paul's sister is out of the country, so she cannot come to the ceremony. Paul ________ his sister ________ (be) here to attend his graduation.
5. The graduation ceremony will be outside. Paul ________ it ________ (will not / rain).
6. Paul's parents would like to buy him a new car, but they can't afford it. They ________ they ________ (can buy) him a new car.
7. Paul wasn't accepted to the university, so he will go to a community college. Paul ________ he ________ (can go) to the university.
8. Paul has applied for financial aid. Paul ________ he ________ (get) financial aid to help pay for his books.
9. It's possible that Paul will be able to transfer to the university in two years. He ________ he ________ (can transfer) in two years.

Listen and check your answers.

CD2, Track 31

B **Talk** with a partner. Read the situations. Make statements with *hope* or *wish*.

Ryan wants to get a new cell phone soon.

Ryan hopes he can get a new cell phone soon.

Soraya can't go home for Thanksgiving.

Soraya wishes she could go home for Thanksgiving.

1. Ryan wants to get a new cell phone soon.
2. Soraya can't go home for Thanksgiving because she has to work.
3. Marla wants to have a big graduation party, but her apartment is too small.
4. Avi is trying to get a plane reservation so he can attend his cousin's wedding in Las Vegas.
5. Karl plans to ask Marta to marry him next weekend. He doesn't know if she will say yes.
6. Maria wants to go to Spain, but she can't afford it.
7. Anton and Ilsa are expecting a baby. They want the baby to be healthy.
8. Jose's wife is in Mexico. He has applied for her to immigrate to the United States. He wants her to come soon.
9. Farid's brother and sister are living in Iran. They cannot come to the United States now. Farid misses them.

Write a sentence for each situation.

Ryan hopes he can get a new cell phone soon.

3 Communicate

A **Write** three holidays or celebrations that you observe. Think about something you wish you could change about each one.

Mother's Day : *I wish I could have the day off to be with my children.*

1. ______________ : ______________________________
2. ______________ : ______________________________
3. ______________ : ______________________________

B **Work** in a small group. Talk about your wishes. Listen to your classmates' hopes for you.

A I don't have Mother's Day off. I wish I could have the day off to be with my children.

B I hope you get the day off next year.

A I hope your children will do something special for you.

USEFUL LANGUAGE
Expressing hope is a common way of ending a conversation.
I hope you feel better soon.
I hope you have a good time.

C **Share** information about your classmates.

Lesson D Reading

1 Before you read

Talk with your classmates. Answer the questions.

1. How are birthdays usually celebrated in your culture?
2. Are some birthdays more special than others? Which ones?

Punctuation can be a clue to meaning. For example, parentheses, commas, and dashes are all used to mark definitions, examples, or explanations. Find two examples in the reading where dashes or commas help define key words.

2 Read

Read the blog. Listen and read again.

CD2, Track 32

www.blogaddress.com

Special Birthdays Around the World

In most cultures, there are certain birthdays that are especially important in a young person's life. If you were an American teenager, for example, you would eagerly look forward to your 16th birthday because in most states that is the age to get a driver's license. Other cultures also have birthdays with special meanings:

Mexico For Mexican girls, the 15th birthday – the "Quinceañera" – symbolizes a girl's transition into adulthood. To celebrate, the girl's family throws a huge party. The girl wears a ball gown similar to a wedding dress. The girl performs a waltz, a formal dance, with her father. A similar custom is celebrated in Brazil.

A girl's Quincaeñera

China On a child's first birthday, parents place their baby in the center of a group of objects, such as a shiny coin, a book, and a doll. Then they watch to see which object the baby picks up first. Most parents hope their child will pick up the coin because, according to tradition, it means the child will be rich.

Nigeria The 1st, 5th, 10th, and 15th birthdays are considered extremely important. Parties are held with up to 100 people. The guests enjoy a feast of a roasted cow or goat.

Saudi Arabia In some countries, such as Saudi Arabia, people don't observe birthdays at all because of spiritual beliefs. According to Muslim traditions, the only celebrations allowed are Eid al Fitr, a feast that signifies the end of Ramadan, and Eid al Adha, which celebrates the end of the annual pilgrimage to Mecca.

Israel A boy's 13th and a girl's 12th birthdays are serious as well as happy occasions. On these birthdays, children become responsible for their own religious and moral behavior.

Adult birthdays also have special significance in many cultures. In the United States, for example, birthdays ending in "0" – 30, 40, 50, etc. – are especially meaningful.

3 After you read

A **Check** your understanding.

1. What is the writer's purpose in writing this article?
2. Why do American teenagers look forward to their 16th birthdays?
3. Birthdays in some cultures symbolize important transitions in one's life. Provide two examples of this from the article.
4. Why are birthdays not celebrated in Saudi Arabia?
5. Underline the word *eagerly* in the first paragraph. Does this word have a positive or negative meaning? What words help you to understand the meaning of this word?
6. Are any of the special birthdays described in the reading similar to traditions in your culture? Which ones?
7. What would be a good concluding sentence to this article?

B **Build** your vocabulary.

1. In the reading passage, underline the words from the chart. Write the meaning from the story.
2. Use a dictionary and write a different meaning for each word.

word in story	Meaning in story	Other meaning
1. states	*areas that are part of a country*	*conditions of the mind*
2. object		
3. rich		
4. transition		
5. throw		
6. ball		
7. pick up		
8. observe		

3. Write sentences using the other meaning of each word on your own paper.

C **Talk** with a partner.

1. How many states or provinces are there in your native country?
2. Do you have a favorite object? What is it? Why do you like it?
3. What transitions have you made in your life?
4. What does *being rich* mean to you?
5. What holidays do you observe?

For college and career readiness practice, see pages 163–165.

Determine the purpose of the text and how it is conveyed through key details and examples; use a dictionary to identify multiple meanings of a word

Lesson E Writing

1 Before you write

A **Talk** with a partner. Answer the questions.

1. Look at the pictures. Can you guess where the people are from and what holiday they are celebrating?
2. What is your favorite holiday or celebration? Why?

B **Read** the paragraph.

My Favorite Celebration

My favorite celebration is the Iranian New Year, *Norouz* ("new day"). This holiday begins on the first day of spring and lasts 13 days. On the Wednesday before Norouz, people build bonfires and jump over them. Iranian people believe that if they do this, they will get rid of their illnesses and misfortunes. On Norouz Eve, the family gathers around a table with seven items that begin with the letter "s" in Persian: an apple, wheat pudding, dried berries, vinegar, a coin, a beautiful flower, and garlic. A bowl of goldfish, a Koran, colored eggs, and a mirror are also on the table. These items symbolize beauty, health, prosperity, and fertility. On Norouz Day, people kiss each other and say, "I hope you will live for one hundred years." We spend the next 13 days visiting each other and eating sweets. Finally, on the last day of the celebration, everyone goes to a park for a big picnic. I wish my whole family lived with me here so that we could celebrate Norouz together.

The conclusion – the last sentence of a paragraph – is an important part of a paragraph. One way to conclude a paragraph is to relate the topic to your personal life.

C **Work** with a partner. Complete the outline of the model paragraph.

I. Topic: *My Favorite Celebration - Norouz*

II. Meaning or symbolism: ______________________

____

III. When celebrated: ______________________

IV. Customs:

A. ______________________

B. ______________________

C. ______________________

D. ______________________

E. ______________________

V. Conclusion: ______________________

____

D **Plan** a paragraph about your favorite holiday or celebration. Make an outline like the one in Exercise 1C. Include at least three customs. Use your own paper.

2 Write

Write a paragraph about your favorite holiday or celebration. Describe its meaning or symbolism. Include at least three customs. Write a conclusion that relates the celebration to your personal life. Use the paragraph in Exercise 1B and the outlines in Exercises 1C and 1D to help you.

3 After you write

A **Check** your writing.

	Yes	No
1. My paragraph describes the meaning or symbolism of my favorite holiday	☐	☐
2. I described at least three customs for my favorite holiday or celebration.	☐	☐
3. I wrote a conclusion relating the celebration to my personal life.	☐	☐

B **Share** your writing with a partner.

1. Take turns. Read your paragraph to a partner.
2. Comment on your partner's paragraph. Ask your partner a question about the paragraph. Tell your partner one thing you learned.

Lesson F Another view

1 Life-skills reading

Mother's Thanksgiving **Pumpkin Pie**

Preparation time: 15 minutes / Cooking time: 50 minutes

Ingredients

1 pre-made pie crust
1 (8-ounce) package cream cheese, softened
2 cups canned pumpkin, mashed
¼ teaspoon salt
1 cup sugar
1 egg plus 2 egg yolks, lightly beaten
1 cup heavy cream
¼ cup (½ stick) melted butter
1 teaspoon vanilla extract
½ teaspoon ground cinnamon
¼ teaspoon ground ginger, optional

1. Preheat the oven to 350 degrees Fahrenheit.
2. Beat the softened cream cheese.
3. Add the pumpkin and beat until blended.
4. Then add the salt and sugar, and beat until blended.
5. Then add the egg mixed with the yolks, cream, and melted butter, and beat until blended.
6. Finally, mix in the vanilla, cinnamon, and ginger.
7. Pour the filling into the pre-made pie crust, and bake for 50 minutes, or until the center is firm.
8. Set the pie on a wire rack, and cool until it is room temperature. Cut into slices and serve with whipped cream or ice cream.

Serves 6–8 people.

A **Read** the questions. Look at the recipe. Fill in the answer.

1. Which ingredient do you need one cup of?
   - (A) heavy cream
   - (B) sugar
   - (C) vanilla
   - (D) both *a* and *b*
2. What should you do after you blend the cream cheese and pumpkin?
   - (A) Add the salt and sugar.
   - (B) Bake the pie.
   - (C) Add the eggs.
   - (D) Pour the filling into the pie crust.
3. Which ingredient is not required?
   - (A) vanilla
   - (B) ginger
   - (C) cinnamon
   - (D) cream cheese
4. According to the recipe, what would be a good synonym for the word *blended*?
   - (A) cooked
   - (B) beat
   - (C) melted
   - (D) mixed

B **Solve** the problem. Give your opinion.

Ana's class is having a *potluck*. Everyone is supposed to bring something. Her classmates are asking her to bring a dish from her country. Ana has very little time and money now and can't afford to make the dish for the potluck. What should she do?

2 Grammar connections: tag questions

Watch

A tag question is a small question at the end of a statement. Use tag questions to confirm what you think is true or not true. A positive statement is followed by a negative question tag, and a negative statement is followed by a positive question tag.

AFFIRMATIVE SENTENCE + NEGATIVE TAG	NEGATIVE SENTENCE + AFFIRMATIVE TAG
You **like** to dance, **don't** you? –Yes, I do. (I like to dance.) –Actually, no. I don't like to dance.	You **don't like** to dance, **do** you? –No, I don't. (I don't like to dance.) –Actually, I do. I like to dance.
You'**re** tired, **aren't** you?	You **aren't** tired, **are** you?
You **went** to a restaurant, **didn't** you?	You **didn't go** to a restaurant, **did** you?

A **Work** with your classmates. Use tag questions. Complete the chart.

A Ivan, you don't like chocolate, do you?
B Actually, I do. I like chocolate.
A Fabiana, you don't like chocolate, do you?
B No, I don't.

Find someone who . . .	**Name**
doesn't like chocolate	*Fabiana*
ate at a restaurant last night	
isn't tired today	
didn't go on vacation last month	
is good at math	
didn't study last night	
has a birthday in June	

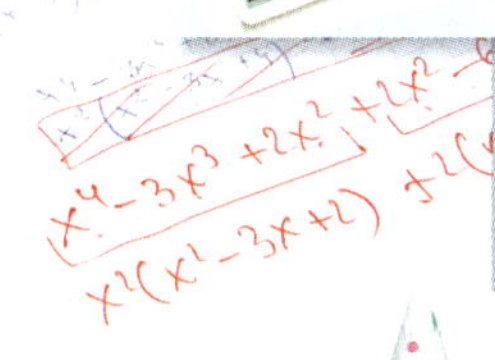

B **Talk** with a partner. Ask questions about your partner's life. Use tag questions. Take turns.

A You like to fish, don't you?
B Yes, I do.

REVIEW

1 Listening

Listen. Take notes on a street interview.

CD2, Track 33

Things that bring good luck	Things that bring bad luck
1. *wear bright colors like red*	4.
2.	5.
3.	6.

Talk with a partner. Check your answers.

2 Grammar

A Write. Complete the story.

A New Year's Eve Celebration

Sergei ___*wishes*___ (1. hopes / wishes) his friend Olga could visit him in New York over the holidays, but she can't get the time off. ______ (2. Therefore / Since), they won't be together on New Year's Eve. If she ______ (3. is / were) in New York, he would take her to Times Square ______ (4. so / because) there is a big celebration there. Every year at one minute before midnight, a large crystal ball starts to drop slowly from high above the street. When it reaches the bottom, everybody goes crazy ______ (5. since / so) it's the beginning of the New Year. Sergei really ______ (6. hopes / wishes) that Olga can come next year. If she comes, she ______ (7. will / would) have a great time.

B Write. Look at the words that are underlined in the answers. Write the questions.

1. **A** ______
   B Sergei would take Olga to Times Square if she were in New York.
2. **A** ______
   B The crystal ball starts to drop at one minute before midnight.
3. **A** ______
   B Sergei hopes that Olga can come next year.

Talk with a partner. Ask and answer the questions.

3 Pronunciation: linking consonant-vowel sounds

When a word ends in a consonant sound and the next word begins with a vowel sound, the words sound like they are linked together. Move the final consonant sound of the first word to the beginning of the second word.

A Listen to the following sentences.

CD2, Track 34

1. Smaller cars would use less energy.
2. Smog is a big environmental problem.
3. If everyone drove less, our air quality would improve.
4. In the future, we will see more electric cars and trucks on our roads.
5. We should all have efficient appliances.
6. We need to protect our environment.

Listen again and repeat. Pay attention to the linked consonant-vowel sounds.

B Listen and repeat. Then underline the linked consonant-vowel sounds.

CD2, Track 35

1. All things in this world are connected.
2. People are concerned about saving this earth.
3. Most of the cars on the highway have only one person in them.
4. People make a lot of unnecessary trips.
5. We should close off unused rooms in our homes.
6. The Internet is a good source of information about global warming.

Talk with a partner. Compare your answers.

C Read the questions and answers. Underline the linked consonant-vowel sounds.

1. **A** What do you think about global warming?
   B Well, I haven't read a lot about it.
2. **A** How can I help clean up the beach?
   B You can pick up trash and put it in garbage cans.
3. **A** What can all of us do to protect our environment?
   B We can all cut down on our energy use.
4. **A** What is an easy way to save energy?
   B Turn off lights when you leave a room.

Talk with a partner. Practice the questions and answers.

D Write four sentences from Units 9 and 10. Underline the linked consonant-vowel sounds. Then work with a partner. Read your sentences using linked consonant-vowel sounds.

Reading Tip: Read the first paragraph. What is the focus of the article? Then read the first sentence in each of the following paragraphs. How is each different?

Promoting Multiple Intelligences in the Classroom

Frank Kimmel's 4th grade class in Seattle, Washington buzzes with activity. Kimmel is a strong believer in Howard Gardner's theory of multiple intelligences. This is the idea that there are several different kinds of intelligence, and people can be intelligent in different ways. "My job as a teacher is to provide my students a variety of learning experiences that will help them use and develop all of their intelligences," he explains. In Kimmel's classroom, students spend part of each day moving around to various learning centers – places where they can work on different skills, individually or in small groups.

For example, in one corner of the classroom there is the "visual center," with art supplies, photo books, building blocks, and a computer that's connected to a 3-D printer. Students can look at photos and use their imagination to draw, paint, build, and create things.

Along one side wall is the "music center" where students can listen to music and nature sounds, look at musical scores, and use a computer program to write their own musical compositions. There are also some simple musical instruments that students can check out and practice at home.

There's the "STEM corner" – Science, Technology, Engineering and Mathematics – where students come to work on math problems and scientific experiments. This area has games and puzzles that require logic and Kimmel sometimes brings in old appliances that students take apart and put back together.

On the back wall is the "word center" with adventure stories and biographies, books on tape, and poetry. In addition, there are crossword puzzles and other word games, dictionaries, and writing materials. This is a popular gathering place for group storytelling.

In one front corner is the "quiet zone" where students can go for quiet reflection and meditation. Here, students can also write in their journals and complete self-assessments.

Finally, the "nature center" is outside, in a corner of the playground. It's a small garden area with raised beds where students can dig in the dirt and learn about planting and caring for vegetables and flowers.

At the end of a busy day, one of the 4th graders summed it up when she said enthusiastically, "I really like Mr. Kimmel's class because there are lots of interesting things to do and I'm never bored!"

UNIT 1

1 Check your understanding

1. What is special about Mr. Kimmel's class?
2. How many learning centers does the article describe?
3. What can students do in the visual center?
4. What can students do in the nature center?
5. Read the last paragraph. Do you think the author agrees with Mr. Kimmel's way of teaching? Explain your answer.

2 Build your vocabulary

A Find the words in Column 1 in the paragraph indicated and underline them. Then write the clue that helped you know the meaning. Finally, write the dictionary definition that matches the meaning in the article.

Word	Clue	Dictionary definition
1. buzzes, **¶1**	*class... buzzes with activity*	*Makes a low humming sound like bees, machinery, or people talking.*
2. learning center, **¶1**		
3.check out, **¶3**		
4. meditation, **¶6**		
5. nature center, **¶7**		
6. enthusiastically, **¶8**		

B Find each of the following academic words in the article and underline the sentence.

create individually journals logic theory

Then, on another piece of paper, copy and complete the chart.

Academic word	Phrase or sentence from article	Part of speech	Dictionary definition	My sentence
create	*Students can . . . use their imagination to create things.*	*verb*	*to make something new or imaginative*	*I like to create my own greeting cards.*

3 Talk with a partner

Answer each question with evidence from the reading. Use one of the phrases in the Useful Language box.

1. What does Mr. Kimmel say about his job as a teacher?
2. What is a popular place for storytelling?
3. What does one student say about Mr. Kimmel's class?

USEFUL LANGUAGE
Phrases to cite evidence:
(name of person) states that . . .
The article states that . . .

Objective: CCR Anchor 9: Analyze how two or more texts address similar themes or topics in order to build knowledge or to compare the approaches the authors take.

4 Analyze the texts

Review the following texts to answer the questions below: (1) p. 12, *Many Ways to be Smart;* and (2) p. 136, *Promoting Multiple Intelligences in the Classroom.*

1. What main idea do both articles share?
2. What intelligence does the "STEM corner" address? What activities take place there?
3. What intelligences does the "word center" address? What activities take place there?
4. What intelligence does the "quiet zone" address? What activities take place there?
5. Do you think that teachers should use a variety of activities in order to address multiple intelligences? Support your answer with examples from your personal experience.

5 Before you write

Copy and complete the graphic organizer on another piece of paper. Fill it in with (1) the main idea, (2) the types of intelligence, and (3) examples of materials in the learning center that support that intelligence. Use information from Exercises 1–4 and evidence from the two articles. Finally, (4) fill in the conclusion with your answer to question five in Exercise 4.

Main Idea:	
Types of Intelligence in *Many Ways to be Smart*	**Supporting Teaching Methodology in *Promoting Multiple Intelligences in the Classroom***
Conclusion:	

6 Write

Write one paragraph explaining multiple intelligences. Include examples for three different intelligences. Use information from your graphic organizer.

7 After you write

A Check your writing. Did you include all the ideas in your graphic organizer?

B Share your writing with a partner.

a. Take turns. Read your writing to your partner.
b. Read your partner's writing to yourself. Compare it to your partner's graphic organizer.
c. Comment on your partner's writing: Ask one question; share one thing you learned.

Reading Tip: Look at the picture. Then read the title and the first sentence in each paragraph. Who is this article about? What happened? Read and find out.

Rafael Salazar

Rafael Salazar was born in 1986 on a small farm in southern Mexico. His family was very poor. He remembers waking up at 5:30 a.m. and going with his father to milk cows before breakfast, then walking one hour to his local elementary school. "I was fortunate because my parents always pushed me to study," Rafael says. "They weren't educated, but they knew that education is the only way out of poverty."

Rafael's parents encouraged him to move to the United States. He arrived in 2004 and moved in with his aunt in San Diego, California. He spoke no English, but he knew he had to learn English to be successful. Right away, he registered for ESL classes at San Diego City College. He started with morning classes, then he joined the afternoon classes and even attended evening classes. Everyone was glad to see Rafael's passion for learning. "I never saw such a determined student," said Amanda Yellin, Rafael's teacher in ESL 1. "He practically lived at the school."

Rafael's career counselor helped him obtain a weekend job as a houseman in a local hotel, where he moved furniture and prepared rooms for banquets, or large dinner parties. His boss noticed his passion to succeed and encouraged him to consider a career in the hospitality industry. Soon, Rafael was promoted to the position of lead houseman, then banquet waiter. Now, he's banquet captain.

Rafael believes strongly in setting goals. "Set a goal and make it happen. When you reach that goal, set another one," he suggests. His next goal is to become a food and beverage manager. He plans to begin a certificate program in hotel management in the fall. Eventually, he wants to be the general manager of a major hotel.

At a recent banquet honoring hospitality employees, Rafael received his hotel's Outstanding Hospitality Worker Award. Speaking fluent English, he gave an encouraging speech in which he thanked his parents, his aunt, his ESL teachers, and his boss at the hotel. He encouraged others like him to set goals, work hard, and, above all, learn English. "Don't allow language to be an obstacle to your success," he told them. "If a poor farmer like me can succeed in America, so can you."

1 Check your understanding

1. Look at the reading tip again. What is the article about?
2. Why did Rafael's teacher, Amanda Yellen, say, "I have never seen a more dedicated student?"
3. What was Rafael's first job? What other jobs has he had at the hotel?
4. What is Rafael's goal? How does he plan to achieve his goal?
5. Read the last paragraph. Why do you think the author wrote this article?

2 Build your vocabulary

A Find the words in Column 1 in the paragraph indicated and underline them. Identify the part of speech: noun, verb, adjective, or adverb. Then use a dictionary to complete the chart with other forms of the word and their parts of speech.

Word in Article	Part of speech	Other forms of the word	Part of speech
1. educated, **¶1**	*verb*	*education* *educational*	*noun* *adjective*
2. encouraged, **¶2**			
3. passion, **¶2, ¶3**			
4. succeed, **¶3, ¶5**			
5. strongly, **¶4**			
6. believes, **¶4**			

B Find each of the following academic words in the article and underline the sentence.

eventually major obtain promoted registered

Then, on another piece of paper, copy and complete the chart.

Academic word	Phrase or sentence from article	Part of speech	Dictionary definition	My sentence
eventually	*Eventually he wants to be the general manager of a major hotel.*	*adverb*	*in the end*	*Eventually she wants to be a doctor.*

3 Talk with a partner

Answer each question with evidence from the reading.
Use one of the phrases in the Useful Language box.

1. How did Rafael show that education was important to him when he was a child in Mexico?
2. How do you know Rafael was determined to learn English in the United States?
3. Why did Rafael's boss encourage him to consider a career in the hospitality industry?

USEFUL LANGUAGE
Phrases to cite an example:
One example from the article is . . .
One example the author gives is . . .

Objective: CCR Anchor 9: Analyze how two or more texts address similar themes or topics in order to build knowledge or to compare the approaches the authors take.

4 Analyze the texts

Review the following texts to answer the questions below: (1) p. 24, *An Immigrant Family's Success Story;* and (2) p. 139, *Rafael Salazar.*

1. What do both articles describe?
2. What is one example from each article about learning English?
3. What is one example from each article about hard work and sacrifice?
4. What is one example from each article about eventual success?
5. Read the quotes from Choi and Rafael from the last paragraphs in each article. Restate your favorite quote in your own words.

5 Before you write

Copy and complete the graphic organizer on another piece of paper. Fill it in with (1) the topic and (2) two examples for each key point. Use information from Exercises 1–4 and evidence from the two articles. Finally, (3) fill in the conclusion with your answer to question five in Exercise 4.

Topic:		
Learning English	**Hard Work and Sacrifice**	**Plan for Success**
Examples **1.** **2.**	**Examples** **1.** **2.**	**Examples** **1.** **2.**
Conclusion:		

6 Write

Write one paragraph that explains how immigrants overcome obstacles to become successful. Use information from your grahic organizer.

7 After you write

A Check your writing. Did you include all the ideas in your graphic organizer?

B Share your writing with a partner.

a. Take turns. Read your writing to your partner.
b. Read your partner's writing to yourself. Compare it to your partner's graphic organizer.
c. Comment on your partner's writing: Ask one question; share one thing you learned.

Reading Tip: Read the title and first paragraph. Identify one problem between immigrant parents and their teens.

Communication Tips for Immigrant Parents and Teens

Parents in the United States face challenges in communicating with their teenage children as the teens struggle to establish their own identities. When the parents are immigrants whose teenagers came to the U.S. at a young age, these challenges are magnified. There are a couple of reasons for this. First of all, the teenagers may have a greater identification with American culture than their parents have. In addition, the teenagers often speak more English than their parents. Trying to be traditional children at home and all-American children at school, the teenagers may feel they lead double lives and the parents may feel they no longer know their children. This leads to conflict and stress.

Professional experts offer several tips to immigrant parents for improving communication with their teenagers.

1. Learn as much English as you can. Free English as a Second Language classes are offered at adult schools, community colleges, and libraries as well as at community-based organizations. For those whose work or family schedules prevent attending classes, there are also online programs, many of them free. Your children will respect you for trying to learn more English.

2. Set regular times for conversation and interaction. Eating meals together is a great way to listen and talk with each other. You can discuss experiences in adapting to the new culture as well as how the new culture is different from the home culture. The more you listen to your teenager the more your teenager will have a sense of self-respect and respect for you.

3. Provide praise. Most teenagers want to be independent, but they also need feedback. Compliment them for their good behavior. For example, even if a report card has a bad grade, before you ask about the bad grade, give a compliment on the good grades.

4. Allow some privacy. As teenagers become young adults, they may not share everything with their parents. For safety reasons, you always need to know where they are, and who they are with, but you don't need to know every detail.

The role parents play in their children's lives is especially important during the teenage years. Teenagers can be difficult as they try to find out who they are and who they want to be. Keep open communication channels with teens so that they don't feel isolated. And remember, the most important way to help your teens is to express your love and appreciation for them as they struggle to adapt to adulthood in a new culture.

1 Check your understanding

1. What is the purpose of this article?
2. According to the article, what are two ways parents can learn more English?
3. Why is it important for parents to set regular times for conversation with their teens?
4. Why is it important to praise teenagers?
5. Of the four tips suggested to improve communication between immigrant parents and their teens, which two tips do you think are the most effective? Why?

2 Build your vocabulary

A Find the words in Column 1 in the paragraphs indicated and underline them. Then complete the chart by writing the phrase in which the word occurs and your guess of its meaning as used in the article. Finally, write the dictionary definition.

Word	Phrase	Guess the meaning	Dictionary definition
1. struggle, **¶1**	*struggle to establish their own identities*	*try*	*to make great efforts*
2. magnified, **¶1**			
3. respect, **¶3**			
4. praise, **¶5**			
5. compliment, **¶5**			
6. express, **¶7**			

B Find each of the following academic words in the article and underline the sentence.

adapt conflict establish isolated stress

Then, on another piece of paper, copy and complete the chart.

Academic word	Phrase or sentence from article	Part of speech	Dictionary definition	My sentence
adapt	*adapt to a new culture*	*verb*	*to adjust to new circumstances*	*Soon you will adapt to the cold weather.*

3 Talk with a partner

Answer each question with evidence from the reading.
Use one of the phrases in the Useful Language box.

USEFUL LANGUAGE
Phrases to cite evidence:
The article states that . . .
According to the article, . . .

1. Why are the challenges of communication between immigrant parents and teens greater than those between non-immigrant parents and teens?
2. What causes teenagers of immigrant parents to feel they are leading double lives?
3. What is the most important way for parents to help teens?

Objective: CCR Anchor 9: Analyze how two or more texts address similar themes or topics in order to build knowledge or to compare the approaches the authors take.

4 Analyze the texts

Review the following texts to answer the questions below: (1) p. 38, *Barriers Between Generations*; and (2) p. 142, *Communication Tips for Immigrant Parents and Teens*.

1. What is the topic of both articles?
2. What is the first barrier described in *Barriers between Generations*? What is a solution for it from *Communication Tips for Immigrant Parents and Teens*?
3. What is the second barrier described in *Barriers between Generations*? What is a solution for it from *Communication Tips for Immigrant Parents and Teens*?
4. Which tips for opening communication channels suggested in the article *Communication Tips for Immigrant Parents and Teens* might help Dolores communicate more effectively with her son?
5. Which tip do you think is the most effective for solving communication barriers between parents and their teens? Use evidence from both articles and your experience to support your answer.

5 Before you write

Copy and complete the graphic organizer on another piece of paper. Fill it in with (1) the topic, (2) one communication problem between immigrant parents and teens, (3) three solutions to the problem, and (4) two details for each solution. Use information from Exercises 1–4 and evidence from the two articles. Finally, (5) fill in the conclusion with your answer to question five in Exercise 4.

Topic:		
Problem	**Solution 1**	**Detail** **Detail**
	Solution 2	**Detail** **Detail**
	Solution 3	**Detail** **Detail**
Conclusion:		

6 Write

Write one paragraph that identifies one communication problem between immigrant parents and teens and two or three solutions for it. Use information from your graphic organizer.

7 After you write

A Check your writing. Did you include all the ideas in your graphic organizer?

B Share your writing with a partner.

a. Take turns. Read your writing to your partner.
b. Read your partner's writing to yourself. Compare it to your partner's graphic organizer.
c. Comment on your partner's writing: Ask one question; share one thing you learned.

Reading Tip: Look at the title, first sentence, and last sentence of the article. What do you think is the main idea of this article? Is it surprising?

Winning the Lottery Can Be Stressful

Stress is defined as our body's reaction to changing events in our lives. We usually think of change as negative, but positive events also produce stress. Here are three stories about people who experienced stress as a result of a positive event – winning the lottery.

Money demand upsets couple. John and Susan Patel couldn't believe their good luck when they won $92 million in their state's lottery. A short time later, however, they were shocked and upset by a demand from a clerk at the convenience store where they bought their lottery tickets. The clerk shouted angrily that the Patels promised to give her $500,000 as a reward for selling them the winning ticket. John Patel says he pledged to "take care of" the clerk, but he never promised her a specific dollar amount. He also says that right after winning the jackpot, he gave the clerk $20,000.

No money left for this winner. Robert Novak, who won almost $14 million in the Pennsylvania state lottery, discovered that it can be very difficult to cope with sudden success. He used the money to start several businesses, including a restaurant and a used-car lot, but they all failed. His own brother tried to steal money from him. Novak's landlady said that Novak owed her half the lottery money. In the end, a court gave her one-third of Novak's winnings. By 1999, Novak was broke and stressed out. Without money, he was living with his parents and seeing a doctor for depression.

Rich man, poor man. The life of Calvin Ross changed overnight when he won $5.6 million in the lottery. He divorced his wife, bought expensive cars, and spent huge sums of money on gifts for his friends. But because of bad investments and excessive spending, Ross always ran out of money before his $191,000 annual checks arrived every October. He now lives by himself and works to pay off his debts.

Of course, most people who win the lottery say that winning has had a positive effect in their lives. The three stories in this article are unusual. However, they show that even a happy event like winning the lottery may bring about new and stressful problems.

1 Check your understanding

1. Look at the reading tip again. What is the article about?
2. How does this article define *stress*?
3. According to the article, do people usually have positive or negative ideas about stress? Underline the sentence that answers this question and restate it in your own words.
4. Who won the most money? What problem did they face?
5. Read the last paragraph. Why do you think the author wrote this article?

2 Build your vocabulary

A Find the words in Column 1 in the paragraphs indicated and underline them. For each, find clues in the words around them to guess their meaning. Then match the words with their meanings.

Word		Clue	Meaning
1. produce, ¶1	b	*as a result*	a. strong request
2. demand, ¶2	____		b. cause
3. pledged, ¶2	____		c. huge amount of something
4. jackpot, ¶2	____		d. without money
5. broke, ¶3	____		e. promise
6. excessive, ¶4	____		f. lottery winnings

B Find each of the following academic words in the article and underline the sentence.

annual defined investments reaction specific

Then, on another piece of paper, copy and complete the chart.

Academic word	Phrase or sentence from article	Part of speech	Dictionary definition	My sentence
annual	*before his $191,000 annual checks arrived*	*adjective*	*every year*	*It's important to get an annual health check-up.*

3 Talk with a partner

Answer each question with evidence from the reading.
Use one of the phrases in the Useful Language box.

1. Why was the paragraph about Calvin Ross called "Rich man, poor man?"
2. Why did Robert Novak end up living with his parents after he won the lottery?
3. Does winning the lottery usually have a positive or negative effect?

USEFUL LANGUAGE
Phrases to cite evidence:
The article pointed out . . .
The author states that . . .

Objective: CCR Anchor 9: Analyze how two or more texts address similar themes or topics in order to build knowledge or to compare the approaches the authors take.

4 Analyze the texts

Review the following texts to answer the questions below: (1) p. 50, *Stress: What You Ought to Know* and (2) p. 145, *Winning the Lottery Can Be Stressful*.

1. What is the topic of both articles?
2. Are the definitions of stress the same or different in both articles? Use information from both texts to support your answer.
3. Reread "What are the signs of stress" in *Stress: What You Ought to Know*. Provide two examples of physical or emotional stress from *Winning the Lottery Can Be Stressful*.
4. Reread "How can you manage stress" in *Stress: What You Ought to Know*. Does this paragraph provide solutions to the people in the three stories in *Winning the Lottery Can Be Stressful*? Why or why not?
5. If you were to win the lottery, do you think it would be stressful? Why or why not? Use evidence from both articles to support your opinion.

5 Before you write

Copy and complete the graphic organizer on another piece of paper. Fill it in with (1) your topic, (2) two examples of how the articles are the same, and (3) two examples of how the articles are different. Use information from Exercises 1–4 and evidence from the two articles. Finally, (4) fill in the conclusion with your answer to question five in Exercise 4.

Topic:	
Stress: What You Ought to Know	***Winning the Lottery Can Be Stressful***
HOW THE SAME?	
HOW DIFFERENT?	
Conclusion:	

6 Write

Write one paragraph that compares and contrasts the two articles that discuss stress. Use the information from your graphic organizer.

7 After you write

A Check your writing. Did you include all the ideas in your graphic organizer?

B Share your writing with a partner.

a. Take turns. Read your writing to your partner.
b. Read your partner's writing to yourself. Compare it to your partner's graphic organizer.
c. Comment on your partner's writing: Ask one question; share one thing you learned.

Reading Tip: Read the proverb. What do you think it means? Can you guess how it is connected to the picture?

"Give a man a fish, and you have fed him for today. Teach a man to fish, and you have fed him for a lifetime."

Heifer International

A well-known Chinese and English proverb says, "Give a man a fish, and you have fed him for today. Teach a man to fish, and you have fed him for a lifetime." This proverb, or statement that gives advice, represents the beliefs of Heifer International, an organization that gives gifts of live animals to poor families all over the world.

Heifer International was started by an American farmer named Dan West. West was a volunteer relief worker in Spain during its civil war, from 1936 to 1939. His job was to decide who would receive the small amount of food aid offered to them. Because there was not enough food, many people died. West realized that it was good to give people food, but it was more important to help them find a way to produce or create their own food. With this simple idea, West founded Heifer International as soon as he returned to America.

The first group of heifers — young female cows -- was shipped to Puerto Rico in 1944. Families used the animals to produce milk, fertilizer (food for plants), and calves, which are baby cows. Also, each family agreed to give its heifer's first female calf to another family. West called this "passing on the gift." In this way, an entire community would benefit from the gift of one heifer.

Today, Heifer International gives gifts of heifers, sheep, goats, and many other animals. Since 1944, it has helped more than 8 million people in 125 countries. The story of Christine Makahumure from Rwanda is typical. After her husband died in a war, Christine had no way to support her parents and young daughter. She applied to Heifer International and received a cow. She used some of the milk to feed her family and sold the rest. With the money she made by selling milk, she was able to buy a small house for her parents. To meet her commitment of "passing it on," she gave her cow's first calf to a neighbor as a gift. She also adopted and took care of four orphans -- local children whose parents had died. According to the Heifer International Web site, "Christine is living proof of the life-changing difference an animal from Heifer can make" to the people of a community.

1 Check your understanding

1. Look at the reading tip again. Restate the proverb in your own words.
2. Explain the saying "passing on the gift" in your own words.
3. What gave Dan West the idea to start Heifer International?
4. How did Christine survive after her husband died in the war?
5. How does Christine's story illustrate the way Heifer International can change the lives of more than one person in a community?

2 Build your vocabulary

A English often uses punctuation, such as dashes and commas, with synonyms and phrases to signal definitions. Find the words in Column 1 in the paragraphs indicated and underline them. Then complete the chart with the punctuation that signaled the meaning, and the definition, explanation or example.

Word	Signal	Definition, explanation or example
1. proverb, **¶1**	*comma*	*statement that gives advice*
2. Heifer International, **¶1**		
3. heifers, **¶3**		
4. fertilizer, **¶3**		
5. calves, **¶3**		
6. orphans, **¶4**		

B Find each of the following academic words in the article and underline the sentence.

aid civil commitment community founded

Then, on another piece of paper, copy and complete the chart.

Academic word	Phrase or sentence from article	Part of speech	Dictionary definition	My sentence
aid	*who would receive the small amount of food aid offered to them*	*noun*	*help, assistance*	*The Red Cross gives aid to people who need help after a disaster.*

3 Talk with a partner

Answer each question with evidence from the reading. Use one of the phrases in the Useful Language box.

1. What can a heifer provide a family?
2. What other gifts does Heifer International give needy people?
3. What are two examples from the reading of "passing on the gift"?

USEFUL LANGUAGE
Phrases to cite evidence:
According to the author, . . .
The author states that . . .

Objective: CCR Anchor 9: Analyze how two or more texts address similar themes or topics in order to build knowledge or to compare the approaches the authors take.

4 Analyze the texts

Review the following articles to answer the questions below: (1) p. 64, *Running with Ropes*; and (2) p. 148, *Heifer International*.

1. What is the main idea of both articles?
2. Both articles describe people who need help and people who give help. Who needed help? Who gave help?
3. Both articles describe people who have received help from others. What help did they need? Why did they need it?
4. For each article, describe the reason for giving help and the benefits the giver identified.
5. The articles describe how Scott, Justin, Dan and Christine's lives changed. Describe in your own words how their lives changed. Who do you think benefited more, the giver or the receiver? Explain why.

5 Before you write

Copy and complete the graphic organizer on another piece of paper. Fill it in with (1) the main idea and (2) answers to the questions for each organization. Use information from Exercises 1–4 and evidence from the two articles. Finally, (3) fill in the conclusion with your answer to question five in Exercise 4.

Main Idea:		
	Running With Ropes	***Heifer International***
1. Who experienced a problem?		
2. What was the problem?		
3. Who helped to solve the problem?		
4. What was the solution?		
5. How did the receiver benefit?		
6. How did the giver benefit?		
Conclusion:		

6 Write

Write one paragraph about the life-changing events described in the articles and the benefits to both giver and receiver. Use information from your graphic organizer.

7 After you write

A Check your writing. Did you include all the ideas in your graphic organizer?

B Share your writing with a partner.

a. Take turns. Read your writing to your partner.
b. Read your partner's writing to yourself. Compare it to your partner's graphic organizer.
c. Comment on your partner's writing: Ask one question; share one thing you learned.

Reading Tip: Look at the picture. Identify the different things in the picture. Read the title. What do you think the article is about?

Multitasking: Time saver or time waster?

Are you a multitasker? Do you watch TV and cook dinner at the same time? Do you often interrupt your work to check your email? Do you talk on your phone while you're driving? If you do these or similar things, then you are one of many multitaskers. According to a survey, or study, by the magazine *Scientific American MIND*, 90 percent of American adults multitask regularly.

Most people say they multitask because they are too busy, and multitasking saves time. Popular electronic devices like tablets and smart phones make it convenient to do several tasks at once, so people feel like they are getting more done. Melissa Brown of Evanston, Illinois, says she has no trouble listening to music, surfing the Internet, and sending text messages to friends while she does her homework.

Recent studies, however, show that Melissa and others like her are perhaps getting less done than they think they are. That's because with multitasking, there are actually many "microinterruptions" in which people stop one task, start another, and eventually return to the first one. These stops and starts make it difficult to concentrate, and so multitaskers actually waste time, according to a study at Microsoft Corporation. In the study, workers who interrupted their work to answer an email or text message took an average of 15 minutes to return to the work they were doing before the interruption.

Some psychologists say that the human brain just isn't good at concentrating on two things at the same time. This doesn't matter if you're only preparing a salad and listening to the radio, they say. But if you're doing a difficult task that requires thinking, like writing a report, then multitasking can slow you down and cause mistakes. It can even be dangerous, as in the case of people who talk on the phone, eat, or even apply makeup while driving.

In short, even though most people believe multitasking saves time, studies show that the opposite is true. Experts, or people who know a lot about saving time, offer some basic advice: try to focus on one task at a time. Check email just once an hour, turn off distracting noise while you're working, and most importantly, avoid talking on the phone while you're driving.

1 Check your understanding

1. Look at the reading tip again. Did you guess correctly? Restate what the article is about.
2. According to the article, why do people multitask?
3. What did the Microsoft Corporation study find out about workers who stopped their work to check emails?
4. Find what some psychologists say about multitasking and difficult tasks. Underline the sentence. Restate it in your own words.
5. Read the last paragraph. What do experts advise about multitasking?

2 Build your vocabulary

A Many English words are based on Latin or Greek prefixes. Find the prefixes in Column 1 in the paragraphs indicated and underline the words that contain them. Then complete the chart by writing the word and your guess of its meaning.

Prefix	Signal	Example from article	Meaning
1. multi, **¶1**	many	*multitasker*	*Someone who does several things at once*
2. micro, **¶3**	small		
3. inter, **¶3**	between		
4. pre, **¶4**	before		
5. psycho, **¶4**	mind		
6. mis, **¶4**	wrong		

B Find each of the following academic words in the article and underline the sentence.

experts concentrate focus requires survey

Then, on another piece of paper, copy and complete the chart.

Academic word	Phrase or sentence from article	Part of speech	Dictionary definition	My sentence
experts	*Experts, or people who know a lot about saving time, offer some basic advice*	*noun*	*specialists*	*It's important to get financial advice from experts.*

3 Talk with a partner

Answer each question with evidence from the reading. Use one of the phrases in the Useful Language box.

1. How many Americans multitask?
2. How does Melissa Brown feel about multitasking?
3. What did the Microsoft Corporation study show?

USEFUL LANGUAGE
Phrases to report ideas or research:
_______ (name of person) indicated that . . .
_______ (name of company or study) reported that . . .

Objective: CCR Anchor 9: Analyze how two or more texts address similar themes or topics in order to build knowledge or to compare the approaches the authors take.

4 Analyze the texts

Review the following texts to answer the questions below: (1) p. 76, *The Impact of Technology*; and (2) p. 151, *Multitasking: Time saver or time waster?*

1. What topic do both articles address?
2. Both articles mention different kinds of technology. Identify two from each article.
3. New technology can have a negative as well as a positive impact. Cite the example of a negative outcome described in the article "*Multitasking: Time saver or time waster?*" and the example of a positive outcome described in the article "*The Impact of Technology.*"
4. Both articles provide research or statistics. Give one example from each article.
5. Do you think the technology featured in these articles makes your life better or causes you more problems? Use your own experience and information from the articles to support your answer.

5 Before you write

Copy and complete the graphic organizer on another piece of paper. Fill it in with (1) the topic and (2) two examples for each key point. Use the information from Exercises 1–4 and evidence from the two articles. Finally, (3) fill in the conclusion with your answer to question five in Exercise 4.

Topic:		
Kinds of Technology	**Research about Technology**	**Advantages / Disadvantages of using Technology**
Examples	**Examples**	**Examples**
Conclusion:		

6 Write

Write one paragraph that discusses different kinds of technology, research about technology, and advantages and disadvantages of using technology. Use information from your graphic organizer.

7 After you write

A Check your writing. Did you include all the ideas in your graphic organizer?

B Share your writing with a partner.

a. Take turns. Read your writing to your partner.
b. Read your partner's writing to yourself. Compare it to your partner's graphic organizer.
c. Comment on your partner's writing: Ask one question; share one thing you learned.

Reading Tip: Look at the title. Then read the first sentence in each paragraph. What is the article about? Read and find out.

Amazing Bargains on Internet Auction Sites

Would you like to buy a new pair of sneakers for $6.99? How about headphones for $3.50 or a leather coat for $20? In the past, you could only find bargains, or discounts, like these at thrift stores, flea markets, and garage sales. Nowadays, however, you can find them easily and conveniently at an Internet auction Web site.

In an auction, people who want to buy the same item bid against each other. That is, they compete, or try to win the item, by offering more and more money. The "winner" is the person who offers the highest price. In 1995, a clever immigrant to the United States named Pierre Omidyar had the brilliant idea of starting an auction site on the Internet. He named it eBay. And eBay has become one of the largest and most successful online auction sites, although there are many others.

You can buy almost anything at an online auction. There is practical everyday merchandise like car parts, children's clothing, laptops, books, and sports equipment. There are collectors' items like rare and unusual stamps, glass animals, valuable old photographs, or comic books. And then there are the strange, off-the-wall items that have sold on Internet auction sites: a ten-year-old grilled cheese sandwich that showed the head of the Virgin Mary, which sold for $28,000 in 2004; and the entire town of Albert, Texas, which sold for $3.8 million in 2007.

You can also sell almost anything at an Internet auction site. Is your garage full of worthless old junk? Sell it online to the highest bidder! Do you have an old smart phone or computer that you aren't using anymore? Price them cheaply and someone is sure to bid on them. Millions of people utilize online auction sites every day to sell their "unwanted items". Many people have even started lucrative online auction businesses that earn hundreds or even thousands of dollars each month.

Since 1995, online auction sites have become enormously popular. As an example, eBay has almost 150 million registered users in 30 countries. Of course, there are some disadvantages to shopping at online auctions. You cannot touch the merchandise you are buying, and after you buy something, there is often a limited refund period. However, the convenience of the sites and the possibility of finding bargains are the reasons why millions of people buy and sell regularly at Internet auctions.

1 Check your understanding

1. What is the main idea of the article?
2. How do Internet auction sites work?
3. Describe one well-known auction site that the article talks about.
4. What are some of the things that people can buy on Internet auction sites?
5. Read the last paragraph. Do you think the author is in favor of Internet auction sites? Explain your answer.

2 Build your vocabulary

A Find the words in Column 1 in the paragraphs indicated and underline them. Which words are positive? Which words are negative? Write the clue that helped you guess.

Word	Clue	Positive	Negative
1. conveniently, **¶1**	*easily*	☑	☐
2. brilliant, **¶2**		☐	☐
3. practical, **¶3**		☐	☐
4. off-the-wall, **¶3**		☐	☐
5. junk, **¶4**		☐	☐
5. lucrative, **¶4**		☐	☐

B Find each of the following academic words in the article and underline the sentence.

enormously equipment immigrant items utilize

Then, on another piece of paper, copy and complete the chart.

Academic word	Phrase or sentence from article	Part of speech	Dictionary definition	My sentence
enormously	*auction sites have become enormously popular*	*adverb*	*to a large degree; extremely*	*He ate an enormously large dinner.*

3 Talk with a partner

Answer each question with evidence from the reading.
Use one of the phrases in the Useful Language box.

1. When did Pierre Omidyar get his idea for eBay?
2. What are some practical things that people can buy on Internet auction sites?
3. What are some of the disadvantages to shopping at online auctions?

USEFUL LANGUAGE
Phrases to cite evidence:
According to the article, . . .
The article states that . . .

Objective: CCR Anchor 9: Analyze how two or more texts address similar themes or topics in order to build knowledge or to compare the approaches the authors take.

4 Analyze the texts

Review the following texts to answer the questions below: (1) p. 90, *The Smart Shopper*; and (2) p. 154, *Amazing Bargains on Internet Auction Sites*.

1. What is the topic shared by the articles?
2. What are some ways that the articles are similar?
3. What are some ways that the articles are different?
4. Which article is more positive about online shopping? Explain your answer.
5. Based on what you have read or based on your experience, do you recommend online shopping? Cite examples from both articles to support your answer.

5 Before you write

Copy and complete the graphic organizer on another piece of paper. Fill it in with: (1) the topic shared by the articles, (2) two examples of how the articles are the same, and (3) two examples of how they are different. Use information from Exercises 1–4 and evidence from the two articles. Finally, (4) fill in the conclusion with your answer to question five in Exercise 4.

Topic:	
The Smart Shopper	***Amazing Bargains on Internet Auction Sites***
HOW THE SAME?	
HOW DIFFERENT?	
Conclusion:	

6 Write

Write one paragraph that compares and contrasts the two articles about online shopping. Use information from your graphic organizer.

7 After you write

A Check your writing. Did you include all the ideas in your graphic organizer?

B Share your writing with a partner.

a. Take turns. Read your writing to your partner.
b. Read your partner's writing to yourself. Compare it to your partner's graphic organizer.
c. Comment on your partner's writing: Ask one question; share one thing you learned.

Reading Tip: Read the last paragraph of the article. What is the article about? What is the main idea?

The Benefits of Telecommuting

Gloria Alvarez gets up at 6:30 a.m. each weekday morning and goes into her kitchen. There, she makes coffee and prepares breakfast for her two teenagers. After the children take off for school, she heads for work. Most days, she gets dressed first, but once in a while, she works in her pajamas. However, no one cares, because Ms. Alvarez is one of a growing number of Americans who telecommute, or telework. That is, they work from home, and they use technology – a computer, phone, and fax machine – to stay in touch with their workplace.

According to Global Workplace Analytics, 3.7 million employees (2.8% of the workforce) now work from home at least half the time. Many commuters are mothers like Alvarez, who work from home full-time as a customer service representative for a major clothing company.

Telecommuting has great advantages for both workers and employers. For workers, the best benefit is the time they save because they don't have to travel. Parents who telecommute can spend more time with their children. Likewise, they are available to take care of additional family responsibilities. Furthermore, working at home is also convenient for disabled people and others who have difficulty traveling. In addition, telecommuting gives workers more opportunities because, thanks to technology, they can work for companies that are not near their homes.

Employers also benefit when workers telecommute. They save money because they don't need as much office or parking space. Moreover, their workers are less likely to leave the company and look for another job because they are more motivated. Also, studies show that telecommuters can often complete more work in less time, because they don't have to deal with office interruptions.

Research shows that almost half of U.S. workers have jobs that they can do at home at least part of the time. Examples are managers, telephone salespeople, writers, computer programmers, artists, and customer service representatives. In the future, if all these people are able to work at home, they can avoid miles of driving and save millions of gallons of gasoline. In this way, telecommuting could help not just workers and companies, but also the earth.

UNIT 8

1 Check your understanding

1. What is the main idea of the text?
2. According to the article, what are the benefits of telecommuting for workers?
3. According to the article, what are the benefits of telecommuting for employers?
4. Where do people who telecommute usually do their work?
5. Do you agree that telecommuting is beneficial? Support your opinion with examples from the article.

2 Build your vocabulary

A Transitions are words and phrases that link ideas between sentences and paragraphs as well as within sentences. Some transitions signal addition of ideas — such as *also*. Other transitions signal contrast between ideas — such as *but*. Find the transition words and phrases in Column 1 in the paragraphs indicated and underline them. Then complete the chart by identifying the two ideas they connect. Finally, identify the purpose of the transition by checking the correct box.

Transition word	**First idea**	**Second idea**	**Purpose**	
			Adds an idea	Contrasts two ideas
1. however, **¶1**	*she works in her pajamas*	*no one cares*	☐	☑
2. likewise, **¶3**			☐	☐
3. furthermore, **¶3**			☐	☐
4. in addition, **¶3**			☐	☐
5. moreover, **¶4**			☐	☐

B Find each of the following academic words in the article and underline the sentence.

available benefit major motivated research

Then, on another piece of paper, copy and complete the chart.

Academic word	**Phrase or sentence from article**	**Part of speech**	**Dictionary definition**	**My sentence**
available	*and are available to take care of family responsibilities*	*adjective*	*free, uncommitted*	*I am available to meet with you tomorrow.*

3 Talk with a partner

Answer each question with evidence from the reading.
Use one of the phrases in the Useful Language box.

1. What do studies show about the productivity of telecommuters versus employees at the workplace?
2. Who are some of the people who benefit the most from telecommunicating?
3. What equipment do telecommuters need to have at home to do their work?

USEFUL LANGUAGE
Phrases to cite evidence:
According to the author, . . .
The author states that . . .

Objective: CCR Anchor 9: Analyze how two or more texts address similar themes or topics in order to build knowledge or to compare the approaches the authors take.

4 Analyze the texts

Review the following texts to answer the questions below: (1) p. 102, *Hard and Soft Job Skills*; and (2) p. 157, *The Benefits of Telecommuting*.

1. What is the topic of both articles?
2. Both articles describe people who work. How is Som's job different from Gloria's job? Give two examples of differences.
3. How is Som's job similar to Gloria's job? Give two examples of similarities.
4. What are a few reasons Som thrives at his job in the workplace and Gloria enjoys telecommuting?
5. The two articles are about working in the actual workplace and telecommuting. Which way do you think is more beneficial? Explain why. Use examples from both articles.

5 Before you write

Copy and complete the graphic organizer on another piece of paper. Fill it in with (1) your opinion based on your answer to question five in Exercise 4, (2) three key arguments and (3) evidence to support each argument. Use the information from Exercises 1–4 and evidence from the two articles. Finally, (4) fill in a conclusion based on your opinion.

Opinion:	
3 Key Arguments	**Evidence to Support Arguments**
1.	1.
2.	2.
3.	3.
Conclusion:	

6 Write

Is working in the workplace more or less beneficial than telecommuting? Write one paragraph that gives your opinion, arguments and supporting evidence. Use information from your graphic organizer.

7 After you write

A Check your writing. Did you include all the ideas in your graphic organizer?

B Share your writing with a partner.

a. Take turns. Read your writing to your partner.
b. Read your partner's writing to yourself. Compare it to your partner's graphic organizer.
c. Comment on your partner's writing: Ask one question; share one thing you learned.

Reading Tip: Before you read, look at the title and headings. What is the article about?

Plastic Bags – Convenience or Catastrophe?

Prior to the invention of plastic bags, shoppers used paper bags. Often these bags would tear easily, and they were not easy to carry from store to store. The first plastic bags were developed in the 1950s. Their simple design with built-in handles offered a strong carrying bag with a high load capacity. Store owners liked plastic bags because they were cheaper to purchase than paper bags, and shoppers thought they were easy to use and much stronger than paper bags. By the 1980s, plastic bags had completely replaced paper shopping bags in grocery chains and stores.

So why are they a catastrophe?
Although other countries use plastic bags, in the United States they are almost an institution. People in the United States throw away almost 100 billion plastic bags every year. Unfortunately, many of these plastic bags fly off garbage trucks and landfills and go into waterways or spoil the landscape. These plastic bags are not biodegradable, so it takes 10 to 20 years for them to disintegrate in landfills. Eventually, they break down into smaller pieces, which then pollute the land and water. Another problem is they are a serious danger to birds and marine mammals that mistake them for food. For example, sea turtles regularly try to eat floating plastic bags because they think they are jellyfish.

What can be done about the problem?
Many businesses have stopped offering customers plastic bags and even some communities have banned them. There are two things that can be done immediately to reduce the use of plastic bags.

<u>1. Switch to reusable shopping bags.</u>
These bags are convenient and come in a variety of sizes, styles and materials. When they aren't using being used, they can be folded up and put into a pocket or purse.

<u>2. Recycle plastic bags.</u>
If people have to use some plastic bags, they need to be sure to recycle them. Many grocery stores have places to recycle plastic bags.

More and more people are questioning whether the convenience of using plastic bags is outweighed by the catastrophe that these bags create for our planet. One frequent shopper concludes, "Sure plastic bags are convenient, but they are not worth the trouble! Every time I carry something in plastic, I think of the plastic littering our parks, the years and years it takes for plastic to decompose, and those poor turtles eating them and dying."

1 Check your understanding

1. Look at the reading tip again. Did you guess correctly? What is the main idea of this article?
2. Why does the author say plastic bags are so convenient?
3. According to the article, why are plastic bags a catastrophe? Underline the three reasons given.
4. What are two suggestions from the article to reduce the use of plastic bags?
5. Read the last sentence of the article. Restate it in your own words. Why do you think the author put that quote in the article?

2 Build your vocabulary

A Many English words are based on Latin or Greek prefixes. Find the prefixes in Column 1 in the paragraphs indicated and underline the full word. Use a dictionary to complete the chart with the meaning of each word.

Prefix	Meaning of Prefix	Word from reading	Meaning of word
1. dis-, ¶2	away	*disintegrate*	*break into fragments*
2. un-, ¶2	not		
3. re-, ¶3 re-, ¶3	again		
4. re-, ¶1 re-, ¶3	back backward		
5. de-, ¶4	not		

B Find each of the following academic words in the article and underline the sentence.

capacity concludes design institution prior

Then, on another piece of paper, copy and complete the chart.

Academic word	Phrase or sentence from article	Part of speech	Dictionary definition	My sentence
capacity	*a strong carrying bag with a high load capacity*	*noun*	*the amount that a container can hold*	*I need a pitcher with one quart capacity.*

3 Talk with a partner

Answer each question with evidence from the reading.
Use one of the phrases in the Useful Language box.

1. Why do turtles try to eat plastic bags?
2. Which country uses the most plastic bags?
3. How long does it take plastic bags to disintegrate in landfills?

USEFUL LANGUAGE
Phrases to cite evidence:
The author reports that . . .
The author points out that . . .

Objective: CCR Anchor 9: Analyze how two or more texts address similar themes or topics in order to build knowledge or to compare the approaches the authors take.

4 Analyze the texts

Review the following texts to answer the questions below: (1) p. 116, *All Things Are Connected*; and (2) p. 160, *Plastic Bags: Convenience or Catastrophe?*

1. What is the topic of both the fable and the article?
2. Both the fable and the article describe a problem. Identify the problem in the fable and the article.
3. Both the fable and the article explain what caused the problem. What are the causes for each problem identified in question #2?
4. What are the effects of the causes identified in question #3?
5. The old woman in the fable always told the chief, "All things are connected." Do you agree or disagree? Use evidence from both the fable and the article to support your opinion.

5 Before you write

Copy and complete the graphic organizer on another piece of paper. Fill it in with (1) the topic, (2) the problems, (3) the causes of each problem and (4) the effect (or what happened) for the fable and the article. Use information from Exercises 1–4 and evidence from the two articles. Finally, (5) fill in the conclusion with your answer to question five in Exercise 4.

Topic:
Fable: *All Things Are Connected*   **Problem** → **Cause** → **Effect**
Plastic Bags – *Convenience or Catastrophe?*   **Problem** → **Cause** → **Effect**
Conclusion:

6 Write

Write one paragraph that identifies two main problems, one in the fable and one in the article, and the causes and effects of each of those two problems. Use the information in your graphic organizer.

7 After you write

A Check your writing. Did you include all the ideas in your graphic organizer?

B Share your writing with a partner.

a. Take turns. Read your writing to your partner.
b. Read your partner's writing to yourself. Compare it to your partner's graphic organizer.
c. Comment on your partner's writing: Ask one question; share one thing you learned.

Reading Tip: Read the title and the first and last paragraphs to find the meaning of the topic. What is the article about?

Kwanzaa

Americans celebrate several holidays in December. These are Christmas, Hanukkah, Kwanzaa, and depending on the year, Eid al-Adha. But unlike Christmas, Hanukkah, and Eid al-Adha, Kwanzaa is not a religious holiday. It celebrates African-American culture, community, and family.

Dr. Maulana Karenga, a professor at California State University, Long Beach, created Kwanzaa in 1966. For many years, he looked for a way to bring African-American people together by connecting them with their African roots, or beginnings. *Kwanzaa* comes from a phrase in Kiswahili, a language spoken in eastern and central Africa, for "first fruits." So the holiday combines traditions from different African harvest festivals.

The number seven is important in Kwanzaa. The holiday lasts seven days, from December 26 to January 1, and there are seven principles, or rules, to follow. The Nguzo Saba, or seven principles, are:

1. *Umoja* (unity): Joining together to form and maintain unity in the family, community, and as African-Americans;
2. *Kujichagulia* (self-determination): To speak for, create for, and take care of ourselves;
3. *Ujima* (collective work and responsibility): Building the community and solving its problems together;
4. *Ujamaa* (cooperative economics): A community building and profiting from its own businesses;
5. *Nia* (purpose): The goal of building and developing African-American communities;
6. *Kuumba* (creativity): Using new ideas to make the community beautiful and successful;
7. *Imani* (faith): Belief in the importance of African and African-American culture, history, family, and leaders.

Each family celebrates Kwanzaa in its own way. Celebrations often include songs and dances, African drumming, storytelling, poetry, and traditional foods. Many people enjoy wearing brightly colored African clothes. On each of the seven nights, the family gathers and a child lights a candle. Then the family discusses one of the seven principles. Kwanzaa also has seven basic symbols that symbolize values and ideas from African culture. The symbols include an ear of corn, a cup, candles, a candleholder, crops (fruits, nuts, and vegetables), a mat, and gifts. A feast of African or African-American foods, called *karamu*, is held on December 31.

Kwanzaa is growing in popularity around the world. It is now celebrated by almost 20 million people with African ancestry in the United States, the United Kingdom, the Bahamas, and Brazil, as well as in Kenya and Zimbabwe.

1 Check your understanding

1. What is the purpose of this article?
2. Why and when was Kwanzaa created?
3. How is Kwanzaa different from the other American holidays in December?
4. What is done on each of the seven nights of Kwanzaa?
5. Which of the seven principles of Kwanzaa do you think is the most important? Explain why.

2 Build your vocabulary

A Suffixes are letter(s) added to the end of a word to change its meaning or part of speech. The suffix *–ity* is added to adjectives to change them to nouns. Find the nouns that end in *-ity* in the paragraph indicated and underline them. Write the words into Column 1 in the chart. Then use a dictionary to complete the chart with the definition of the noun and the adjective form of the word.

Nouns	Definition	Adjective
1. **¶1**, community	*Any group living in the same area or having common interests.*	*communal*
2. **¶2**, ___________		
3. **¶3**, ___________		
4. **¶3**, ___________		
5. **¶3**, ___________		
6. **¶5**, ___________		

B Find each of the following academic words in the article and underline the sentence.

cooperative maintain principles symbolize traditions

Then, on another piece of paper, copy and complete the chart.

Academic word	Phrase or sentence from article	Part of speech	Dictionary definition	My sentence
cooperative	*cooperative economics*	*adjective*	*acting or working together with others*	*Cleaning up after the party was a cooperative effort.*

3 Talk with a partner

Answer each question with evidence from the reading. Use one of the phrases in the Useful Language box.

1. What is *umoja*?
2. What is *karamu*?
3. How many people around the world celebrate Kwanzaa?

USEFUL LANGUAGE
Phrases to cite evidence:
The article defines . . . as . . .
The article estimates that . . .

Objective: CCR Anchor 9: Analyze how two or more texts address similar themes or topics in order to build knowledge or to compare the approaches the authors take.

4 Analyze the texts

Review the following texts to answer the questions below: (1) p. 128, *Special Birthdays Around the World;* and (2) p. 163, *Kwanzaa*.

1. What topic do the two articles share?
2. What are two similar activities that happen during Kwanzaa and birthday celebrations around the world?
3. Both articles describe symbols used in celebrations. Give an example from each article.
4. Give an example from each article about the significance of numbers in the celebrations.
5. Both articles describe holidays or celebrations that bring families or communities together. What holiday or celebration in your culture brings families or communities together? How is it similar or different from those described in the two articles?

5 Before you write

Copy and complete the graphic organizer on another piece of paper. Fill it in with (1) the topic and (2) details about Kwanzaa and birthday celebrations in two different countries. Use information from Exercises 1–4 and evidence from the two articles. Finally, (3) fill in the conclusion with your answer to question five in Exercise 4.

Topic:			
	Kwanzaa	**Birthday celebration**	**Birthday celebration**
1. Where is it celebrated?			
2. What is it?			
3. When is it celebrated?			
4. What are two customs?			
5. What are two symbols that are part of the celebration?			
Conclusion:			

6 Write

Write one paragraph that describes Kwanzaa and birthday celebrations from two different countries. Use information from your graphic organizer.

7 After you write

A Check your writing. Did you include all the ideas in your graphic organizer?

B Share your writing with a partner.

a. Take turns. Read your writing to your partner.
b. Read your partner's writing to yourself. Compare it to your partner's graphic organizer.
c. Comment on your partner's writing: Ask one question; share one thing you learned.

AUDIO SCRIPT

Welcome

Page 3, Exercise 2A – CD1, Track 2

A Hi, Mark. I see you're studying for the vocabulary test. You did so well on the last one. What's your secret?
B I make vocabulary cards. I write the vocabulary words on one side of the card and then write the definition on the other side. I also write an example sentence with the word in it and draw a picture for some words. I test myself and ask others to test me, too.
A Oh, that's a creative way to study, and I can see that you're artistic, too.
B Thanks! And you always do well on math tests. What strategies do you use for studying math?
A I like to study with other people. We form a small group and test each other on equations and formulas. We have fun while we study so the time goes by fast.
B You're so outgoing and fun-loving – I can see how that fits your personality. Who do you study with?
A I often study with Juan. He's an active person and likes to study while moving – sometimes we memorize formulas while bouncing a basketball. It's a good way to remember something.

Page 4, Exercise 3A – CD1, Track 3

1. Mohammed was listening to the radio.
2. Yoko heard a loud noise.
3. Last night at 8:00 p.m., the Martinez family was watching television.
4. I woke up at 6:00 a.m. this morning.
5. Merin was playing her violin this morning.
6. Isabella and Jeremy were doing their homework.
7. Marcos drove to the supermarket.
8. Nur vacuumed the house yesterday.

Page 4, Exercise 3B – CD1, Track 4

Last summer, my sister and I drove from Tucson to Phoenix. On our way, it was very windy, and there were dark clouds in the sky. We were traveling slowly when suddenly we saw huge clouds of dust in the air. The sky turned brown, and we couldn't see anything. It was very scary. While we were driving, we were looking for a place to turn off the road. Finally we came to an exit and got off the main road. We went into a restaurant. The dust finally went away while we were waiting at the restaurant.

Page 5, Exercise 4A – CD1, Track 5

1. Angelica hasn't been to Mexico recently.
2. I've been to Niagara Falls a few times.
3. Claudia and Paul haven't gone camping lately.
4. Sabrina has volunteered at the Humane Society several times.
5. She hasn't cooked Korean food yet.
6. My father has already shown his confidence.
7. Peter has enjoyed socializing since his graduation.
8. Roberta has already traveled all over the United States.
9. Monica has spoken Spanish since preschool.
10. Manuel has already taken several English classes

Page 5, Exercise 4B – CD1, Track 6

1. **A** Have you practiced English outside of class lately?
   B No, I haven't. I'm too shy.
2. **A** How many times have you texted your friends today?
   B I have texted my friends at least seven times so far today.
3. **A** How many times have you eaten Mexican food?
   B I have eaten Mexican food many times. I love it!
4. **A** Has Daniel done his homework yet?
   B No, he hasn't. He needs to finish it before tomorrow.
5. **A** How long have you studied in this school?
   B I have studied at this school for three months.

Unit 1: Personal information

Page 7, Exercises 2A and 2B – CD1, Track 7

A Come on in. The door's open!
B Hi, Nina!
A Emily! Come on in. Have you been jogging?
B Yeah, I was just coming back from my run, and I thought I'd see what you're – whoa! Look at this kitchen!
A Yeah, it's a mess, isn't it? We're having 14 people for dinner tonight, and I'm going to be in the kitchen all afternoon!
B It smells great already! Hey, I just heard that Brenda got first place in the high school math contest. Is it true?
A Yes, it's true! She's really good at math. She just loves it.
B Brenda's such a "brain." I'm sure you're really proud of her!
A Yeah, she's very intelligent. But I have to say that Gerry and Danny are bright, too – they're just smart in different ways.
B What do you mean?
A Well, take Gerry. He's not mathematical like Brenda, but he's really musical. He plays four different instruments, he sings really well – he's even writing some of his own songs.
B I guess that's Gerry?
A Yeah.
B So Brenda's gifted in math, and Gerry's good at music. What about Danny? What's he good at?
A Well, he's good at fixing cars. He's the mechanical one in the family.
B Oh, I remember he bought that old, old car when he was 16. How's that coming? Is he still working on it?
A Emily, you should see that car now! It's gorgeous! He fixed everything, and it runs perfectly!
B Amazing! You know, it's really interesting how your kids are all smart in different ways. And, Nina, you're pretty smart, too!
A Me?
B Well, look at you! Maybe it's easy for you to cook for 14 people, but I could never do it. I have absolutely no aptitude for cooking!
A Gee, Emily. No one ever told me that I'm smart!
B Well, Nina, you are smart! And the smart thing for me to do is to go home and let you do your work. I'll talk to you tomorrow.
A Bye, Emily. Thanks for stopping by!

Page 7, Exercise 3A – CD1, Track 8

Emily stops by Nina's house on her way home from jogging. They talk about Nina's three children. Brenda is very mathematical. She's just won a math contest at school. When Emily calls Brenda a brain, Nina says that all her children are bright, but in different ways. Gerry isn't gifted in math, but he's very musical. He plays and sings very well and even writes music. Danny is the mechanical one in the family. He's good at fixing old cars. Emily thinks that Nina is also smart because she is such a good cook. Emily has no aptitude for cooking.

Page 8, Exercise 2A – CD1, Track 9

1. Carol speaks very intelligently. She's a bright girl.
2. That isn't a bad guitar, but he's playing it badly.
3. Benny is an excellent cook. His dinner last night was fantastic.
4. The mechanic did a good job on my car. Now it runs perfectly.
5. You danced very skillfully in the dance contest. You're a wonderful dancer!
6. I don't type very fast. I can't move my fingers very quickly.
7. That writing test was hard. Writing isn't an easy subject for me.
8. You sang that song beautifully! I didn't know you could sing so well!
9. Your report is great. You wrote it very clearly.
10. I work slowly. I'm a careful worker.

Page 10, Exercise 2A – CD1, Track 10

1. Do you believe that there are many kinds of intelligence?
2. I think Nina has an interesting family.
3. Brenda's teachers agree that she is very gifted.
4. Do you think that Nina cooks very well?
5. Many people believe Gerry will become a famous musician.
6. I didn't realize that Danny has an aptitude for fixing cars.
7. Do you feel that mechanical skills are very important?
8. Nina knows that her children are very different.

Page 12, Exercise 2 – CD1, Track 11

Many Ways to Be Smart

Josh is a star on the school baseball team. He gets Ds and Fs on all his math tests. His brother, Frank, can't catch, throw, or hit a baseball, but he easily gets As in math. Which boy do you think is more intelligent? Howard Gardner, a professor of education at Harvard University, would say that Josh and Frank are both smart, but in different ways. His theory of multiple intelligences identifies nine different "intelligences" to explain the way people understand, experience, and learn about the world around them.

Verbal / Linguistic Some people are good with words. They prefer to learn by reading, listening, and speaking.

Logical / Mathematical These people have an aptitude for math. They like solving logic problems and puzzles.

Musical / Rhythmical These people are sensitive to sound, melodies, and rhythms. They are gifted in singing, playing instruments, or composing music.

Visual / Spatial These "picture people" are often good at drawing or painting. They are sensitive to colors and designs.
Bodily / Kinesthetic Some people are "body smart." They are often athletic. Kinesthetic learners learn best when they are moving.
Interpersonal Certain people are "group smart." They easily understand other people. They are good at communicating and interacting with others.
Intrapersonal Some people are "self smart." They can understand their own feelings and emotions. They often enjoy spending time alone.
Naturalist These people are skilled in working with plants and animals in the natural world.
Existential Certain people are gifted in exploring deep questions about the meaning of life and death and ways to find inner peace.
According to Gardner, many people have several or even all of these intelligences, but most of us have one or two intelligences that are primary, or strongest.

Unit 2: At school

Page 19, Exercises 2A and 2B – CD1, Track 12

Part 1

Do you like to work with people? Do you enjoy traveling? Are you bilingual?
Then La Costa Community College's Hospitality and Tourism certificate program is for you. Our graduates find high-paying jobs with hotels, restaurants, airlines, travel agencies, and more! This growing industry needs leaders – it needs you!
For more information about La Costa's certificate program in Hospitality and Tourism, call 866-555-6868 today!

Part 2

A Mrs. Ochoa?
B Oh, hi, Vasili. How's it going?
A Pretty well. Um, I was in my car this morning, and I heard an advertisement about a certificate program in hospitality and tourism.
B Yes, it's a great program. Are you interested?
A Yeah, but I have some questions.
B Well, I'll try to answer them for you.
A OK. So first, what are the requirements for the certificate? How many courses are required?
B There are six required courses, plus an internship.
A An internship? What's that?
B You work at a local tourism business for three months. There's no pay, but it's a great way to learn about the industry – you know, see if you like it.
A I see. Are the classes in the daytime or at night? Because you know, I can't quit my job, and . . .
B No problem, Vasili. Classes are scheduled at different times, and some of them are even offered online.
A Oh, yeah? That's great. Um, how long does it take to complete the program?
B Well, it depends. I'd say – with the internship – between one and two years. Some people just take one class at a time, so it takes them longer.
A OK, that's good. How much does the program cost?
B Well, let's see. There are six classes, and they're three units each. It's $50 a unit, so that's $900 for the certificate. Books are another $100 per class, and then there's parking and health fees. So the total is about $1,600.
A $1,600? Wow! That's a lot of money.
B Don't worry. There's financial aid for students who qualify.
A OK. You know, I think I'd like to apply. When's the registration deadline?
B Let's see. Looks like it's December fifteenth for the winter semester. You have time.
A But my English, is it good enough?
B Well, you're required to take an English placement test, but I'm sure you'll do fine, Vasili. You're bilingual, you're very motivated, and you have good interpersonal skills. Hospitality and tourism could be a really good career for you.

Page 19, Exercise 3A – CD1, Track 13

Vasili hears a radio ad about the Hospitality and Tourism certificate program at La Costa Community College. The ad says graduates can find high-paying jobs in the tourism industry. Vasili goes to see his ESL counselor, Mrs. Ochoa. She tells him about the program requirements, which include an internship in a local tourism business. She also tells him about the deadline for registration, and she says there is financial aid for students who qualify. Vasili is concerned about his English, but Mrs. Ochoa tells him not to worry. Vasili is bilingual, he's very motivated, and he has good interpersonal skills.

Page 20, Exercise 2A – CD1, Track 14

1. **A** When is the English placement test given to new students?
   B The English placement test is administered a week before the first day of class.
2. **A** Is a math placement test also required?
   B No, a math placement test is not needed.
3. **A** Where is the financial aid office located?
   B It is located next to the admissions office.
4. **A** Where are the classes held?
   B Most of the classes are held in the business building.
5. **A** Are classes offered at different times?
   B Yes. Both day and evening classes are offered.
6. **A** Are job placement services provided to graduates?
   B Yes. Job help is offered to students who qualify.

Page 22, Exercise 2A – CD1, Track 15

1. Applicants are expected to meet all application deadlines.
2. New students are told to come early for registration.
3. Are all new students required to take a writing test?
4. Some students are advised to enroll in an English composition class.
5. Are students expected to attend every class?
6. Students are encouraged to meet with a counselor regularly.
7. When are participants expected to complete their internships?
8. Students are required to earn a grade of C or better in each course.
9. Students are told to study with a partner and to go to tutoring often.
10. Are students allowed to retake the course if they don't pass?

Page 24, Exercise 2 – CD1, Track 16

An Immigrant Family's Success Story
Choi and Lili Wei left China with their baby boy in the early 1990s. They were poor field workers in their native country, and they wanted their child to have the opportunities they lacked. They arrived in New York and found a one-bedroom apartment in a poor, unstable area. They could only afford a bicycle for transportation, yet they felt fortunate to have the chance to begin a new life in the United States.
Choi and Lili faced many obstacles because they couldn't speak English and had no skills. They found night work cleaning businesses and restaurants. They saved every penny, and after six years, they were able to buy a small restaurant of their own.
They were determined to learn English, get an education, and make a good life for their son. The couple sacrificed a great deal. They never went to the movies, never ate out, and hardly ever bought anything extra. In their free time, they attended English and citizenship classes. Both of them eventually earned their GED certificates. Choi then enrolled in college while Lili worked in the restaurant.
This past spring, Choi fulfilled a lifelong dream of graduating from college. Now he is registered in a master's degree program in business beginning this fall. And what about their "baby" boy? Their son, Peter, now 21, received a scholarship to a private university, where he is working on his own dream to become an architect.
Choi and Lili are proud to be models of the "American dream." Choi has this advice for other new immigrants: "Find your passion, make a plan to succeed, and don't ever give up."

Review: Units 1 and 2

Page 30, Exercise 1 – CD1, Track 17

A Hey, Faisal! I haven't seen you in a while. What's new?
B Hi, Angela. Um, I just talked to Mr. Ortiz, my career counselor. He gave me some information about a certificate program in automotive technology.
A Is that like car repair?
B Well, yeah, but these days, you know, cars are a lot more complicated than they used to be. Everything is computerized now. I've always liked fixing up cars, but . . .
A I remember back in high school when you fixed the transmission on my dad's truck. He said you had a real aptitude for mechanical things.
B Yeah, I guess so. But I need more education if I want to get a high-paying job in the auto industry.
A So what did Mr. Ortiz tell you?
B Well, there are eight required courses, plus two more courses that you're allowed to choose.
A That's a lot of classes. How long will it take to complete them all?
B Four semesters. It's pretty fast. And the classes are scheduled at all different times, you know – daytime and evening, and even on weekends.
A How much will it cost?
B Each course is $60. And I need ten courses. So the total is $600, not including books and tools. Plus financial aid is offered to students who qualify.
A You sound really motivated.
B I am. I think this is the right program for me.

Page 31, Exercise 3A – CD1, Track 18

/t/
1. He has always liked playing number games.
2. She has worked as an accountant for ten years.

/d/
3. Emily has realized that Brenda has a good brain.
4. Naturalists are skilled in working with plants.

/ɪd/
5. The little boy started counting when he was two.
6. She is gifted in singing and dancing.

Page 31, Exercise 3B – CD1, Track 19

1. Classes are located at various elementary schools.
2. All students are advised of the school rules.
3. An application is required for admission.
4. A math test is needed as well.
5. The test is administered once a week.
6. The students are expected to pay their fees soon.
7. Lucas hasn't talked with a counselor yet.
8. But he is finished with all his tests.

Unit 3: Friends and family

Page 33, Exercises 2A and 2B – CD1, Track 20

Part 1

A You have one new message.

B This call is for Mrs. Wen Lee. This is the attendance office from Central High School calling on Tuesday, March 10th, at 2:00 p.m. We're calling to report an unexcused absence for your daughter, Lan, from her 7th period class today. Please call the office at 619-555-2300 to explain why your daughter missed class. Thank you.

Part 2

C I can't believe we're at the mall on a school day!

D Yeah. Do you think anyone at school is going to miss us?

C No way. There's a substitute teacher in my last period class.

D Mine, too! So, how's everything at home?

C It's the same old thing. I'm so frustrated. My mother won't let me do anything! She is so strict.

D Strict? Like how?

C Well, I'm not permitted to go anywhere without my parents or my brother. And my mom says I can't go out on a date without a chaperone until I'm 18!

D That's so unfair! I wonder why your mother's so strict.

C I don't know. I think she's trying to bring me up like she was raised in China. She just doesn't understand the customs here in the United States.

Part 3

C Hi, Mom.

E Hi, Lan. How was school today?

C Um, fine. Is something wrong?

E The school called and said you were absent from your 7th period class. Where did you go?

C Come on, Mom. Don't get excited.

E Tell me where you went!

C Mary and I just went to the mall right across the street from school, OK?

E But what about your last class?

C There was a substitute teacher, OK? I didn't miss anything!

E I don't understand how you could do this!

C Well, it's your fault! You're so strict that I had no choice. Everybody's allowed to go to the mall except for me. Why can't you trust me?

E This is not about trust. You broke the school rules. You're on restriction for the next two weekends.

C On restriction?! What about Celia's birthday party next Saturday?

E I'm afraid you'll have to miss it. Next time, maybe you'll think before you act.

Page 33, Exercise 3A – CD1, Track 21

Mrs. Lee received a phone message from her daughter's school saying Lan missed her 7th period class. Lan left school early to go to the mall with her friend Mary. At the mall, Lan tells Mary that her mother is too strict. Lan thinks it's because her mother wants to bring her up the same way she was raised in China. That's why Lan needs a chaperone to go out on a date. At home, Lan and her mother have an argument. Lan is angry because she's not permitted to go to the mall alone. She thinks her mother doesn't trust her. Mrs. Lee is upset because Lan broke the rules. As a punishment, she says Lan is on restriction for two weeks.

Page 34, Exercise 2A – CD1, Track 22

1. **A** Do you know what the student's name is?
   B Her name is Lan.
2. **A** Can you please tell me what class she missed?
   B Mr. Latham's 7th period English class.
3. **A** I wonder who Lan went to the mall with.
   B She went to the mall with Mary.
4. **A** I would like to know why she broke the rules.
   B I don't know why. Perhaps she was bored in class.
5. **A** Can you tell me when she and her friend left the school.
   B They left after 6th period.
6. **A** I want to know what they did at the mall.
   B They talked and went window-shopping.
7. **A** Do you know when they came home from the mall?
   B I don't know when they came home.
8. **A** Could you please tell me what Lan's punishment was?
   B Her mother put her on restriction for two weeks.

Page 36, Exercise 2A – CD1, Track 23

A Can I go to a party at Joe's house?

B Maybe. First I need to know if you finished your homework.

A Yes, I finished it an hour ago.

B Do you know if the party starts at 5:00 or 6:00?

A It starts at 6:00.

B OK. Can you tell me if his parents will be home?

A Yes, his parents will be there.

B That's good. I wonder if you need to take a birthday gift.

A No, I don't. It's not a birthday party.

B I wonder if they're going to serve dinner.

A Yes. They're going to grill chicken for us.

B What about your friend John? Do you know if he's invited to the party?

A Yes, I think so.

B Do you know if John's parents can bring you home?

A I'll ask them.

B I am wondering if you can text us when you are on the way home.

A Sure. I'll do that.

Page 38, Exercise 2 – CD1, Track 24

Barriers Between Generations

In immigrant families, language differences and work schedules often create barriers to communication between the generations. Dolores Suarez, 42, and her son, Diego, 16, face both kinds of barriers every day. Dolores is an immigrant from Mexico who works seven days a week as a housekeeper in a big hotel. She doesn't use much English in her job, and she has never had time to study it. Consequently, her English is limited. Her son, on the other hand, was raised in the United States. He understands Spanish, but he prefers to speak English. When his friends come over to visit, they speak only English. "They talk so fast, I can't understand what they are saying," says Dolores. To make the situation more complicated, Diego and Dolores live with Dolores's father, who speaks Nahuatl, a native language spoken in Mexico. Diego can't understand anything his grandfather says. Dolores's work schedule is the second barrier to communication with Diego. Because she rarely has a day off, Dolores isn't able to spend much time with him. She doesn't have time to help him with his homework or attend parent-teacher conferences at his school. In 1995, when Dolores immigrated to the United States, her goal was to bring up her son with enough money to avoid the hardships her family suffered in Mexico. Her hard work has permitted Diego to have a comfortable life and a good education. But she has paid a price for this success. "Sometimes I feel like I don't know my own son," she says.

Unit 4: Health

Page 45, Exercises 2A and 2B – CD1, Track 25

Part 1

A Cindy, have you seen Sara?

B No. I don't think she's here yet.

A She should have been here 25 minutes ago. Did she call to say she'd be late?

B No, she didn't.

C Oh! Uh, good morning, Mr. Stanley.

A Good morning, Sara.

C I'm sorry, I know I'm late, but the buses are so unreliable.

A I don't know about the buses, Sara, but I do know that if you're late one more time, I'm going to have to fire you.

Part 2

C Thanks for picking me up, Mike.

D No problem.

C We have to hurry – my driving test is in half an hour.

D We have plenty of time. The DMV is just ten minutes from here.

C All right.

D Are you OK? You seem tense.

C Yeah, I'm pretty stressed out.

D How come?

C I was late to work again this morning . . .

D Oh, no!

C And the boss said that if it happens again, he's going to fire me.

D No wonder you're stressed out.

C I'm so worried about losing my job, I can't sleep, I can't eat, I can't concentrate . . .

D You know, Sara, if you're not feeling well, you don't have to take the driving test today.

C Yes, I do, Mike. I have to pass this driving test so I can get my license and buy a car and stop depending on buses.

D OK, OK, I understand. But if you want to pass the test, then you have to calm down. Try to relax. Take a few deep breaths.

C OK.

D Now think positive thoughts. Tell yourself, "I'm a good driver. I'm going to pass my driving test."

C "I'm a good driver, I'm going to pass my driving test."

D Seriously, Sara. You ought to learn some techniques for coping with anxiety.

C Like what?

D Simple stuff. Like I said, deep breathing is good, um, thinking positive thoughts. And I find that it helps me to meditate every day.

C Meditation. Let's talk about it later. Here's the DMV.

D Good luck, and don't forget: You're a good driver!

C Thanks, Mike. You're a good friend.

Page 45, Exercise 3A – CD1, Track 26

Mike is driving Sara to the Department of Motor Vehicles (DMV) to take her driving test. He notices that she's very tense. Sara says she's stressed out because she was late to work again. She's worried that her boss will fire her if she's late one more time. She's so afraid of losing her job that she can't eat, she can't sleep, and she can't concentrate. Mike says that she has to calm down if she wants to pass her driving test. He suggests three techniques to help her cope with her anxiety. One is deep breathing. The second one is thinking positive thoughts, and the third one is meditation.

Page 46, Exercise 2A – CD1, Track 27

Ana and Bill just got engaged, and they are planning to get married in four weeks. Because the wedding is so soon, they are feeling a lot of pressure. Ana's mother wants a big wedding, but Ana and Bill don't. Because they are paying for the wedding themselves, they believe they should do what they want. Another pressure is all the things Ana and Bill have to do before the wedding. For example, Ana has to buy a dress, choose her bridesmaids, and send out the invitations. Bill has to plan the reception and order the food. Most importantly, they have to decide where the wedding will be. Ana wants to get married outdoors, but Bill thinks they shouldn't plan an outdoor wedding because it might rain. Now Bill has a different idea. He realizes that they shouldn't get married so soon. Maybe they should postpone the wedding by a few months. That way, they don't have to feel so much pressure.

Page 48, Exercise 2A – CD1, Track 28

1. She should have talked to someone about her problems.
2. She should have gone out with friends.
3. She shouldn't have stayed home alone all the time.
4. She should have made new friends.
5. She should have exercised.
6. She should have eaten regular, balanced meals.
7. She shouldn't have eaten lots of junk food.
8. She shouldn't have slept so much.
9. She should have called her family.

Page 50, Exercise 2 – CD1, Track 29

Stress: What You Ought to Know

What is stress?

Stress is our reaction to changing events in our lives. The reactions can be mental – what we think or feel about the changes – and physical – how our body reacts to the changes.

What causes stress?

Stress often comes when there are too many changes in our lives. The changes can be positive, like having a baby or getting a better job, or they can be negative, such as an illness or a divorce. Some stress is healthy. It motivates us to push forward. But too much stress over time can make us sick.

What are the signs of stress?

There are both physical and emotional signs of stress. Physical signs may include tight muscles, elevated blood pressure, grinding your teeth, trouble sleeping, an upset stomach, and back pain. Common emotional symptoms are anxiety, nervousness, depression, trouble concentrating, and nightmares.

How can you manage stress?

To prevent stress, you should eat right and exercise regularly. When you know there will be a stressful event in your day – such as a test, a business meeting, or an encounter with someone you don't get along with – it is really important to eat a healthy breakfast and to limit coffee and sugar. When you find yourself in a stressful situation, stay calm. Take a few deep breaths to help you relax. Roll your shoulders or stretch to loosen any tight muscles. And take time to think before you speak. You don't want to say something you will regret later!

We all have some stress in our lives. It is important for us to use strategies to handle it, so that the stress doesn't overwhelm us.

Review: Units 3 and 4

Page 56, Exercise 1 – CD1, Track 30

A Hi, Sue. This is Blanca.
B Hi! How are you?
A Well, to be honest, not so good.
B Why? What's wrong?
A I'm really worried about Yesenia. Lately she's been different. She seems tense and too quiet. It's hard for her to concentrate on her schoolwork.
B She's 13 now, isn't she?
A Yeah. She just had a birthday last week.
B That's a hard age.
A You know, we raised her to always talk to us about her problems, but last night, I got angry at her. I shouldn't have shouted at her, but she wouldn't answer my questions.
B Do you know if she's having any problems at school?
A That's what I was asking her about. I don't know what's going on with her.
B You know, Blanca, when my daughter was 13, I took a parenting class at the middle school. It really helped me learn how to cope with teenagers.
A A parenting class? I don't know. I'll have to think about that.
B I also think you ought to call Yesenia's counselor at school. The counselor can talk to Yesenia and to her teachers and find out how she's doing.
A OK.
B And one more thing. You sound pretty stressed out, too. Why don't you and Yesenia take an exercise class together? It will help both of you to calm down and relax.
A That's a great suggestion, Sue. I'll ask her tonight. Thanks a lot.

Page 57, Exercise 3A – CD1, Track 31

A Where did he go?
B Can you tell me where he went?

Page 57, Exercise 3B – CD1, Track 32

1. **A** What does Ann do to reduce stress?
   B She listens to music.
2. **A** Why are you so tense?
   B I have my driver's test today.
3. **A** Do you know what Rodolfo does to calm down?
   B He walks or jogs.
4. **A** When did Ivan miss his class?
   B He missed his class on Tuesday.
5. **A** Can you tell me where Andy lives?
   B He lives on East Fifth Street.
6. **A** Do you know why they're always late?
   B No, I don't know.

Unit 5: Around town

Page 59, Exercises 2A and 2B – CD1, Track 33

A Hi! Are you the volunteer coordinator?
B Yup, Steve Jones. And you're Almaz? Did I say it right?
A Yes, exactly, Almaz Bekele. Nice to meet you.
B You, too. Please have a seat. I was just looking over your application to volunteer here at Quiet Palms, and it looks really good. Is it OK if I ask you some questions?
A Of course. Go ahead.
B OK, let's see. You wrote that you've been a volunteer before. Can you tell me about that?
A Sure. I volunteered last summer at the public library downtown.
B What did you do there?
A I worked with adults who wanted to learn how to read. I also taught a little writing, and on Saturdays, I read stories to the kids.
B Did you enjoy that?
A Yeah, but what I really liked was working with the older people. It felt like I was doing something really worthwhile.
B Uh-huh. So now tell me why you want to volunteer in a nursing home.
A Well, I think I might want to work in the healthcare field someday, but I won't know for sure until I get some experience.
B I see. Well, we'd love to have you volunteer here.
A Great! When can I start?
B I like your enthusiasm, but we have some health requirements. First, you need to take a blood test and a TB test. You can start as soon as we get the results. It usually takes two or three days.
A OK. I'll take care of that right away. Also, um, I was wondering – can you tell me what my responsibilities will be?
B Sure. One thing volunteers do is, uh, they help residents with their meals. You might encourage them to eat, or just keep them company during mealtime.
A Yeah, my grandmother always eats more when I'm with her. She likes having people around.
B Then I'm sure you understand that you need to be patient and compassionate with the residents.
A I know.
B Volunteers also deliver mail and flowers, and they take residents for walks. You'll get more responsibilities as soon as you feel more confident.
A Sounds good.
B There's an orientation next Monday at 8:30.
A I'll be there!
B One more thing. You'll need to make a commitment to volunteer at least three hours per week.
A No problem! I can't wait to start.

Page 59, Exercise 3A – CD1, Track 34

Last summer, Almaz volunteered at the public library downtown. She liked working with the older people because she felt that she was doing something worthwhile. Today, she is meeting with Steve, the volunteer coordinator at Quiet Palms, a nursing home. She wants to volunteer there to find out if she likes working in the healthcare field. Steve tells her about some of her responsibilities at Quiet Palms. He says it's very important for volunteers to be compassionate and patient when they are working with the residents. He asks Almaz to make a commitment to volunteer at least three hours per week. Almaz agrees to attend an orientation. She says she can't wait to start volunteering.

Page 60, Exercise 2A – CD1, Track 35

1. **A** Mr. Shamash is in pain. When will he start to feel better?
   B He'll feel better as soon as he takes his medication.
2. **A** How long will Mr. Shamash stay at Quiet Palms?
   B He'll stay until his broken hip heals.
3. **A** When can Mr. Shamash begin exercising again?
   B As soon as Mr. Shamash feels stronger, he can start doing moderate exercise.

4. **A** When does Mr. Shamash get ready for his walk?
   B He gets ready as soon as Almaz arrives.
5. **A** How long will Mr. Shamash and Almaz play cards?
   B They'll play cards until it is time for lunch.
6. **A** How long did Mr. Shamash nap yesterday?
   B He napped until Almaz came to visit him.
7. **A** When is Mr. Shamash going to go to sleep?
   B As soon as his visitors leave, he'll take his medicine and go to sleep.
8. **A** When did the nurse assistant help Mr. Shamash with his shower?
   B As soon as Mr. Shamash woke up, the nurse assistant helped him with his shower.

Page 62, Exercise 2A – CD1, Track 36

Sharing with Sally

Jake, a college student, volunteered all last year. He called elderly people on the phone once a week and talked to each person. He said it was a very valuable experience. Betsy, a 35-year-old mother of two, has volunteered for two years so far and loves it.

Page 64, Exercise 2 – CD1, Track 37

Running with Ropes

Imagine running with your eyes closed. How do you feel? Insecure? Afraid? Justin Andrews knows these feelings very well. Justin is a former long-distance runner who lost his vision because of a grave illness. For the past six months, he has been running twice a week with the help of volunteer runners at Running with Ropes, an organization
that assists blind and visually impaired runners. "Running with Ropes has changed my life," Justin says. "Until I heard about it, I thought I'd never run outside again."
Volunteers at Running with Ropes make a commitment to volunteer two to four hours a week. Scott Liponi, one of the running volunteers, explains what they do. "We use ropes to join ourselves to the blind runners and guide them around and over obstacles, such as holes in the road and other runners." Scott has learned how to keep the rope loose so the blind runner has more freedom. He deeply respects the blind runners' tenacity. "They are incredibly determined," he says. "It doesn't matter if it's hot, raining, or snowing – they are going to run." Scott says it is gratifying to share in the joy of the runners and to feel that they trust him. "The four hours I spend at Running with Ropes are the most rewarding part of my week," he says. "It's really a worthwhile Commitment."

Unit 6: Time

Page 71, Exercises 2A and 2B – CD2, Track 2

Part 1

A Excuse me, ma'am?
B Yes?
A I'm a reporter for KESL Radio, and today we're asking people for their opinions about technology and timesaving devices. Do you have a minute to answer some questions for me?
B Sure.
A May I have your name?
B Jean Rosen. Mrs. Rosen.
A Do you have a favorite time-saving device?
B Let me see. . . . I guess it's this – my address stamper.
A Oh. I expected something electronic, not manual! Does it really save you time?
B Absolutely. It takes about a minute to handwrite a return address. The address stamper just takes seconds, even though it's not electronic.
A Thank you for your time, Mrs. Rosen.

Part 2

A Excuse me, sir. Do you have a minute?
C Well, I'm in a bit of a hurry.
A I'm a reporter for KESL Radio. I'm asking people for their opinions about how technology helps them save time.
C Technology – a time-saver? I'm afraid you're talking to the wrong man. I'm not a fan of technology.
A Why is that?
C Well, take e-mail, for example. Half the time it's spam. And it's distracting, too. It interrupts my work.
A But isn't it convenient?
C Not that I can see. If you ask me, most of this electronic stuff wastes more time than it saves. I still write letters by hand although I have a perfectly good computer at home.
A I see. Could I get your name before you go?
C Ronald Chung.
A Thank you for your time, Mr. Chung.

Part 3

A Good morning, ma'am. I'm a reporter for KESL Radio.
D Yes?
A I'm asking people their opinions about technology and time-saving devices.
D Oh, that sounds interesting.
A Do you have a favorite time-saving device?
D Oh, yes. I just love my cell phone.
A I guess it saves you lots of time because you can use it anywhere.
D That's right. You see, I go to lots of sales to buy clothes for my daughter. I take pictures with my camera phone of clothes I think she might like.
A Really?
D Yeah. Then I send her the pictures while I'm still in the store. She sends me a text message back. It says "Buy" or "Don't buy."
A Now that's innovative.
D Yeah. Not a bad idea, huh?
A I'm sure our listeners will enjoy hearing about such an unusual use.
D Happy to share. It really is a time-saver. But not a money-saver.
A I see what you mean! Oh, I didn't get your name.
D Patricia Morales.
A Well, thank you, Ms. Morales, for sharing your favorite time-saving device.

Page 71, Exercise 3A – CD2, Track 3

Today, a reporter from KESL Radio asked three people about technology and their favorite time-saving devices. Mrs. Rosen's favorite device is manual. She says it saves time, even though it isn't electronic. Mr. Chung isn't a fan of technology. In fact, he says technology wastes more time than it saves. For example, he says he doesn't like email because he gets lots of spam. He also finds email distracting. He doesn't think it is convenient. Ms. Morales loves technology. She uses the camera on her cell phone in a very innovative way – to send her daughter pictures of clothes that are on sale. Her daughter sends a text message back: "Buy" or "Don't buy. "

Page 72, Exercise 2A – CD2, Track 4

1. Mrs. Sanchez can't operate her digital camera although she read the directions many times.
2. Although Mrs. White's car has a GPS system, she gets lost all the time.
3. Mr. Green doesn't use his microwave although he paid a lot of money for it.
4. Although email is fast, Mr. Chung doesn't like to use it.
5. I prefer to read paperback and hardcover books although e-books are very popular.
6. Although Ms. Kaye had urgent business 1000 miles away, she refused to travel by plane.
7. I prefer to use a fan when it's hot although my house has central air-conditioning.
8. Although Ben never sets his alarm clock, he still gets to work on time.
9. I play my CDs on my CD player at home although all my music is available online.

Page 74, Exercise 2A – CD2, Track 5

Although Pam and Beth are sisters, they are very different. Pam is very modern. She loves electrical appliances because they are fast and convenient. For example, she loves her microwave because she can use it to thaw meat quickly. She enjoys shopping for the latest kitchen devices, although some of them are very expensive. Beth has a different attitude about modern technology. She prefers not to use electrical appliances. For instance, she never uses a microwave because she thinks the radiation is bad. She dries her clothes outside on a line because she likes their smell after they've been in the fresh air. She washes her dishes by hand because she says dishwashers waste energy. Pam doesn't understand why Beth is so old-fashioned. But although the sisters have different lifestyles, they appreciate and enjoy one another very much.

Page 76, Exercise 2 – CD2, Track 6

Changes in technology can change people's lives.

The development of transportation— trains, cars, and planes - provides us with one example. Before the 19th century, most people lived within walking distance of work. In the 20th century many people began to commute between home and work because trains and cars connected cities with suburbs. Today, because of airplanes, many people travel great distances for their work. Some, because of the Internet, don't need to travel at all.
Technological changes have also impacted the media – for example, how we get the news. Newspapers were once people's primary source for the news: in 1965, 72 percent of Americans reported that they read a newspaper on an average day. By 2005, that number was down to 50 percent. In the past, a common way people got news was by listening to the radio. I suppose nearly everyone had a radio then. By the 1950s, television was overtaking radio. Now even the number of people watching the news on television has declined, dropping from 60 percent in 1993 to 28 percent in 2006. So what's the latest source for news? The Web. The number of Americans who use the Internet to get the news is increasing. Most people access the news on their smartphones.
Media has also changed the way we get jobs. We used to look for job openings in the classified ads of a newspaper. Then we'd mail an application through the US Postal Service (now called *snail mail* by some). Finally, if we were lucky enough to get an interview, we'd go to the job site. Today we can find notices for jobs online and we can submit our applications over the Internet. The employer can even interview us over the Internet using programs, such as Skype, that provide voice over and video over calls. These changes save time for both the employer and the applicant.

Another example of the impact of technology is how we pay for goods and services. Until the mid-1940s, people had to carry large amounts of cash in their purses and wallets. Then, one day in 1949, a man named Frank McNamara took some business associates to dinner, but he left his wallet at home. He had to call his wife to bring him money to pay the bill. Mr. McNamara vowed to find a way to avoid carrying cash. Although some stores already had their own charge cards, there was no single, multi-purpose credit card. A year later he returned to the same restaurant with the same people but paid with the credit card he had created, called "Diner's Club." Today, people don't even need to carry a credit card. They can pay with their smartphones. In what other ways do you think technology may change our lives in the future?

Review: Units 5 and 6

Page 82, Exercise 1 – CD2, Track 7

A Good afternoon, listeners. Today we're talking with Rebecca Ford, Coordinator of Adult Literacy Services at our downtown library. Thank you for joining us, Ms. Ford.
B It's a pleasure to be here.
A To start off, could you describe your job for us?
B Sure. I'm responsible for training and supervising all the volunteer literacy tutors at the library.
A How many tutors are there?
B We have between 20 and 30 volunteer tutors at a time.
A And who are the students that they work with?
B The students are adults who don't have good reading and writing skills. Some of them are immigrants who can't read and write very well, even though they've been in this country for many years.
A I see. Could you tell us more about your tutors? What kind of people are they?
B Well, our tutors are all different ages, and they have different backgrounds. Some of them are volunteering for the first time, and some have volunteered many times in their lives. But in one way, they're all the same: they're very compassionate. They really care about helping other people. Also, they're very generous with their time.
A I suppose they also have to be very patient if they're teaching adults to read.
B Yes, that's right.
A What are the requirements for becoming a literacy tutor?
B OK. First, they're required to have 12 hours of training in tutoring techniques. Then, as soon as they complete their training, we match each tutor with a student. They're required to meet their student for at least one and a half hours per week, and the library requires a minimum commitment of six months.
A That's good to know. Ms. Ford, if any of our listeners are interested in volunteering, who should they contact?
B They can call my office. The number is 914-555-6700.
A OK, listeners, that number again is 914-555-6700 if you want to volunteer. We appreciate your taking the time to talk with us today, Ms. Ford.
B I enjoyed it. Thank you for having me.

Page 83, Exercise 3A – CD2, Track 8

1. Pam loves electrical appliances because they save her time.
2. She wants to volunteer in the healthcare field.
3. Even though computers are timesavers, some people don't use them.
4. Will he go to sleep as soon as his visitors leave?

Page 83, Exercise 3B – CD2, Track 9

1. She delivers meals to seniors.
2. Volunteers should be patient and compassionate.
3. Do you walk to work or drive?
4. Mr. Chung isn't a fan of e-mail.

Unit 7: Shopping

Page 85, Exercises 2A and 2B – CD2, Track 10

Part 1

A Excuse me. Do you work here?
B Yes. Do you need some help?
A Where do I take this thing?
B What have you got there?
A It's a camera, a digital camera. I'd like to get my money back, if possible.
D OK, if you want a refund, you need to talk to somebody in Customer Service. See that guy who's wearing a red tie over there? He'll help you.
A Thank you.

Part 2

C Who's next?
A Hi. I want to return this camera that I bought. I'd like to get my money back.
C You bought it here? Do you have the receipt?
A The receipt? Just a minute. Here it is.
C OK. That's good. Is the camera defective?
A What do you mean – "defective"?
C Well, is there something wrong with it? Doesn't it work?
A Oh, no – it's not broken or anything. I just don't like it.
C What's the problem?
A It's the screen.
C The screen?
A Yeah. The screen is too small. A few days ago, I was taking pictures. It was a sunny day, and I couldn't see the picture in the screen! Maybe it's my eyes.
C No, I don't think it's your eyes. That screen is kind of small. So, did you want to exchange it for another camera?
A I'm not sure. Is it possible to get my moneyback?
C Well, let me look at that receipt again. You got this on the 5th, and today is the 20th. So it's been 15 days. Our policy for a refund is that you have to bring it back within 10 days. So, sorry – no refund.
A Oh. I didn't know about the 10 days.
C Now, for an exchange: You have 30 days – if the merchandise is in perfect condition.
A Oh, it's just like new! I only used it a couple of times. Here, see for yourself.
C Yeah, you're right. Looks OK to me. Is everything in the box?
A I think so. Like I said, I hardly used the camera. Here's the case that came with it. And here's the instruction book, and the warranty card, and all the papers that –
C OK, great. Why don't I keep this camera here while you look around the store?
A You mean, I have to choose another camera today? I'm kind of in a hurry.
C Well, if you want, I could just give you a store credit instead. With a store credit, you can come back and shop anytime.
A Oh, that's a good idea. Maybe I can bring my nephew with me next time I come. He knows a lot about cameras.
C OK, let me get you a store credit.
A I really appreciate all your help.
C No problem.

Page 85, Exercise 3A – CD2, Track 11

Rosa wants to return the camera that she bought and get a refund. She is told that she needs to speak with someone in customer service. The clerk there asks Rosa if the camera is defective, and she says it isn't. The clerk tells her about the store policy for returns and exchanges. It's too late for Rosa to return the camera, but she can exchange it if the merchandise is in perfect condition. Rosa still has the camera box with the instruction book and the warranty card. Since Rosa is in a hurry, she decides to get a store credit, and she will use it at a later time.

Page 86, Exercise 2A – CD2, Track 12

1. I want to buy a camera which is not too expensive.
2. I'd like to get a good camera which will last for many years.
3. Many people who are looking for cameras shop online.
4. My friend told me about a camera store which sells used merchandise.
5. Customers who appreciate good service like to shop at Super Camera.
6. The clerk who works in customer service is very helpful.
7. These days, many people want an expensive camera which has separate lenses.
8. Sometimes people need to return merchandise which is defective.
9. Buyers who don't ask about a store's return policy may be sorry later.
10. Many people now have smart phones which have excellent cameras.

Page 88, Exercise 2A – CD2, Track 13

1. A good friend that I've known for several years needed a new car.
2. She used to drive an old car that she got from her father.
3. Last January, the old car that she was driving stopped working.
4. The mechanic that her neighbor recommended couldn't fix it.
5. Finally, she decided to buy a used car from a man that she knew at work.
6. He's an honest person that she trusts completely.
7. The price that he named was really good.
8. The used car that he sold her is only three years old.
9. It's a reliable car that she can drive for a long time.
10. Suzy is happy to have a vehicle that she doesn't have to worry about.

Page 90, Exercise 2 – CD2, Track 14

The Smart Shopper

Dear smart shopper,

I'm a jewelry lover, and I enjoy shopping online. Unfortunately, I just bought a pair of gold earrings that I don't like. When I tried to return them, I learned that the seller has a no-return policy. Don't I have the right to get a refund?

– Mad Madelyn

Dear Mad Madelyn,

If the merchandise is defective, the seller must return your money or make an exchange. However, if the merchandise was in good condition when you received it, and if the retailer has a no-return policy, there is nothing you can do. This is true for store purchases as well as Internet purchases. In the future, here are some questions you should ask before you buy anything:

- Does the seller say "satisfaction guaranteed or your money back"?
- Is there a time limit on returns, such as two weeks?
- Who pays the shipping costs on items that are returned?
- Do you need to return the merchandise in its original package?
- Is the original receipt required?
- Does the retailer give a store credit instead of a cash refund?
- If the retailer has a store in your area, can you return the merchandise to the store instead of shipping it?

Next time, find the return policy on the merchant's Web site and print it, or ask the merchant for the return policy in writing. It's important to get all the facts that you need before you buy!

– Smart Shopper

Unit 8: Work

Page 97, Exercises 2A and 2B – CD2, Track 15

Part 1

A David, can I talk to you for a second?
B Yeah, sure.
A Um, you know, you've been leaving early a lot lately, and when you do that, I have to stay later and close up the shop by myself.
B Oh, come on, Yolanda. That doesn't happen very often.
A Well, it happened twice last week, and it's happened once so far this week. I'd say that's pretty often. Plus, sometimes the shop is full of customers, and you're in the back room talking on your cell phone. So I feel like I've been doing my job and yours, too. It's not fair. Something's wrong here. We have to figure out a better system here so we divide the work more equally.
B OK, whatever – but I have to go now. See you!

Part 2

C Yolanda, over here!
A Hi, guys.
D Whoa, Yolanda – what's wrong?
A I'm exhausted. I've just finished work.
D Don't you usually finish at 4:00?
A Yeah, Teresa, but the other guy on my shift, David, he's going to night school, and lately he's been leaving early a lot. So then I have to clean up the shop and close up by myself. Sometimes I don't get out of there until 4:45 or 5:00. It's really frustrating.
D That's really unfair.
C I think you should quit that job!
D Quit? That's crazy, Julie. She can't quit – it's hard to find another job!
C Well, have you tried talking to David?
A Yeah, I talked to him, but it didn't help.
D What about your boss? Have you told her?
A No, not yet. I'd really like to try to work something out with David first.
C Listen, I have an idea. What about making a chart?
A A chart? How does that work?
C It's simple. You make a list of all the duties in your shift. You know – open up, make coffee, whatever. Then you negotiate with David and decide who's going to do which tasks.
A OK . . .
C And then, every day, as soon as you finish a task, you write your initials on the chart.
A I get it. So then if David isn't doing his share, it's easy to see.
C And if the problem continues, you can show the chart to your boss and let her deal with it.
A I like that idea, Julie. Especially the part about negotiating with David. I really hope we can work this out together.

Page 97, Exercise 3A – CD2, Track 16

Yolanda and David work at Daria's Donut Shop. Lately, David has been leaving work early, and Yolanda has to close up the shop by herself. Tonight, Yolanda is having coffee with her friends. She is exhausted. Her friends give her advice. Teresa thinks she should talk to her boss, but Yolanda wants to try to work things out with David first. Julie thinks Yolanda should make a chart of their duties. Then she should negotiate with David and decide who is going to do which tasks. When they finish a task, they should write their initials on the chart. If David isn't doing his share of the work, it will show in the chart. Then Yolanda can show the chart to their boss and let her deal with the situation.

Page 98, Exercise 2A – CD2, Track 17

1. Daria Thompson is the owner of Daria's Donut Shop. She has been selling donuts at this location for more than 20 years.
2. It's 7:00 a.m. Daria has been making donuts for three hours.
3. It's 7:30 a.m. Daria has just opened the shop for customers.
4. It's 10:30 a.m. Daria's son has been helping her all morning.
5. He has just finished cleaning the counters and shelves. Everything is spotless.
6. Daria needs more help in the shop. She has decided to hire Yolanda.
7. Yolanda's shift begins at 6:00 a.m. today. She has been waiting for the bus for 30 minutes. She's worried that she's going to be late.
8. It's 6:05 a.m. Yolanda has just called to say she will be late.
9. It's 6:30 a.m. Yolanda has just arrived at the store. Daria is really glad to see her!
10. It's noon. Yolanda has been working for several hours and she's ready to take a break.

Page 100, Exercise 2A – CD2, Track 18

1. **A** I heard that Juan and his friends went to a party after work. How was the party?
   B It was really exciting.
2. **A** What did Juan and his friends like the most about the party?
   B There was a lot of interesting music from different countries.
3. **A** How did Juan feel the next day at work?
   B He was exhausted.
4. **A** How long did he have to work?
   B He had to work from 9:30 to 6:30. It was a tiring day.
5. **A** Does Juan usually start working at 9:30?
   B No, he overslept! He was shocked that he didn't hear the alarm clock.
6. **A** How did his boss react when he showed up late?
   B His boss was irritated.
7. **A** What did his boss say to him?
   B He told Juan that he was disappointed in him.
8. **A** How did Juan feel after his boss told him that?
   B He felt embarrassed.
9. **A** Juan didn't have a good day, I guess. What did he do later that night?
   B He stayed home and had a relaxing night in front of the TV.
10. **A** So, is Juan going to go out again on a weeknight?
    B I don't think so. He said it was an exhausting experience.

Page 102, Exercise 2 – CD2, Track 19

Hard and Soft Job Skills

Som Sarawong has been working as an automotive technician at George's Auto Repair for over five years. Today was a special day for Som, a 35-year-old Thai immigrant, because he received the Employee of the Year award. According to Ed Overton, Som's boss, Som received the award "because he's a great 'people person' and he has superb technical skills. I even have him work on my own car!" Som has the two kinds of skills that are necessary to be successful and move up in his career: soft skills and hard skills. Soft skills are personal and social skills. Som gets along with his co-workers. He has a strong work ethic; in five years, he has never been late or absent from work. Customers trust him. Hard skills, on the other hand, are the technical skills a person needs to do a job. Som can repair cars, trucks, and motorcycles. He learned from his father, who was also a mechanic. Then he took classes and got a certificate as an auto Technician. Soft and hard skills are equally important, but hard skills are easier to teach and assess than soft skills. People can learn how to use a machine and then take a test on their knowledge. However, it's harder to teach people how to be cooperative and have a good work ethic. George Griffith, the owner of George's Auto Repair, explains, "I've been working in this business for over 30 years, and most of the time when I've needed to fire someone, it was because of weak people skills, not because they didn't have technical abilities." Soft skills and good technical knowledge are a winning combination, and today, Som Sarawong was the winner.

Review: Units 7 and 8

Page 108, Exercise 1 – CD2, Track 20

A Good evening, class. I've invited two business owners to our class to describe job skills that are important for their businesses. I'd like to introduce Len Sullivan, the owner of Sullivan's Electronics, and Cora Zimmer, the owner of Zimmer's Restaurant. First, let's hear from Mr. Sullivan.
B Thanks. It's a pleasure to be here. So, talking about job skills, I would say that first and most importantly, my employees need to have good communication skills. That's true for the salespeople on the floor as well as the ones working in customer service. And at the same time, I expect my people to be good listeners. I've been working in this business for 25 years, and I've hired a lot of people in that time. And I can tell you, my best employees are the ones who really know how to listen to customers and respond to their needs. And now the third important skill is that my employees need to be good problem solvers. They have to deal with all sorts of problems every day, and I expect them to work things out and find good solutions.
A Thank you, Mr. Sullivan. Now let's listen to Ms. Zimmer and find out what skills are important in the restaurant business.
C Thank you so much for inviting me. One important skill my employees need is to manage their time effectively. Restaurant work is very fast-paced and exhausting, so the waiters and also the cooks have to be good time managers. Another important job skill for my employees is good communication skills, just as Mr. Sullivan said. I want my employees to understand instructions and also be able to talk to our

customers. Finally, I need employees who can train others in their job duties.

A Thank you both. I know the class is very interested in your comments. And now, I'd like to open this up for questions. Class, do you have questions that you would like to ask?

Page 109, Exercise 3A – CD2, Track 21

1. **A** Is the camera defective?
   B It's defective and too small!
2. **A** Don't you usually finish at 5:00?
   B I do usually finish at 5:00, but not today.
3. **A** Why aren't you applying for that job?
   B I am. I'll go there tomorrow.
4. **A** I don't trust the man who sold you this car.
   B Well, I do! It's my decision, not yours.
5. **A** Is he excited about his new job?
   B No, but his wife is.
6. **A** Did you put the returned merchandise on my desk?
   B No, I put it in your desk.

Page 109, Exercise 3B – CD2, Track 22

1. **A** I'd like to exchange this sweater.
   B Why?
   C It's too big, and it has a hole.
2. **A** You can't leave early again!
   B Yes, I can and I will.
3. **A** Why don't you clean the counters?
   B Why don't you?
4. **A** Let's talk about a raise after you've worked here for six months.
   B Can we talk before six months?

Unit 9: Daily living

Page 111, Exercises 2A and 2B – CD2, Track 23

A Mei! Dinner!
B I'll be right there! Sorry I'm late. I was just checking something on the computer.
A OK. Sit down. We've been waiting for you.
B I know. I'm sorry, but I was looking at a website that describes ways to save our planet.
C Save our planet? What does that mean? What's the matter with our planet?
B Dad, it means taking responsibility for saving the earth.
C Saving it from what?
B From global warming! We had a guest speaker today in biology class, and he mentioned a whole bunch of stuff – simple steps we can take to reduce our energy use and protect the environment.
A Like what?
B OK, well, first of all, he said we need to cut down on driving, so we should walk, ride a bicycle, carpool, or take public transportation.
C I'd do those things if I could. But my job is an hour away, and there's no bus service that goes there. And there's nobody for me to carpool with.
B I see your point, but how about recycling? I think we could do a better job of recycling bottles, cans, glass, paper . . .
A You're right. We could do that if we tried.
B Another idea was to turn off unnecessary lights. Look at this house: lights on in every room.
C I like that idea. It'll help cut down on the electric bill.
A What else did the speaker suggest?
B Let me think. Oh, he said that we should wash our clothes in cold water.
A Really? I'm not sure the clothes will get clean, but I suppose we can try.
C That'll save money on the electric bill, too.
B But isn't our washing machine really old? If we bought a new one that's more energy-efficient, it could help the environment and our electric bill!
A I don't think we can afford to buy new appliances right now.
B OK. But what about energy-efficient light bulbs? We could switch to those, right?
A That sounds pretty simple, Mei.
B Cool!
C I have to say, I love your enthusiasm. I never realized how simple it can be to . . . what did you say. . . save our planet?
B Yeah, the speaker said that if everyone did even one of these things every day, it would do a lot to reduce global warming.
C Speaking of warming, can we eat before the food gets cold?

Page 111, Exercise 3A – CD2, Track 24

Mei was late to dinner because she was looking at a website about saving the planet. She wants to take more responsibility for saving the earth from global warming. Mei tells her parents about the guest speaker who came to her biology class. The speaker suggested simple things people could do to reduce their energy use and protect the environment. For example, they could carpool instead of driving alone,
recycle their bottles and cans, and use energy-efficient light bulbs. Mei's parents agree that it is important to cut down on energy use since it would also help them save money. However, they can't afford to buy new appliances right now.

Page 112, Exercise 2A – CD2, Track 25

1. Many people put their newspapers in the trash can. If everybody recycled newspapers, we would save millions of trees.
2. Noah never takes his car in for a tune-up. Noah's car would use less gas if he tuned up his car regularly.
3. Mr. Brown drives his own car to his job downtown. Mr. Brown would save money on gas if he carpooled to work.
4. Many items in the supermarket are packaged in plastic. If you bought products that are packaged with recycled paper, you would help to reduce global warming.
5. Jessica always stays in the shower for a very long time. If Jessica took shorter showers, she would save water.
6. Some kinds of fish contain large amounts of lead, a poisonous metal. You would be healthier if you stopped eating fish that contains lead.
7. Energy-efficient appliances use less electricity. If Mei's family bought a new washing machine, they would save money on their electric bill.
8. Kristina never puts enough air in her tires. If Kristina put more air in her tires, she would buy less gasoline.

Page 114, Exercise 2A – CD2, Track 26

1. Since there is a buildup of harmful gases in the atmosphere, global warming is increasing.
2. Warm water is expanding in the oceans, so the sea level is rising.
3. Since the sea level is rising, towns near oceans are in danger of flooding.
4. Since global warming changes weather patterns, many places will have less rainfall.
5. The mosquito population will increase, so there will be an increase in diseases like malaria.
6. Since the ocean water is getting warmer, typhoons and hurricanes are becoming more frequent.
7. Cities are growing, so many plants and animals may lose their natural habitats.
8. Summer temperatures will continue to rise, so there will be longer periods of no rain and increased days of very high temperatures.

Page 116, Exercise 2 – CD2, Track 27

All Things Are Connected

Long ago, there was a village chief who never allowed anyone to disagree with him. Whenever he wanted to do something, he asked the members of his court for their advice. But whether the chief's idea was wise or foolish, his advisors always said the same thing: "Indeed, it is wise." Only one old woman dared to give a different answer. Whenever the chief asked for her advice, she always replied, "All things are connected."
One night, the chief was awakened by the sound of frogs croaking in the swamp. It happened again the next night and the next and the next. The chief decided to kill all the frogs in the swamp. When he consulted the members of his court, they replied as usual: "Indeed, it is wise." But the old woman kept silent. "And you, old woman, what do you think?" the chief demanded. "All things are connected," she replied. The chief concluded that the old woman was a fool, and he ordered his servants to kill all the frogs. Therefore, the chief slept peacefully.
But soon the mosquitoes in the swamp began to multiply since there were no frogs to eat them. They came into the village and made everyone miserable. The chief ordered his servants to go into the swamp and kill the mosquitoes, but it was impossible. Furious, the chief summoned the members of his court and blamed them, saying, "Why didn't you tell me that killing the frogs would make the mosquitoes multiply and everyone would be miserable? I should have listened to the old woman."
Because the mosquitoes were there, all the people of the village were forced to go away. Finally, the chief and his family left, too. Until he died the chief never forgot the old woman's words: "All things are connected."

Unit 10: Free time

Page 123, Exercises 2A and 2B – CD2, Track 28

A Hi, Cathy. What are you doing this weekend?
B Oh, Thanh. I'm glad you asked. I was invited to Bao and An's wedding. It's Saturday night, and I haven't bought them a gift yet.
A So?
B Well, I don't know what to get them. They aren't registered at any stores.
A Registered? What's that?
B Well, for many American weddings, the bride and groom sign up with a gift registry service at a store. They make a list of what they want, and then people can go to the store or the store's website and buy something on the couple's list.
A I've never heard of that custom. At a Vietnamese wedding, guests just bring cash in an envelope.
B Really?
A Yeah, and during the reception, the bride and groom walk from table to table, greet the guests, and collect the envelopes. If I were you, I would just take an envelope.
B OK. Thanks for the advice. I guess customs are really different- across cultures, aren't they?
A That's for sure. Do you know what really surprised me the first time I went to an American wedding?
B No, what?

A As the bride and groom were leaving the reception, the guests threw rice at them. What a waste of food! Where does that custom come from?
B Oh, that's a really old tradition. Rice is a symbol of fertility and longevity, so throwing rice represents the hope that the couple will have children and live a long life together.
A That's really interesting.
B Yeah. So, Thanh, what else happens at a Vietnamese wedding?
A Well, for one thing, it's traditional for a Vietnamese bride to wear a red dress.
B Red? Not white, like in this country?
A That's right. In our culture, red symbolizes good fortune. In fact, one of the traditional foods at a Vietnamese wedding is red sticky rice.
B Interesting. Let me ask you something else. My invitation was just for the wedding reception in the evening. What about the ceremony?
A Well, traditionally, the ceremony takes place at the bride's home, with just the family and close relatives. It's usually held in the morning. The reception in the evening is actually a huge party, with all the couple's friends and acquaintances, lots of dancing, and lots of food. Be prepared for a seven- or eight-course dinner.
B Wow! I guess I won't eat anything beforehand. So, will I see you at Bao and An's wedding?
A I wish I could go, but I have to go to my nephew's graduation party. I hope you have a great time.
B I hope so, too. I'm really looking forward to it.

Page 123, Exercise 3A – CD2, Track 29

Cathy and Thanh are talking about wedding customs. Cathy is invited to a Vietnamese wedding, and she is surprised that the bride and groom are not registered for gifts at any stores. In contrast, Thanh is surprised by the American tradition of throwing rice at the bride and groom. Next, they talk about clothes. Thanh says a Vietnamese bride wears a red dress because the color red symbolizes good fortune. Then Cathy asks why she was invited only to the wedding reception, not the ceremony. Thanh explains that traditionally the ceremony is only for the family. The couple's friends and acquaintances are invited to the evening reception. In fact, Thanh says the evening party will include seven or eight courses of food. Cathy says she is looking forward to the wedding.

Page 124, Exercise 2A – CD2, Track 30

1. The Patels are from India, but they live in the United States now. They are planning a wedding for their daughter, Parveen. If they lived in India, the groom's family would pay for the wedding.
2. The wedding will be in the United States. If the Patels had the wedding in India, the wedding celebration would last three days. Here it will last for one day.
3. The Patels don't have a lot of money. If they were rich, they would invite 300 people; instead, they will invite about 150.
4. The Patels are planning to have music for the reception. If a band doesn't charge too much, they will have live music.
5. It's possible that the weather will be nice on the day of the wedding. If the weather is nice, they will have the ceremony outside.
6. It's possible Parveen and her husband will get some vacation time from work. If Parveen and husband get enough time off from work, they will take a trip to Hawaii for their honeymoon.
7. They don't have a lot of time off from work. If they had more time, they would go to India for their honeymoon.
8. Parveen and her new husband will live in their own apartment. If they were in India, they would live with the groom's parents.

Page 126, Exercise 2A – CD2, Track 31

1. Paul's high school graduation is tomorrow. His friend Luis has to work. Luis wishes he could go to Paul's graduation.
2. Paul's father has asked for the day off so that he can attend his son's graduation. He hopes he gets the day off.
3. Paul's grandfather has been sick. He's not sure if he will attend the graduation. Paul hopes his grandfather will attend the ceremony.
4. Paul's sister is out of the country, so she can't come to the ceremony. Paul wishes his sister were here to attend his graduation.
5. The graduation ceremony will be outside. Paul hopes it will not rain.
6. Paul's parents would like to buy him a new car, but they can't afford it. They wish they could buy him a new car.
7. Paul wasn't accepted to the university, so he will go to a community college. Paul wishes he could go to the university.
8. Paul has applied for financial aid. Paul hopes he gets financial aid to help pay for his books.
9. It's possible that Paul will be able to transfer to the university in two years. He hopes he can transfer in two years.

Page 128, Exercise 2 – CD2, Track 32

Special Birthdays Around the World
In most cultures, there are certain birthdays that are especially important in a young person's life. If you were an American teenager, for example, you would eagerly look forward to your 16th birthday because in most states, that is the age to get a driver's license. Other cultures also have birthdays with special meanings:
Mexico For Mexican girls, the 15th birthday – the "Quinceañera" – symbolizes a girl's transition into adulthood. To celebrate, the girl's family throws a huge party. The girl wears a ball gown similar to a wedding dress. The girl performs a waltz, a formal dance, with her father. A similar custom is celebrated in Brazil.
China On a child's first birthday, parents place their baby in the center of a group of objects, such as a shiny coin, a book, and a doll. Then they watch to see which object the baby picks up first. Most parents hope their child will pick up the coin because, according to tradition, it means the child will be rich.
Nigeria The 1st, 5th, 10th, and 15th birthdays are considered extremely important. Parties are held with up to 100 people. The guests enjoy a feast of a roasted cow or goat.
Saudi Arabia In some countries, such as Saudi Arabia, people don't observe birthdays at all because of spiritual beliefs. According to Muslim traditions, the only celebrations allowed are Eid al Fitr, a feast that signifies the end of Ramadan, and Eid al Adha, which celebrates the end of the annual pilgrimage to Mecca.
Israel A boy's 13th and a girl's 12th birthdays are serious as well as happy occasions. On these birthdays, children become responsible for their own religious and moral behavior. Adult birthdays also have special significance in many cultures. In the United States, for example, birthdays ending in "0" – 30, 40, 50, etc. – are especially meaningful.

Review: Units 9 and 10

Page 134, Exercise 1 – CD2, Track 33

A This is Grace Leong, for KPFX News. I'm standing on the busy corner of Pacific Avenue and Grant Avenue in San Francisco's Chinatown. Tomorrow is the beginning of Chinese New Year, and with me I have two people who can give us some interesting information related to good luck in the coming year. Could you tell us your name, please?
B Angela Kwan.
A Angela, what are some things we can do to bring good luck?
B Well, it's traditional to wear bright colors, such as red. Red is a very bright and happy color, so it symbolizes a bright and happy future. Another thing is, at midnight on New Year's Eve, you should open all the doors and windows of your house. That's to let the old year out and make room for the new. And on New Year's Day, one good thing to do is to eat a lot of candy. If you do that, the new year will be very sweet.
A Very interesting, Angela. I think I'll go shopping for a new red dress, and I'm definitely looking forward to eating all that candy! And what's your name, sir?
C Hi. My name's Martin Chan.
A Martin, Angela told us some things that bring good luck. What are some things that we should not do on New Year's?
C Well, you shouldn't sweep the house on New Year's Day because you might sweep away your family's good fortune. That's why people sweep the house very carefully before the start of the holiday. And it's bad luck to buy a pair of shoes, because . . .
A Not even red shoes?
C No. The word for "shoes" sounds like the word for "evil" in Mandarin, so you don't want to buy shoes. And you shouldn't use knives or scissors on New Year's Day because if you do, you might cut off your good fortune.
A Thank you, Martin and Angela, and I hope you both have a very happy new year.

Page 135, Exercise 3A – CD2, Track 34

1. Smaller cars would use less energy.
2. Smog is a big environmental problem.
3. If everyone drove less, our air quality would improve.
4. In the future, we will see more electric cars and trucks on our roads.
5. We should all have efficient appliances.
6. We need to protect our environment.

Page 135, Exercise 3B – CD2, Track 35

1. All things in this world are connected.
2. People are concerned about saving this earth.
3. Most of the cars on the highway have only one person in them.
4. People make a lot of unnecessary trips.
5. We should close off unused rooms in our homes.
6. The Internet is a good source of information about global warming.